Agreement and the Stability of Democracy

Agreement and the Stability of Democracy

Ian Budge

University of Essex

Markham Publishing Company / Chicago

Markham Series in Empirical Democratic Theory

Deane E. Neubauer, Editor

(

Owing to Judith
and Charles

ACKNOWLEDGEMENT

The ideas behind this investigation first developed under the benevolent criticism of Charles McCall and R. A. Dahl. The extent of my intellectual drawings on Professor Dahl's writings are indeed evident at every point in the book. What does not appear is his helpfulness in securing financial support for the research and in proffering good advice in various emergencies in which I have turned to him.

When I found myself a stranger in London Dr. Mark Abrams very generously oriented me towards the British survey situation. I also received indispensable help from Donald Monk, to whose wise advice, unstinted attention, and time I owe a workable questionnaire. At this stage Jim Sharpe gave valuable background information from his Clapham survey.

Methodological difficulties at various stages threatened completion of analysis. For help in the resolution of these I stand greatly indebted to Professor D. E. Stokes of the Survey Research Center, University of Michigan; John Nimmo of the Usher Institute of Public Health, Edinburgh; and Dr. William Howie, of the Department of Mathematics, University of Strathclyde. For the laborious processing that produced the final data I most heartily thank Merrill Shanks and the Inter-University Consortium for Political Research; Mrs. Maureen Thompson; Miss Eileen Turner; and the Data-Processing Unit of the Faculty of Arts and Social Sciences of the University of Strathclyde.

In preparing various drafts of this book I have, as always, greatly benefited from the comments of Professor Dahl and also from the informed criticisms of A. M. Potter, Michael Margolis, Kenneth Alexander, R. R. Alford, F. I. Greenstein, and Anthony King. The editorial interventions of L. W. Milbrath, Deane Neubauer and Jane Hadley also preserved discussion from numerous infelicities of style and interpretation; for those which remain I must affirm sole responsibility.

For typing of various drafts I owe a great deal to Mrs. Elizabeth Banks, Mrs. Elisabeth Elder, Miss Ann Marie McEleney, Mrs. T. Appleton, Mrs. Margaret Parkinson.

The sinews of research were very generously provided by grants from the Ford Foundation and the University of Strathclyde.

Finally I must express my deepest appreciation for the cooperation extended to me by the fifty-nine busy MPs and candidates, and the 147 electors who agreed to be interviewed. The validity of the ensuing discussion rests entirely on their willingness to provide information. From both Conservative and Labour Party organizations and officials I received much assistance at different stages of research. BBC-Television and ABC-Television kindly provided statistics on their coverage of political issues. I trust that all these individuals and organizations will find some recompense for their trouble in the partial light which this study sheds on British democratic processes.

I. B.

TABLE OF CONTENTS

INTRODUCTION

THE PROBLEM

Considered in one light democracies are the countries where political conflict is most endemic and widespread. At regular intervals the population is mustered into opposing groups whose spokesmen proclaim their opposition to the other groups. A whole class of full-time opponents of the Government is maintained at public expense to denounce the shortsightedness and malice of official decision-makers. The most successful and obstructive of these critics are rewarded with office, and their ousted competitors in turn given the chance to arouse popular hostility against their policies. The internal disunity of democracies can be contrasted with the unanimous approval that has greeted official action in such countries as Soviet Russia, Nazi Germany, contemporary Spain and Saudi Arabia.

Considered in another light, certain democracies are the countries with the most stable political processes of all. Constitutions are not swept away with discredited governments. Disagreements are debated and settled without the aid of guns. Those who have the control of arms and of the police abide by rules which proscribe their use against most political opponents. Those opponents in turn act according to procedures which forbid appeals to violence or revolution against government policies which have passed through prescribed stages.

This contrast between the flux and struggle exemplified by party competition in elections and in the legislature, and, on the other hand, the relatively undisturbed stability of the procedures by which competition is carried on has perplexed countless political analysts. For two thousand years it was maintained that democratic processes could not possibly work. From Plato, founder of the systematic study of politics, to Rousseau, often cited as the most eminent modern theorist of democracy, the classical writers reverted to the view that the opposing and voracious desires of individuals and groups would tear apart any political system which tried to give them free play. But the unexpected success of some countries in maintaining just such a political system for some generations has foreclosed this rapid exit from the theoretical maze. Accepting the fact that democracies can survive the conflicts which their freedoms generate, the problem is now to explain how they survive. This book represents part of a cumulative attempt to advance the understanding of this central problem of politics, a problem whose importance has been under'ined so ominously by the events of the past forty years.

EXPLANATIONS

Two types of causal factors can be drafted to explain the continuance of constitutional rights and freedoms in a democratic system. It is possible to look at the phenomenon in terms of socioeconomic influences or in terms of the psychological prerequisites of the democratic citizenry.

The socioeconomic approach is exemplified in the pioneering study by S. M. Lipset which linked the general level of affluence and the extent of disparities between rich and poor to the existence of constitutional government and prevalence of revolution over most countries of the world.[1] Economic factors like the ones pinpointed by Lipset have obvious effects on the politico-economic cleavages inside a political system and less obvious effects on the educational opportunities and communication levels necessary for democracy.[2]

Examples of the explanation of democratic stability in terms of psychological attributes appear in the hypotheses formulated by R. A. Dahl[3] and V. O. Key[4] about the link between actual implementation of constitutional procedures and the uneven distribution of agreement

---

[1] S. M. Lipset, *Political Man* (Garden City, N.Y.: Doubleday, 1960), Chap. 2. See also P. Cutright, "National Political Development: Economic and Social Correlates," in N. W. Polsby, R. A. Dentler, and P. A. Smith, eds., *Politics and Social Life* (Boston: Houghton Mifflin, 1963), pp. 569–82.

[2] For the link between communications and democracy, see D. Lerner, *The Passing of Traditional Society* (New York: Free Press of Glencoe, 1958), and L. Pye, *Aspects of Political Development* (Boston: Little, Brown, 1966). For the effects of education on civic dispositions, see G. A. Almond and S. Verba, *The Civic Culture* (Princeton, N.J.: Princeton University Press, 1963).

[3] R. A. Dahl, *Who Governs?* (New Haven, Conn.: Yale University Press, 1961), Chap. 28.

[4] V. O. Key, Jr., *Public Opinion and American Democracy* (New York: Knopf, 1961), pp. 536–43.

between activists and general population in a democracy. In Dahl's and Key's theories the greater support of the politically involved for constitutional procedures allows them to be put into practice regardless of whether they have the undivided support of the relatively apathetic.

The extent to which psychological explanations for democratic stability complement socioeconomic is shown by Neubauer's demonstration that above a certain "threshold" of development the more democratic countries are not necessarily the most economically flourishing.[5] Underdevelopment certainly inhibits democratic freedoms by holding down educational and communication levels. But marked fluctuation in these freedoms among developed countries themselves can be explained only by different degrees of socialization into democratic procedures.[6]

Psychological factors thus seem to mediate the gross impact of society and the economy upon democratic politics. The precise nature of such mediation is discussed in Chapter 12. Because psychological variables seem likely, on the basis of the available evidence, to be more closely and sensitively related to democratic stability, this study is almost exclusively concerned with the correspondence between the distribution of psychological attributes and adherence to constitutional procedures within one democracy.

DEFINITIONS

The term "democracy" has been used ten times in the preceding pages and will appear with equal frequency in following chapters. It will clarify discussion to give some indication of the meaning attaching to the term before we enter the detailed argument of the book. In the present context 'democracy' is regarded as a political system in which power to make policy decisions is allocated basically as the result of free competitive elections in which every citizen's vote is weighted identically and all have relatively equal access to information about the competing alternatives. The definition is a summary of the ten conditions of the political system termed polyarchy by R. A. Dahl.[7] One

---

[5] D. E. Neubauer, "Some Conditions of Democracy," *American Political Science Review*, 61 (December 1967), 1002–9. The *American Political Science Review* is hereafter cited as *APSR*.

[6] *Ibid*, pp. 1002, 1008.

[7] R. A. Dahl, *Preface to Democratic Theory* (Chicago: University of Chicago Press, 1956), p. 84. The ten definitional characteristics of polyarchy stated by Dahl are: (Continued)

must, however, take heed of the crucial rider that Dahl adds to his definition. He notes that none of the conditions he specifies for poly-archy have ever been met or are ever likely to be met in any human organization.[8] In order to make use of the definition in analyzing the real world, therefore, it is necessary to modify it by adding that the conditions need exist only to a relatively high degree.[9] In fact it is more useful to regard the general definition given above and each of the ten conditions that it summarizes as the upper limits of continua or scales. Complete absence of these characteristics forms the lower limits of each scale. Actual political systems can be ranked on such scales in terms of their relative distance from complete attainment of polyarchy. The upper chunk may be called 'polyarchies,'[10] in our terms, 'democracies'. The countries which fall into this 'chunk' include the United States, Great Britain, most of the older Commonwealth and the Scandinavian countries, France and Italy.[11]

A system's adherence to democratic procedures, the central con-cern of this work, is termed "democratic stability" in the ensuing dis-cussions. Again following Dahl, democratic stability is taken here to

---

During the voting period:

1. Every member of the organization performs the acts we assume to consti-tute an expression of preference among the scheduled alternatives, *e.g.*, voting.

2. In tabulating these expressions (votes), the weight assigned to the choice of each individual is identical.

3. The alternative with the greatest number of votes is declared the winning choice.

During the pre-voting period:

4. Any member who perceives a set of alternatives, at least one of which he regardes as preferable to any of the alternatives presently scheduled, can insert his preferred alternative(s) among those scheduled for voting.

5. All individuals possess identical information about the alternatives.

During the post-voting period:

6. Alternatives (leaders or policies) with the greatest number of votes dis-place any alternative (leaders or policies) with fewer votes.

7. The orders of elected officials are executed.

During the inter-election stage:

8. (*a*) Either all inter-election decisions are subordinate or executory to those arrived at during the election stage (*i.e.*, elections are in a sense controlling), (*b*) or new decisions during the inter-election period are governed by the seven preceding conditions, operating, however, under rather different institutional cir-cumstances, (*c*) or both.

[8] Dahl, *Preface to Democratic Theory, op. cit.*, p. 71.

[9] *Ibid.*, p. 84.

[10] *Ibid.*, pp. 73–74, 87.

[11] *Ibid.*, p. 74. Neubauer, in the article cited in Footnote 5 above, has formed an index, based on Dahl's ten conditions of democratic performance, which com-bines indicators for percentage of the adult population eligible to vote, equality of representation, information equality, and party competition. His Table 3 shows the countries mentioned in the text, with others, as scoring highly on his index.

mean the persistence of the definitional characteristics given for the term democracy.[12] Such a vigorous and straightforward definition hides some difficulties however. The definitional characteristics of democracy are thought of as the upper ends of certain scales. A country can therefore be regarded as moving up and down the scale from time to time. So long as it moves within the permitted range of variation— *i.e.*, above 0.5 on the scale for all conditions—we may continue to regard it as a polyarchy or democracy.[13] But if adherence to democratic procedures is fluctuating markedly (*e.g.*, from 0.5 on the scale to 0.8), it is impossible to conclude that democratic procedures are persisting unchanged.

Possibly it is not necessary to think of democratic procedures as persisting quite unchanged: here, too, we can introduce "relativity" into the discussion and speak of democratic stability as the relative persistence of democratic procedures. Relative persistence, and, hence, democratic stability, can now be operationally defined to mean that the practice of democratic rules does not decline at any time to below 0.5 on our scales.

This formulation is satisfactory in principle. In practice too little research has been done on the persistence of democratic processes over time in the different countries of the world to isolate some countries as indubitably stable democracies. We do know that Britain and most other English-speaking countries, as well as the Scandinavian and Low Countries, emerge in the mid-sixties as among the most democratic countries of the world.[14] The history of these countries does not disclose any fundamental alteration in the percentage of all adults

---

[12] Dahl, *Who Governs?, op. cit.*, p. 311.

[13] Dahl, *Preface to Democratic Theory, op. cit.*, p. 87.

[14] Neubauer, *op. cit.*, Table 3. On Neubauer's combined index of democratic performance Britain actually emerges as most democratic of all countries considered. This result may, however, be unduly influenced by the effects on Neubauer's component indicator of information equality of the national character of most British newspapers, which compete over the whole country and are not confined to specific regions. Neubauer's operational measure of information equality takes the following form:

$$\text{number of separately owned papers in capital city} \times \frac{\text{average circulation}}{\text{size of capital}}$$

If only capital cities are compared, the highly concentrated British Press may indeed score highly on this formula, by virtue of the fact that all national newspapers circulate in London. It would score less highly if nations as a whole were compared, since in contrast to other democracies there are few regional papers of importance and since many of these come under the same ownership. There seems little doubt, however, that even with amendments to this component measure, Britain would score highly on the combined index.

eligible to vote, equality of voting, or party competition since the franchise was extended to women fifty or more years ago. And these political features are basic indicators of democracy in the sense we have given the word. It is harder to assess changes in information equality, a fourth basic indicator, but impressionistically it would seem that all these countries have had a variegated, independent and vigorously circulating Press over the same time period.[15] Combining the results of contemporary research and historical inference, it seems plausible to assert that Britain and the other countries mentioned above are not only democracies, but stable democracies. Further definitional problems will be discussed in Chapter 3 after they have emerged from the discussion of the first two chapters.

PLAN OF DISCUSSION

The investigation that follows has as its focus one particular explanation of democratic stability—the Dahl-Key theory of differentiated agreement—and as its purpose the testing this theory, using British survey data that have been collected expressly for this purpose. In the following chapters discussion follows the roughly chronological stages of the project itself. In Chapter 1 the current status of other psychological theories and research findings is discussed, and reasons are given for choosing the Dahl-Key theory for investigation. In Chapter 2 the leading assertions of that theory are analyzed in detail and put into testable form, while certain extensions are explained and predictions advanced. In Chapter 3 other key terms of the discussion are defined and operationalized. In Chapter 4 to 11 predictions are tested by comparing replies of a sample of London politicians with those of a sample of London electors. The replies are elicited by questions concerning various aspects of current political issues, attitudes towards government, the political parties and party leaders, and support for democratic procedures.

The success or failure of the theory as a whole together with modifications suggested by data and the implications of unanticipated findings are assessed in Chapter 12. Five appendices then deal with a further investigation of 'agreement' in the data, survey design, the background to political issues discussed in the text, and construction of various measures used in the analysis. It is hoped that this layout will

---

[15] See the chapters on the political development of these listed countries in R. A. Dahl, *Political Oppositions in Western Democracies* (New Haven, Conn.: Yale University Press, 1966).

simulate for the reader the thought-processes involved in selecting and preparing predictive theory for empirical tests, in checking whether predictions correctly anticipate the actual data, and in deciding over-all whether the theory has been upheld or refuted by the minimal but searching test[16] offered by the British evidence.

SURVEY EVIDENCE

The predictions derived from the subsequent discussion describe patterns of agreement which will be encountered in the responses of politicians and electors in any stable democracy, if assumptions on which the predictions are based are, in fact, true. Just such a check against empirical evidence is made possible by the result of a survey conducted among London politicans and electors in the first half of 1962. The survey is described fully in Appendix A, but some of its out-standing features may be summarized here. The politicians (eighty in the original sample, fifty-nine interviewed) were drawn at random from backbench M.Ps. (Members of Parliament) and from Parliamentary candidates of the Conservative and Labour parties for the whole Greater London area. The systematic sample of electors (203 origi-nally, 147 interviewed) was drawn from a narrower area inside Greater London, which was, however, representative of the whole in terms of social class. To ensure strict comparability between the samples they were interviewed concurrently and with identical schedules. Since the questions ranged over all the topics mentioned above, the replies are capable of revealing the full range of political agreement which may exist in the stable democracy of Great Britain at one point in time. Because the data relate to events only up to mid-1962, however, sub-sequent discussion will not seek to comment on developments after that time.

Although in a study such as the present one tends to generalize from the London data actually being analyzed to the state of affairs in Britain as a whole, the substantial social and political differences ex-isting between London and more distant regions should be kept in mind. Social influences on voting habits for example are known to differ from one part of the United Kingdom to another, as do certain polit-ical attitudes and identifications.[17] Urban-rural differences as well as variations in size among cities themselves may have some effective upon

---

[16] See the first section of Chapter 2 for a full discussion of how far British data on agreement offer a test of the Dahl-Key theory.

[17] I. Budge and D. W. Urwin, *Scottish Political Behaviour* (London: Long-mans, 1966), Chaps. 5 and 9.

feelings of political efficacy.[18] Not enough work has been done in areas directly related to the present research to say with any certainty how the London setting affects the findings. One presumption argued more fully in Appendix A is that the relatively homogeneous environment of the electoral sample increases its issue-agreement *vis-à-vis* politicians and that this slightly biases data against the predictions. It may furthermore be assumed that London life subjects electors to many more social changes and strains—brings them, for example, into closer contact with immigrants—than is the case in less urbanized areas of Britain. Thus findings on their tolerance of minorities and regard for Government may underestimate the levels found elsewhere and again constitute a severer test of the theoretical predictions. But these assumptions remain essentially speculative: their confirmation awaits further empirical research. Bounded as they are by time and place, the London data cannot be said to offer a final and conclusive test of the theories discussed hereafter—no one data-set can. But it does provide a minimal test which the theories must pass to be given even provisional acceptance.

---

[18] Almond and Verba, *op. cit.*, pp. 167, 234.

1

THEORETICAL BACKGROUND

SYNOPSIS

If we concentrate on psychological approaches, the theories advanced to explain democratic stability fall into three main types which are discussed separately below. All seek to show why the conflicts that admittedly emerge between various parties and groups in a democracy and that are freely vocalized as a result of the various freedoms which exist in that type of political system do not generally spread to include the essential constitutional procedures in terms of which conflicts are waged. This general immunity of the central procedures from factional conflict is intriguing because parties and pressure groups in stable democracies are perfectly capable, as experience has shown, of fighting over topics that have at previous times been considered outside politics. Economics, religion, the family, matters of personal privacy have all been drawn in, but not major procedures. Why does party competition usually eschew this one topic in stable democracies when in other systems it is capable of repeatedly bringing established procedures into the very center of controversy?

The theories reviewed in this chapter differ in the type of explanation they provide for the generally non-controversial status of procedures. The first theories we consider stress the differences that occur between patterns of cleavage found in stable democracies compared with patterns of cleavage in other systems. The second group emphasize the role played by unconscious and instinctive political reactions —by habit and apathy—in stabilizing democratic politics. The third kind of theory suggests a linkage between levels of agreement and stability. Proponents of consensus theories differ on the precise nature of this linkage, but the most plausible account seems to be provided by Dahl and Key, who consider that stability is ensured through the greater support given to democratic procedures by the people who lead the parties and, hence, who take the main part in setting the terms on which parties compete. These are the political activists. This Dahl-Key theory of differentiated agreement is spelled out in detail in Chapter 2; in Chapter 1 its relationship to the other psychological theories is examined, together with its development from previous research.

CONFLICT THEORIES

A. The Conflict Consolidation Theory

This first type of explanation for democratic stability sees in democratic conflict a force which itself limits the spread of conflict to essential constitutional arrangements. It tends to emphasize the predominance of conflict in democratic society. It stresses the multiplicity of divisions running through democratic political life and the impossibility of suppressing them without destroying democracy itself. Bypassing the larger question of how the system holds together at all, it asks more immediately how even a simple majority can be created to decide a single issue. Attention thus becomes focused on the replacement of multiple conflicts by one general conflict. It seems to be assumed that the creation of a majority solves the great problem of how democratic procedures can remain outside the partisan battle.

Thus E. E. Schattschneider speaks of the democratic political process as a management of conflict, with the government itself taking sides and defining the alternatives to its own advantage.[1] Conflict itself resolves many conflicts, for the issues which the government promotes and on which feeling is most intense crowd out lesser issues. Moreover any widespread division promotes a consolidation of forces in the opposed camps, and this contributes to a general unification of political feeling in the democracy.

B. The Theory of Cross-Cutting Cleavages

A different theory similarly focuses on conflict as the major reality of democratic politics. This is the idea that cross-cutting conflicts weaken each other. Madison, in Paper 10 of *The Federalist*, may be regarded as the classical exponent of a similar view.

In a complex modern democracy there are large numbers of competing or overlapping interests and a large number of issues being de-

---

[1] E. E. Schattschneider, "Intensity, Visibility, Direction and Scope," *APSR*, 51 (1957), 935, 936, 937, 940.

bated at any one time. Given this situation, most individuals are liable to become members of the majority on some issues and members of the minority on others. The effect is to restrain them as members of the majority from flagrantly breaking any procedural rules, lest they suffer from similar breaches by another majority in a case where they are members of the minority. According to such an interpretation democracy can function very well so long as conflicts do not become linked into the same profound cleavage over a variety of questions. For in that case members of the majority would have no reason to exercise political self-restraint, never being likely to become members of a minority.[2]

Schattschneider criticises this theory on the ground that it too easily assumes the equal intensity of conflict, *i.e.*, assumes that all cleavages are equally important to participants in the political process. Only on that condition would cross-cutting cleavages actually inhibit majorities from crushing minorities. Otherwise they would take the chance of losing procedural guarantees on their less strongly held preferences for the sake of gaining procedural advantages on what they considered the central issue.

The theory can easily meet Schattschneider's criticism however by changing the argument outlined above so that it refers not simply to cross-cutting conflicts of any kind, but only to cross-cutting conflicts which are felt to be of equal importance. A situation where two or more issues of equal importance produce cross-cutting distributions of opinion would in this reformulated argument be taken as favoring the persistence of democratic procedures.

Even so, both conflict theories offer a somewhat limited solution to the puzzle of viable democracy. Conflict seems to form the only factor that need be taken into account, and it provides a remedy to its own ills. Either the politicians promote a major conflict to crowd out all others, as Schattschneider implies, or, on the contrary, the coexistence of several cross-cutting conflicts of equal intensity promotes self-restraint and respect for procedural guarantees among members of the shifting majorities.

Certainly one ought to recognize the essential truth contained in both these explanations. Cleavages are not necessarily cumulative and reinforcing. Concentration on one issue involves neglect of others. Concurrent membership in majorities and minorities probably fosters habits of political self-denial necessary for the operation of democ-

---

[2] Current proponents of this theory include S. M. Lipset. See his *Political Man* (Garden City, N.Y.: Doubleday, 1960), p. 88.

racy.[3] Yet Schattschneider offers no reason why politicians who create a majority on their one overriding division stop short of using it to create a dictatorship or check the feelings engendered by it short of civil war. Nor do the theorists of cross-cutting divisions proffer any factor that could explain the resolution of disputed issues. Everyone has veto power through his membership in some majority, a condition conducive to *immobilisme* and the breakthrough to binding decisions by violent means.[4]

But if conflicts do not automatically impose their own limits upon the process of division in stable democracies, what other factors can explain the undoubted coexistence of political disputes with a relatively stable constitutional framework?

THEORIES OF HABITUAL BEHAVIOR AND APATHY

The second group of theorists who attempt to account for democratic stability are sufficiently impressed by the extent to which conflict pervades politics to be skeptical about the existence of any agreements on fundamental political procedures. In contrast to the theorists just discussed they do not, however, trust solely to conflict to keep the process of controversy and division from bringing the system down.

A. The Theory of Habitual Behavior

One theorist of this school, C. J. Friedrich, invokes unconscious habits of democratic behavior as checks upon conscious controversy.[5] In his view respect for civil liberties is such a behavior pattern. Even the central "agreement to disagree" is simply a way of acting. When circumstances change, as in time of emergency, the behavior changes too. Thus many democratic freedoms are suspended for the duration of a war. If any agreements do exist in a democracy, they are temporary and limited coalitions formed to get immediate action, like the ones envisaged by Schattschneider. But the population continues to be

---

[3] R. A. Dahl explicitly considers these characteristics of issue cleavages, together with the modality of opinion distributions, in the context of other factors making for democratic stability. See R. A. Dahl, *Political Oppositions in Western Democracies* (New Haven, Conn.: Yale University Press, 1966), Chap. 12.

[4] Dahl, in fact, considers that a "low coincidence [of opinion distributions], if of equal salience, strengthens incentives for pressing conflicting opinions." *Ibid.*, p. 381.

[5] C. J. Friedrich, *The New Image of the Common Man* (Boston: Beacon Press, 1950), Chap. 5 *passim*.

divided on more fundamental topics such as religion, questions of so-cial class and of culture.

One has to take the theory of habitual behavior seriously because it underlines the essential truth that a participant in the democratic process is not perpetually examining his conscience to see whether actions taken to gain concrete political ends infringe upon the grand ideals of democracy. Taking his political end for granted, he pursues it through strategies which are largely determined by the patterns of behavior already existing inside the democratic society. Nor is it a valid objection to the theory of habitual behavior to say that habits by themselves explain nothing unless we also know what caused the habit: over short periods of time it is perfectly legitimate to associate the existence of certain habits with the stability of one democratic system and the instability of another.

One can, however, legitimately object to Friedrich's position on the grounds that it contradicts present knowledge about the interplay between acts and attitudes in human behavior. The most detailed and systematic analyses of such interplay in a political context are con-tained in the voting studies. Certainly these studies reveal that "habits" —such as the "habit" of voting the same way as one's social group—may influence voting more than some conscious attitudes to political ques-tions.[6] But they also reveal that where a widespread behavioral pattern exists, large numbers of people are aware that it does exist.[7] It there-fore seems unrealistic for Friedrich to maintain that large masses of people can act in the same way without being aware of their behav-ioral agreement and without inferring from it an attitudinal agreement on certain norms of conduct.

The voting studies also demonstrate that certain conscious atti-tudes—such as the feeling that one belongs to a certain political party[8] or to a particular social class[9]—affect voting more directly than mem-bership of demographic groupings demarcated by income or occupa-tion which are not the focus of conscious loyalties. Many participants

---

[6] B. Berelson, P. F. Lazarsfeld, and W. McPhee, *Voting* (Chicago: University of Chicago Press, 1955), pp. 66–67.

[7] *Ibid.*, pp. 77–78.

[8] For the influence of "party identification" and its superiority to demographic characteristics as a predictor of voting choice, see A. Campbell, G. Gurin, and W. Miller, *The Voter Decides* (Evanston, Ill.: Row, Peterson, 1954), pp. 73, 85–86, 109.

[9] For the stronger influence of "self-assigned class" on voting than member-ship in a social class assigned on the basis of income, see (for Britain) M. Benney, A. P. Gray, and R. H. Pear, *How People Vote* (London: Routledge, 1956), p. 115. Evidence for the United States is given in H. Eulau, *Class and Party in the Eisen-hower Years* (New York: Free Press of Glencoe, 1962), p. 66.

in the political process are quite conscious, therefore, of the meaning and implications of their political habits; these participants do many times form opinions and express them at the polls. Thus one cannot say with certainty whether unconscious habits or conscious attitudes are more important in explaining adherence to democratic processes. Perhaps their relative importance varies according to circumstances, but the evidence shows that cognitive processes cannot be ignored.

In times of peace and stability people may indeed pursue their political ends according to settled habits without reflecting very much upon their conduct. But in periods of stress and upheaval, when many settled habits are being disrupted, people's pro-democratic preferences and perceptions of shared agreements may be held at a much more conscious level and may act as powerful forces supporting adherence to established processes. Otherwise any temporary suspension of democratic practices would become permanent, since once the old habits had been disrupted, people would settle down to new habits of non-democratic behavior and would feel no impulse to return to the old. In Britain during the Second World War, for example, many democratic safeguards were suspended. This suspension did not continue after the end of the War, although by that time many new habits of behavior had evolved. Full democratic procedures were restored, and the most obvious explanation for their restoration is surely that people believed that they ought to be restored, rather than that they blindly and unconsciously reverted to old habits once the emergency was over. Thus an explanation that ignores people's own opinions and that makes democratic behavior merely a blind response to circumstance does not adequately account for the continuance of democratic processes after periods of emergency suspension.

B. The Patriotism-Apathy Theory

It has also been argued that the unconscious attitudes that buttress democracy are not really agreement on its superiority to other political systems. These supportive attitudes may largely consist of apathy and a sense of political ineffectiveness on the part of large segments of the population, feelings that discourage them from challenging established institutions. On the other hand, those persons most inclined to challenge democratic procedures for reasons of personality (such as authoritarian tendencies) may be discouraged from so doing out of a feeling of nationalism and of contempt for other countries.[10]

---

[10] H. McClosky, "Consensus and Ideology in American Politics," *APSR*, 58 (1964), 361–82, esp. 378.

However neither apathy nor patriotism in themselves explain the continuance of democratic processes and the defeat of internal attempts to replace them by more authoritarian procedures. For during internal crises of the democratic order the apathetic would presumably remain apathetic, and those temperamentally inclined to sympathy with anti-democratic movements would not be hampered by patriotic motives from aiding any anti-democratic initiative. Patriotism is an attitude common to democracies and authoritarian regimes alike. It could stimulate opposition to external attempts to subvert the democratic system, but it is hard to see that it would necessarily operate against purely domestic subversion.[11]

CONSENSUS THEORIES

The third type of theory invokes an agreement upon some sort of democratic norms as the most likely explanation for democratic stability. Since the whole of the present study is devoted to discussing and testing a theory of this type, it is as well to clarify immediately what the implications of such theories are and to set forth in detail the criticisms which can be levelled against them.

In many ways this type of theory is the most obvious and simple of the explanations which have been advanced in connection with the phenomenon of viable democracy. If violence is not employed to gain political ends, one naturally expects to discover the existence of an understanding that violence will not be employed. If certain procedures are followed before decisions become binding, one looks for an agreement to abide by such procedures. Speculation on the existence and nature of such "democratic agreements" has always been prominent in the writings of analysts of American politics; celebrated ex-

---

[11] Figures from Almond and Verba's five-nation study indicate, however, that the aspect of the nation in which pride is felt may vary between stable and unstable democracies. In Britain and America feelings of patriotism include pride in existent political institutions, whereas in Italy pride is directed to the country itself and achievements in art. See G. A. Almond and S. Verba, *The Civic Culture* (Princeton, N.J.: Princeton University Press, 1963), p. 102. However, certain American survey findings indicate that the actual operation of such institutions is not very well understood by a large part of the population. See J. W. Prothro and C. M. Grigg, "Fundamental Principles of Democracy: Bases of Agreement and Disagreement," *Journal of Politics*, 22 (1960), 276–94, and McClosky, *op. cit.* Thus pride in American political institutions seems to be felt toward the symbols rather than toward the actual operating institutions. The experience of the Roman Empire and of the French Second Empire suggests that democratic institutions (such as equal voting rights for all citizens) may be used as symbols to generate loyalty toward an authoritarian regime. The patriotism experienced by authoritarian elements in a stable democracy would, therefore, not necessarily hinder them from subverting actual democratic procedures while retaining the formal symbolic institutions.

amples are Toqueville and Bryce.[12] British scholars have also viewed such agreements as necessary to democratic stability.[13]

Recently a powerful attack has been mounted on any theory which would regard the existence of agreement as prerequisite to the smooth functioning of democratic processes. What makes the criticism even more penetrating is the fact that it has originated with investigators who have done a great deal to explore the distribution of democratic agreements among the population of the United States.[14] Briefly, the challenge relates to the most fundamental assumption of the theory: that there is a direct relationship between what people say they believe and what they actually do. Prothro and Grigg point to the discrepancy between the view of 42 percent of their sample of Tallahassee (Florida) electors that "a Negro should not be allowed to run for mayor of this city" and the fact that a few months before the survey a Negro actually did conduct an active campaign for that office without any attempt being made to stop him. McClosky very convincingly criticizes the tendency of highly articulate and verbally skilled academics to place more value than the facts warrant upon such factors as ideas, rational choice and consensus.[15] This criticism seems to be a generalization from the considerable discrepancies, inconsistancies and disagreements which he discovered to exist in attitudes to democracy displayed by the American population to the conclusion that such attitudes exert little or no effect on their actual behaviour.

Leaving aside the question of whether any democratic beliefs are entirely rational, the existence of a complete hiatus between pro- or anti-democratic beliefs and action would invalidate any consensual explanation of democratic stability. If agreement on statements of belief has no relevance to on-going political processes then one must seek other explanatory variables which have such relevance.

There is little direct evidence on the carryover from statements of beliefs and intentions about democracy to actual behaviour, except for the negative finding on anti-Negro sentiments cited by Prothro and Grigg. However the voting studies offer much evidence about the carryover from popular statements to behaviour associated with the general political processes of functioning democracies. There are the findings already cited in the previous section of the discussion on

---

[12] Alexis de Tocqueville, *Democracy in America*, 1 (New York: Vintage Books, 1960), 298–337, 397–439, and James Bryce, *The American Commonwealth* (New York: Macmillan, 1918), Chaps. 78–85 *passim*.

[13] E. Barker, *Reflections on Government* (New York: Galaxy, 1958), p. 63.

[14] Prothro and Grigg, *op. cit.*, pp. 293–94, and McClosky, *op. cit.*, p. 375.

[15] *Ibid.*, pp. 378–79.

the political effects of feelings of warmth toward a party or of a sense of belonging to a particular class. Voters' own feelings about political candidates and about broad issues and the information available to them on specific issues affect their voting choice more immediately than any factors not perceptible to them, such as their membership of purely demographic groups. Voters' own statements of how they intend to vote, taken a month or more before the election, are strongly correlated with their actual vote.[16] Perhaps even more immediately related to this argument is the discovery that voters' own feelings about their moral duty to vote directly affect their actual turnout at the polls.[17]

These examples all demonstrate how beliefs and opinions do prompt political action. There seems no good general ground, therefore, for denying that shared beliefs and opinions about democracy could affect political action.

No doubt the relationship between statements of intention and actual behavior may vary enormously with the ability of the individual to put his beliefs into action. It rests very much with the single person whether he will vote or not and in what way he will vote. He will probably look for a lead or for group support before he indulges in riotous or illegal action or takes steps against political threats to the institutions of which he approves. Sometimes he may not get a lead or may fail to take action as a consequence of doubts about the extent to which his beliefs are shared. To say this is not to agree that beliefs are unimportant in influencing collective action, but to point to conditions under which they may assume more or less prominence as motivating factors in such behavior. And one of these conditions is itself a cognition: namely, the perception that one's beliefs are in fact challenged or that a large group of people share one's views.

Moreover critics of the agreement or consensus theories of democratic stability have themselves demonstrated in their empirical research that democratic agreements do exist in varying degrees among different sections of the population of at least one stable democracy, the United States. It is an inference that goes beyond the immediate evidence to argue that such agreements are necessarily prerequisites for the stability of American democracy, but it is an inference going

---

[16] A. Campbell, P. Converse, W. Miller, and D. Stokes, *The American Voter* (New York: Wiley, 1960), Chaps. 4 and 8, esp. pp. 65 and 74. Campbell and his associates point out that voters' own statements of their intentions have usually been vastly more accurate in predicting voting choice than any other—and especially "objective"—indicators.

[17] Campbell, *et al.*, *The Voter Decides, op. cit.*, Appendix B.

even further beyond the findings to contend that such agreements are not essential to the continuance of democratic procedures.[18]

The arguments of McClosky and Prothro and Grigg and the survey evidence cited from the voting studies bear on the relationship of ideas to action among the whole of a democratic population. As will be seen, however, not all consensual theories attribute equal weight in the functioning of stable democracy to agreement among all sections of the population. The Dahl-Key theory discussed in ensuing chapters, in fact, attaches most importance to agreement on democratic procedures among practising politicians and the better educated and politically aware elements generally. The relationship between opinion and action, as McClosky points out, is likely to be most consistent among highly articulate and verbally skilled persons.[19] It is on the relationship of agreement to action among just such groups that the Dahl-Key theory places greatest weight.

The balance of the evidence cited above indicates that democratic beliefs and opinions are capable of affecting behavior, particularly among the politically involved. Consequently it appears plausible to speculate that the existence of some sort of agreement about the desirability of democratic practices is necessary for the good functioning of democracy. But the premises of this statement should be clearly understood. There is no implication that agreements are the only prerequisites for stable democracy. Habitual behavior, cross-cutting conflicts of equal intensity, the limited coalition-building of pragmatic politicians, the low political effectiveness of potentially hostile elements, unthinking patriotism—all or some of these factors may have to be present before democratic stability can be assured. Some may even have to be present to generate agreement in the first place. All that is being maintained is that agreement is a necessary condition for democratic stability. Nothing has been said about agreements being sufficient of themselves to attain democratic stability.[20]

The Distribution of Democratic Agreements

To conclude that agreements are necessary is not to have mapped out their distribution in democratic societies. Theorists who subscribe to the general explanation differ markedly in their answers to the specific question of who must agree on what with whom?

---

[18] As Prothro and Grigg note in *op. cit.*, p. 293.

[19] McClosky, *op. cit.*, p. 378.

[20] The bearing of the survey evidence on the relationship between the various factors discussed up to this point, democratic agreement and democratic stability, is assessed at the end of Chapter 12.

If the stability of democratic society rests upon some sort of agreement, it seems plausible to maintain that agreement must be focused on basic democratic principles (must include, for example, a belief in freedom) and that it must extend to all, or at least to a majority, of members of the democratic population. Something like this position is held by Griffiths and Pennock in their discussion of "Cultural Prerequisites to a Successfully Functioning Democracy."[21] Although the participants differed on the point of what factors brought about such agreement, they were at one in stating that a fundamental, pervasive and relatively intense agreement was necessary for the maintenance of democratic procedures.

As mentioned above C. J. Friedrich speculates on the existence of quite a different type of democratic agreement. If agreements do exist in democratic society, they refer to limited, concrete objectives, not to the great fundamentals—religion, class, culture, constitutional arrangements—of political or non-political life. The politician brings people together on specific issues, in spite of their disagreements on more general matters.[22]

These grand alternatives can be debated indefinitely in the abstract; however, empirical research provides a test of their claims. The basic work of Prothro and Grigg shows that widespread agreement existed between samples drawn from two regions of the United States when they were confronted with highly generalized statements of the democratic creed (such as "the minority should be free to criticize majority decisions"). There was considerable divergence, however, on the way in which such principles should be applied to situations in which the minority was Communist or Negro.

Prothro and Grigg point out that two explanations can be offered for their findings. One can maintain that agreement on the most general beliefs is a more powerful determinant of behavior than disagreement on more specific beliefs. This interpretation would account for the discrepancy between the anti-Negro sentiments of large numbers in Tallahassee and their failure to take action against the Negro who ran for mayor. According to this view adherence to the general principle that "people in the minority should be free to try to win majority support for their opinions" is stronger than the feeling that a Negro should not be allowed to run for mayor. Equally, however, the discrepancy between widespread endorsement of the anti-Negro statement and the absence of anti-Negro action could be accounted for by

---

[21] E. S. Griffiths, J. Plamenatz, and J. R. Pennock, "Cultural Prerequisites to a Successfully Functioning Democracy," *APSR*, 50 (1956), 101–37.

[22] Friedrich, *op. cit.*, Chap. 5.

Friedrich's view that habits of democratic behavior direct action independently of belief. The latter interpretation is favored by Prothro and Grigg themselves.[23]

The first possible explanation of the findings—that general beliefs are the most powerful determinants of behavior—would seem to offer support to Griffiths' and Pennock's assumption of the existence of a pervasive agreement on democratic fundamentals.[24] But the assumption behind their assumption was surely that most people are capable of accurately applying general beliefs on fundamental democratic principles to the specific situations in which they find themselves. Democracy would benefit remarkably little from general agreements to tolerate minorities if the persons who agreed did not tolerate the Negroes or Communists who constitute the actual minority in real life situations. Thus the hiatus in many people's logical processes which Prothro and Grigg reveal is acutely embarrassing for the assumptions behind Griffiths' and Pennock's discussion.

But the fact that the population disagreed on the examples of concrete, limited action with which they were confronted is equally embarrassing for Friedrich's contention that the only agreements which can possibly exist among a democratic population are on such concrete limited action with specific objectives. Similarly the alacrity with which the population endorsed general abstract principles of democracy hardly bears out his contention that there is no agreement on political fundamentals.

There are findings other than those of Prothro and Grigg which bear on the discussion. V. O. Key[25] presents survey data which show a reasonably high level of electoral agreement on specific (although wide) issues, *e.g.*, support of public education. This high level of agreement also existed on a kind of issue on which Prothro and Grigg did not find agreement: the majority of a national sample examined by Key disagreed strongly with a proposal to fire government workers suspected of communism. This reaction shows that a democratic population is capable of agreeing in support of democratic practices on

---

[23] Prothro and Grigg, *op. cit.*, pp. 293–94. Of course there are other possible explanations for the discrepancy, *e.g.*, that the incentives to anti-democratic action were not in this case great enough.

[24] Griffiths, *et al.*, *op. cit.*, pp. 104, 106, 129–30.

[25] V. O. Key, Jr., *Public Opinion and American Democracy* (New York: Knopf, 1961), pp. 38, 50. On the basis of Prothro and Grigg's research, Key discounts the existence of an agreement on political fundamentals which is anything more than a recognition of the legitimacy of the regime. For an interpretation corresponding to that in the text, see R. A. Dahl, *Who Governs?* (New Haven, Conn.: Yale University Press, 1961), p. 316.

some specific policy matters. But in itself such a finding does not settle the question of whether some sort of agreement on fundamentals as opposed to specific agreements is necessary for democratic stability.

From a survey designed to contrast the attitudes of community leaders with those of the general population, Stouffer[26] shows that leaders were more ready to tolerate non-conformists and to support civil liberties and civil rights than their followers no matter what kind of group was examined. Moreover the leaders came closer to one another's views than did their respective followings. Supporting evidence for these findings comes from A. M. Rose's comparison between the leaders of state-wide organizations in Minnesota and a sample of the population.[27] A greater proportion of leaders than ordinary respondents were satisfied with democratic processes and, predictably, leaders were more active in the community.

Stouffer's research introduces a new dimension into the discussion. He attempts to answer the 'who' parts of the original question of who agrees to what, with whom?, whereas Griffith and Friedrich tended to talk exclusively of the "what."

Undoubtedly the most comprehensive investigation to date of the distribution of various kinds of agreement among a democratic population is that of Herbert McClosky.[28] Briefly summarized McClosky's research shows that agreement to procedural rules of democracy is higher among the political activists than among the American population as a whole. Moreover, activists' sense of political futility is less and their trust in government greater. Even among the population, however, agreement with some democratic principles is very high (for example, 85 percent of the general electorate expressed their "faith in freedom" as measured by some very specific cases indeed). On the other hand activists turned out to be very much divided among themselves on the principle of equality, whether this referred to equal status

---

[26] S. Stouffer, *Communism, Conformity and Civil Liberties* (Garden City, N.Y.: Doubleday, 1955), *passim.*, esp. Chap. 3.

[27] A. M. Rose, "Alienation and Participation," *American Sociological Review*, 27 (1962), 836–38. Rose warns the reader, however, that the response rate to the survey of group leaders was extremely low.

[28] McClosky, *op. cit.* The questions employed by McClosky to measure democratic beliefs were dichotomized alternatives (agree-disagree) of the type: "The majority has the right to abolish minorities if it wants to." "People who hate our way of life should still have a chance to talk and be heard," etc. They are grouped under "Responses to Rules of the Game," "Responses Expressing Faith in Freedom," "Responses on Specific Applications of Freedom of Speech, Procedural Rights, and Other Civil Liberties," "Responses Expressing Belief in Equality," "Responses Expressing Trust, Distrust and Cynicism Toward Government, Politics and Politicians."

for all regardless of color, the equal capability of all to take part in government, or questions of providing for all according to their needs. Since McClosky regards belief in equality as one constituent of democratic beliefs, he is inclined, as noted earlier, to discount the importance of agreement among any section of the population in the functioning of a stable democracy. He is confirmed in this opinion by the fact that his activists, to a much greater extent than the population at large, seem to divide strongly on political issues.

McClosky's discussion makes two points which bear upon the argument as it stands at the moment. First, he finds that different groups in the population do vary in the extent to which they endorse democratic norms. In McClosky's, Stouffer's and Rose's surveys persons occupying leadership positions of various kinds were revealed as more democratic in their beliefs than the general population. McClosky further divided the general population into educational and occupational strata and distinguished groups by their intellectual interests. Those with more education, better jobs, and intellectual interests tended to give more support to democratic procedures.[29] Prothro and Grigg also discovered that those electors with more education were on the democratic side in specific situations to a significantly greater extent than those with less education, as were richer electors when compared with poorer.[30]

McClosky's study also shows that the general population does agree with the democratic position in certain very specific cases. This particular finding accords with that cited by V. O. Key and contradicts to some extent those of Prothro and Grigg.

Thus there are minor discrepancies between the findings of different investigators. Generally however, all empirical research points to the conclusion that agreements on democratic procedures do differ in their extent and content (and by implication, in their intensity) between the members of strata distinguished on the basis of education, income and political activity.

Why should this be so? There is in fact a plausible explanation of how such contrasts develop. Official political ideology sufficiently permeates the outlook of most citizens to make commitment to highly abstract principles of democracy widespread. The most powerful instruments of socialization—the educational system and the family—pass this ideology on to children. The principle that the majority should decide and the minority be tolerated also lies behind a great many utter-

---

[29] *Ibid.*, p. 372.
[30] Prothro and Grigg, *op. cit.*, pp. 287–88.

ances of the mass media in all sorts of non-political contexts. All these agencies of socialization thus instil in most citizens a reasonably consistent commitment to democracy at an abstract level. On the other hand, when the media describe real-life situations, their message tends to mirror the contradictions of actual democratic society, where some minorities such as Communists appear as dangers to the political system which practices the toleration of minorities, and where the popular verbiage of politics expresses strong feelings against political opponents wishing to carry a controversial program even if they do constitute a majority. Conflicting and disturbing emotions of class hostility, grievances against employers and Trade Union chiefs, discrimination against foreign immigrants, undercutting wage levels and housing standards are all assimilated by the child at the same time as the fine clear simple message of abstract democracy. Intolerance towards certain specific groups is learned simultaneously with abstract ideals of general tolerance.

In these circumstances it seems easy for the mass of ordinary people to accept double standards. Asked about democratic principles in the abstract they utter unimpeachable sentiments of support for majority rule and minority rights. Confronted with a specific situation which involves particular majorities or particular minorities they are apt to respond to its substantive content as it affects their immediate interests. If they feel their interests threatened they are likely without reflecting on whether or not it conforms to general democratic principles, to favour any course of action which would protect them. Since they have been oriented to both abstract and specific responses simultaneously, it is difficult for them to perceive any inconsistency. Besides, most people are not trained to bring specific situations under general principles.

The persons who tend to more consistency in their political outlook are by contrast those whose training or circumstances do cause them to reason from general principles to actual situations and back again. Education is designed to emphasize this habit and it probably also infects those who mix with better educated people even if they have had little education themselves—that is to say, the wealthier groups regardless of education. Political activists are more likely to have come from these groups in any case, and, moreover, they are constantly concerned with the regulation of specific courses of action by general legislation. It is therefore quite natural for them to regulate their specific political reactions by general principles. Since the general principles to which they adhere are highly democratic—for the same reasons as those influencing the general population—their greater consistency leads to greater support of democracy in specific cases, which is precisely the empirical finding.

Following this reasoning, the most promising approach is now to explore the differing and possibly complementary forms which the agreement to democratic norms takes among leaders and different groups in the general population. R. A. Dahl and V. O. Key have followed this line of argument in considerable detail.

Differentiated Agreement: Dahl and Key

For the purpose of explaining democratic stability Dahl regards three groups as particularly relevant: the body of citizens generally uninterested in politics; the political stratum (those more interested and involved); and the professional politicians.[31] He assumes on the evidence provided by Prothro and Grigg that the uninterested citizens believe in the very general assumptions of the democratic system and accept that American institutions embody such assumptions.[32] He argues further that the politically involved citizens share a higher measure of agreement on both the general norms of the system and the way they are currently applied to concrete situations. But he regards the politicians as the great bulwark of democratic procedures. Not only are they more keenly aware of what democratic operating rules are, and more agreed on their interpretation, but their vested interest in and attachment to the system which keeps them at the center of affairs and utilizes their peculiar skills prompts them to support it against any threats of disruption. Their superior resources and political skills are usually successful in crushing opposition to the prevailing regime whether it comes from deviants in their own ranks or challengers from outside. In a struggle they can rely on the majority of the political stratum and can appeal to the general beliefs held by the rest of the population. Dahl cites as examples of struggles among politicians over existing norms Roosevelt's proposal of 1937 to change the composition of the Supreme Court; McCarthy's activities in 1954; and the struggle

---

[31] Dahl's explanation for democratic stability is a simplified model of reality. There are, of course, many other groups in the political system than those mentioned here, and there are many different shades of involvement. Dahl's point is that the phenomenon of stability can be understood in terms of the reactions of these three groups alone. Following from this, the relevant reactions of members of each of these groups are assumed to resemble those of other members more than they do those of non-members. (These are not Dahl's own comments, but rather are implications that emerge from his *Who Governs?*, *op. cit.*, pp. 90–94, 315–25.)

[32] The authors of *Voting* note the tendency to accept the actual result of the presidential election as the best possible one. See Berelson, *et al.*, *op. cit.*, p. 192.

over charter reform in New Haven, Connecticut in 1958. But these are exceptional crises. Normally the politicians agree on the question of political procedures out of a genuine belief in their merits.

V. O. Key starts from a concern to examine opinion among the general population on the everyday issues of politics, such matters, for example, as proposals to reduce taxation or to extend government social welfare services. He finds that the distribution of opinion on such matters reflects some widespread agreements as well as disagreements among the ordinary public, and that sometimes the public may not have opinions. On the issues examined by Key the percentage of "don't knows," *i.e.* those with no opinion on an issue, varied from twelve to sixty per cent.[33] The same distributions of opinion may have radically different consequences in cases where opinions are widely held and where they are held only by a minority.

The persons who do have opinions are not different people on different issues; rather, they are an identifiable group. Following Almond,[34] Key notes the presence of an "attentive public," well-informed and critical, within the general population. There is a great contrast between this "attentive public" and the rest of the general population. The latter constitutes a "mass public" whose members may or may not feel themselves to be affected by an issue but who, in any case, respond emotionally rather than critically.[35] The "attentive public" follows issues consistently and reasonably intelligently.

Pursuing this indication that different sections of the population may respond differently to issues, Key selects electors according to the best indicators of political involvement and interest he can find and demonstrates that their familiarity with issues is higher than that existing among those electors with medium and low orientations towards politics.[36] The highly involved electors in fact correspond to Dahl's "political stratum." Like Dahl, Key considers that among this "upper-activist stratum" agreement about democratic norms may exist at a relatively specific level;[37] for example, they are less likely to approve dismissal of government servants accused (without proof) of Communism.[38]

The discovery among the general population of a political stratum which is relatively more committed than others to democratic beliefs

---

[33] Key, *op. cit.*, pp. 78–79.
[34] G. A. Almond, *The American People and Foreign Policy* (New York: Praeger, 1960), pp. 139, 151, 228, 233.
[35] Key, *op. cit.*, pp. 15–16, 85ff.
[36] *Ibid.*, p. 185.
[37] *Ibid.*, p. 550.
[38] *Ibid.*, p. 188.

does not convince Key that he has found the mortar which binds together the divided fabric of democracy. In his discussion of the various distributions that opinion may take on an issue, he distinguishes multiple consensus, that is, the development of simultaneous concurrence by several groups within a public-supportive and permissive consensus and the consensus of decision.[39] The latter is the only type of agreement that may even loosely be considered to have a direct effect on policy formulation. There is, as he entitles the first section of his conclusion, "a missing piece of the puzzle." Policy can be concretely formulated and executed only by leaders. Public opinion itself is the result of an interplay between the actions and beliefs of such leaders and the beliefs of the population.[40] And these leaders are the active politicians, the "professionals" of Dahl's discussion.[41] It is their agreement on the essentials of the democratic system which enables it to operate as if there were general agreement on these questions. Thus Key's detailed analysis of electoral survey data brings him to a position which hardly differs from Dahl's theoretical formulation (although the latter is inclined to put more stress on the uninterested citizen's highly generalized attachment to democracy).[42]

Possible Criticisms of the Dahl–Key Theory of Differentiated Agreement

In effect Dahl and Key are saying that strong support for specific democratic procedures exists somewhere, and if it is shown by Prothro and Grigg not to exist among the general population, then it must occur among the politicians. But can strong democratic agreement plausibly be said to exist only among politicians, or on quite such specific and detailed matters as Dahl and Key seem to imply? Such implications are certainly necessary to support their explanation. But they are open to three possible criticisms.

1. The studies that have been made show agreements among legislators[43] to be rather general role-orientations. Certainly these orienta-

---

[39] *Ibid.*, pp. 536, 29–39.

[40] *Ibid.*, pp. 29–76.

[41] *Ibid.*, p. 51.

[42] Political participants are also divided into three groups, and a similar stress is laid on the role of leaders (in any type of political system) in H. D. Lasswell and A. Kaplan, *Power and Society* (New Haven, Conn.: Yale University Press, 1950), p. 201.

[43] D. R. Matthews, "Folkways of the U.S. Senate: Conformity to Group Norms and Legislative Effectiveness," *APSR*, 53 (1959), 1064–89, and J. Wahlke, H. Eulau, C. Buchanan, L. Ferguson, *The Legislative System* (New York: Wiley, 1962), Chap. 7.

tions stress the mutual tolerance and compromise necessary to the work of the chamber, but the limits that they impose on individual freedom of action in specific cases seem very broad. The crucial point is that one could adhere to all the general requirements of courtesy, reciprocity and institutional patriotism mentioned by Matthews in his study of the Senate or embodied in the "rules of the game" discovered by Wahlke and his associates in American State legislatures and still reject the specific democratic norms advanced by Prothro and Grigg. In the United States many Southern legislators do reject some of these specific applications of democratic norms, particularly when they entail Negro rights.

Conversely, the general population, while rejecting Prothro and Grigg's specific democratic norms, might well endorse role-orientations similar to those discovered among legislators. The general public has already been shown by Key and McClosky to adhere to some quite specific operating norms of democracy in any case, and this finding is borne out by the voting studies (for example, the finding that electors do agree to accept the results of elections).[44]

2. Any rules of the game peculiar to politicians may be so general and imprecise that it would be difficult to agree exactly on them in any case. For example Wahlke and his associates received hundreds of specific answers from the legislators they interviewed. Coded for the purpose of the study, they fell into very general role-orientations. But would the individual legislator be aware of the concordance between his answers and those of his fellows in the absence of a researcher who could devise categories to combine his answers with theirs? Would he consider such general agreement more important than points of disagreement? It is quite probable that the very uncertainty emphasized by Dahl and Key as surrounding the actions of the politician[45] shrouds not only the content of tacit agreements with his fellows but also the very question of whether they are agreed at all.

3. Following on this argument, one can allude to Matthews' remark that the Senate folkways that he discusses are obeyed no more perfectly than traffic laws.[46] The analogy appears imperfect, however, because such "rules" as courtesy and reciprocity are much more like road etiquette than like traffic laws. Like motorists, legislators are open to retaliation if they commit breaches of etiquette, but no automatic sanctions attend them. Politicians subject to multiple and unanticipated pressures from all sections of their society could hardly afford to

---

[44] Berelson, *et al., op. cit.,* p. 192.

[45] Dahl, *Who Governs?, op. cit.,* pp. 321–22, and Key, *op. cit.,* pp. 264–65.

[46] Matthews, *op. cit.,* p. 1086.

commit themselves more fully than others to a detailed and binding code. Yet this is an implication of Dahl's and Key's arguments.

The speculative nature of these three criticisms is worth noting. All extrapolate from the limited evidence at present available and point to the likely effect on agreement among leaders and electors. But no data exist at the time of writing that directly contradict the assertions of the Dahl-Key theory. Perhaps the uncertainty in which politicians live precludes their agreement relative to electors. On the other hand, the unavoidable intimacy in the legislative chamber and its committees and the many shared experiences that differentiate them from even their own most faithful party followers seem capable of promoting strong consensus among politicians in many areas. Perhaps politicians are unconscious of their agreements and perhaps not. Perhaps electors agree more than the evidence from Prothro and Grigg seems to show, but perhaps also politicians agree on more detailed matters than would appear from Wahlke's investigation.

Since agreement is the explanation for democratic stability that seems most promising for initial investigation, and since agreement does not seem to appear at a very specific level among the population, the logical next step in research is to postulate just such a theory of differentiated consensus as Dahl and Key have advanced and to investigate it as the ensuing discussion will do. None of its competitors among the consensual theories of stability explain the actual research findings so fully or consistently as this theory. Of course in selecting it for investigation, we run the risk common in empirical research of barking up the wrong tree. Consensus may not in fact be an influence on democratic stability, and differentiated consensus at least may be irrelevant. But in any case it will be something to have shown that it is irrelevant, and this can be done by the empirical test to which we propose to subject it.

EXTENSIONS OF THE DAHL–KEY THEORY OF DIFFERENTIATED AGREEMENT

1. Political Issues

One of the hardest points for any consensual theory of democracy to explain is the obvious fact that bitter political disagreements do exist in democracies. Such disagreements are often taken up by the political parties and very often become widely discussed political issues. On such issues the leaders themselves divide and, as far as their words can indicate, divide even more bitterly than the mass of the population. What then becomes of their hypothesized agreement on procedural rules? Dahl mentions cases where politicians have divided on major procedural issues, but he also points out that in the United States such cases are of rare occurrence.[47] This also seems to be true of other stable democracies.

But what do the consensual theorists say about substantive, non-procedural issues such as proposals to extend welfare legislation? It is obvious that in democracies leaders do divide for and against such proposals, often on a party basis. Dahl does not talk explicitly about such issues. Key mentions the implications that agreement or disagreement among leaders might have for electors' internal agreement or disagreement in these cases.[48] One can envisage four possible situations:

1. both leaders and electors agreed on an issue;
2. leaders are agreed on an issue and electors are divided;
3. leaders are divided on an issue and electors are agreed; or
4. both leaders and electors are divided on an issue.

Key can envisage the possibility of each of these situations' arising. The initiative toward agreement or disagreement is regarded as coming more often from leaders to electorate than vice versa; *i.e.*, leaders seem usually to divide first on such issues, and electors follow. But Key adds the rider that such straight comparisons of leaders and electorate assume that the issues in question are widely known and widely debated. Otherwise the interaction would take place only between leaders and citizens highly oriented to politics.

Evidence as to which of the four situations is actually most common in a stable democracy comes from a comparison by McClosky and associates of the stands taken by party activists and the general population on a range of political issues.[49] These investigators found more disagreements occurring among activists than among electors. Thus they concluded that the normal distributions of opinion on substantive issues in the United States at any rate was that envisaged under situation 3 above, where leaders were more divided among themselves on issues than were electors. This situation prevailed in the overwhelming majority of issues studied. McClosky and his colleagues, in fact, seem to generalize their results beyond the scope of political issues by remarking that little foundation was discovered for the belief that deep disagreements among the general population are ignored by leaders. In the later article already cited, McClosky revises this conclusion in

---

[47] Dahl, *Who Governs?*, *op. cit.*, pp. 320–21.

[48] Key, *op. cit.*, pp. 73–76.

[49] H. McClosky, P. J. Hoffman, and R. O'Hara, "Issue Conflict and Consensus among Party Leaders and Followers," *APSR*, 54 (1960), 406–27.

view of the greater agreement of his activists on most democratic values. He now attributes both the sharper cleavage over issues and greater consensus over democratic values to the superior ideological sophistication of the activists.[50]

But even if it is said that a sharp cleavage among leaders exists only on substantive issues, the statement may perhaps be queried. The issues with which McClosky and his associates dealt were without exception topics disputed between the parties, topics on which leaders had already divided.[51] Only situations 3 and 4 above—situations entailing some sort of division among leaders—were thus possible since an issue was defined in terms of party and, hence, activist division upon a topic. Since the leaders had in all cases necessarily taken a prior part in defining the issues about which they disagreed, while electors were not as committed, it was, in fact, likely that situation 3 would be more common.

But issues do exist on which divisions of opinion are not coincidental with party lines. There are even some issues on which party leaders do not disagree at all, *e.g.*, the prevention of outright private monopolies. In such a case there is some possibility that both leaders and electors may agree (situation 1 above) or that leaders agree and electors do not (situation 2 above). The findings of McClosky and his associates, therefore, seem to apply to one type of issue—issues on which the parties are clearly opposed—and not to all possible types.

The argument that at least some greater agreement on issues exists among politicians than among electors carries all the more weight if we ask how long an agreement to abide by (general and specific) procedural rules would survive prolonged and consistent controversy on all issues confronting the body politic. Empirically it seems likely that a considerable number of substantive agreements would have to exist simply to make the continuation of procedural agreements possible. It is unlikely, for example, that the results of elections would be accepted if they carried the threat of severe deprivation in every sphere of political activity. Dahl develops this point in another discussion.[52] And McClosky himself remarks that "democratic ideas and rules of the

---

[50] McClosky, *op. cit.*, p. 374.

[51] One should also note that of the 6,848 delegates and alternates to the Democratic and Republican conventions, whom McClosky took as his political leaders, only 3,020 returned usable questionnaires; and of 2,917 adult voters contacted in two successive national cross-section surveys, only 1,610 returned questionnaires. The self-selection of leaders particularly would seem to entail the danger of obtaining responses from the more active (and presumably more zealous) delegates. See McClosky, *et al.*, *op. cit.*, p. 408.

[52] R. A. Dahl, *Preface to Democratic Theory* (Chicago: University of Chicago Press, 1956), p. 77. See also Berelson, *et al.*, *op. cit.*, Chap. 9.

game are ordinarily encountered not in their pure form or in isolation but in substantive contexts that are bound to influence the ways in which we react to them."[53]

A further piece of evidence that supports the hypothesis of some greater issue agreements among politicians is offered by a study of resolutions put forward by English activists at the two major parties' Annual Conferences.[54] Fifty percent of the resolutions proffered at the Conservative Conference and 42 percent of those put forward at the Labour Conference were "non-partisan," *i.e.*, "tending to reflect pressure group concerns or general cultural values."[55] In other words many of these resolutions referred to non-controversial issues, *e.g.*, the desirability of increasing old age pensions. The other resolutions coming under this category referred to non-controversial points on issues that were generally disputed; *e.g.*, on secondary education, a major point of difference between the parties, 64 percent of Labour and 56 percent of Conservative resolutions were void of partisan content.[56]

In brief, even on issues disputed between the parties there are points of agreement among activists (who may be taken as the top level of Dahl's political stratum mixed with some politicians). A later investigation will be made of the exact nature of these points of agreement (Chapter 2). But the important fact is that there are whole issue areas that, far from dividing party activists, may bring them together in substantive agreements that could take some of the strain off procedures.

2. American Stability and Democratic Stability

The theory of differentiated agreement was evolved by Dahl and Key to account for the fact of American political stability in the face of what surveys revealed to be extensive procedural disagreements among the population. No comparable evidence exists on the extent of procedural consensus in other stable democracies. Yet it is natural to start from the assumption that what has been found true of one stable democracy will apply to others, and in particular to the United Kingdom with which subsequent discussion will be concerned.[57] It should be

---

[53] McClosky, *op. cit.*, p. 376.

[54] R. Rose, "Politicial Ideas of English Party Activists," *APSR*, 56 (1962), 360–71.

[55] *Ibid.*, pp. 362, 364.

[56] *Ibid.*, p. 366.

[57] On such institutional features as the legal system, highly organized pressure groups, their two-party systems and legislative arrangements, and on such cultural features as their common language, perceived character of the government, the aspects of the nation in which pride is expressed, the expectation of equal treatment

made clear, however, that any extension of the theory to stable democracies in general breaks the voluntary limitation to American democracy accepted by the two original proponents.[58] Any extended theory must explicitly assume that the populations of all stable democracies are divided on specific democratic procedures and such a theory should, moreover, be referred to as the generalized Dahl-Key theory in order to distinguish it from the more limited original version.

Discussion of the theory has revealed several possible weaknesses and limitations. But this discussion has also suggested that of all the explanations for democratic stability that have been reviewed, the Dahl-Key theory best accounts for existing findings and offers the best leads for further investigation. At its present stage, therefore, the discussion is best continued by provisionally accepting the general explanation that the theory gives of the workings of stable democracy, by extracting its implications, and by then testing against new data both the original assertions and the hypotheses that they suggest. Whether this test casts doubt upon or lends support to the theory, further light will have been shed on the ways in which consensus is linked to democratic stability.

---

by bureaucracy and police, frequency of discussing politics, feelings of civic competence, willingness to indulge in political and civic activity and numerous others, Britain and the United States resemble each other to a much greater extent than either resembles Italy, Germany, or Mexico, for example. See Almond and Verba, *op. cit.*, pp. 82, 102, 108, 120, 219, 267.

[58] Key's subject was specifically public opinion and *American* democracy. Dahl has commented in a personal communication to this author that he propounded his theory with regard to American conditions only.

2

THE GENERALIZED DAHL-KEY THEORY: EXTENSIONS AND PREDICTIONS

The General Form of the Dahl–Key Theory

Essentially the Dahl-Key theory deals with relationships between three different types of participant in the democratic political process. These consist of (a) professional full-time politicians (b) politically interested and involved citizens (the "political stratum"), and (c) politically uninterested and uninvolved citizens (the "general population"). The last group probably comprises the majority of citizens. Although all three groups overlap to some extent in real life, at different times and on different political questions they may be clearly distinguished for analytical purposes.[1]

The theory asserts that:

1. The politicians agree on quite specific operating norms of democratic behavior, as well as on more abstract norms, and are deeply committed to both.

2. The politically oriented citizens agree on the more abstract norms of democratic behavior and also on relatively specific procedures derived from the general norms. It is implied, I think, by both Dahl and Key that those norms are not held at quite the detailed level

---

[1] It should be noted that although members of the political stratum are distinguished from other electors for analytical purposes in this chapter, the comparisons with politicians reported later involve *all* electors in the "general population." The principal reason for using all electors in these comparisons lies in the small numbers of the electoral sample—147 in all. But it is also true that the inclusion of the more politically involved electors in these estimates of comparative agreement forms a conservative assumption in the analysis. If politicians were to be contrasted only with the politically uninvolved electors, it would be no wonder if they were discovered to agree much more, or to support democratic procedures to a much greater extent. When the electorate includes a group that resembles politicians in many respects, the contrasts between politicians and the body of electors become more striking and interesting.

⚥ of the politicians. Their commitment to the specific norms at any rate is not quite so intense as the politicians', though still strong.

3. ⸢The politically uninterested citizens agree on the more abstract norms of democratic behavior (Dahl). They tend, however, to disagree about specific applications of these norms. Although in isolated cases they may reach a consensus about some specific applications (Key), it seems that they are much less consistent in relating their abstract democratic beliefs to their everyday behavior.⸣ Intensity of feeling about democracy is probably least among this group, certainly where specific applications of abstract democratic principles are involved.

4. On the non-procedural political issues that constantly arise over substantive questions of public policy (in areas such as education, defense, foreign affairs etc.), it seems probable that any distribution of agreement or disagreement among the leaders may be accompanied by any distribution of agreement or disagreement among the general population. More specifically, any of the four situations outlined by Key and described above may occur on any issue.

5. ⸢However at any one time in a stable democracy, it does seem that a fair number of substantive issues will be subjects of agreement among the electorate and among the politicians⸣ (Key's permissive, supportive and multiple concensus). These, however, may not be the same issues for the politically uninterested citizens and the politically oriented citizens, or for either of these groups and the politicians.

6. ⸢The system works in normal times because those participants who are most attached to democratic ideals at the specific as well as at the general level are the very people who have most weight in the discussion and resolution of issues because of their high interest and activity in politics. Equally important, there is no sizable segment of the population alienated from the democratic system which feels intensely about issues⸣ (Key).[2] ⸢In case of a challenge to democratic norms, the most ardent defenders of the system are the most influential and skillful men in it—the politicians⸣(Dahl).

The theory is stated in the comparative terms of one group being more or less agreed than another partly because of the difficulty of measuring "high" or "low" absolutely.[3] This point will be discussed

---

[2] V. O. Key, Jr., *Public Opinion and American Democracy* (New York: Knopf, 1961), pp. 229, 230. This stress upon the apathy of alienated elements clearly links the theory of differentiated agreement with the patriotism-apathy theory described above.

[3] For the general advisability in surveys of comparing one group's characteristics with those of another group rather than relying upon some absolute (and probably arbitrary) standard of measurement, see H. Hyman, *Survey Design and Analysis* (Glencoe, Ill.: Free Press, 1955), pp. 126–31.

fully in Chapter 3. Another powerful reason for focusing attention on relationships among the three groups derives from Dahl's remark that consensus is a process, not a static condition of society, and typically stands subject to growth and decay. What the generalized theory predicts, therefore, is not an invariant "high" level of agreement among the politicians and an invariant "low" level among the less politically involved; rather it is an invariant *higher* level of agreement among politicians *relative* to that among the less politically involved. Such a way of stating the theory allows for the flow and ebb of agreement among all groups, while hypothesizing that it is the relatively greater agreement of one compared to the other which so powerfully affects the stability of democracy.[5]

It can be seen from this summary that the Dahl-Key theory does not simply discuss the distribution of democratic agreements among the various strata of the population. It also speculates about the ways in which these agreements prompt the professional politicians and the political stratum to action when they feel that democratic procedures are threatened. Such hypotheses on the behavior of politicians and activists in a crisis are difficult to test directly. But, in any case, the predictions about crisis behavior cannot hold true unless the logically prior assumptions on which they are based, assumptions relating to the distribution of agreement among the population, are upheld under analysis. Politicians can hardly be prompted to defense of democratic procedures through their agreement on democratic norms if such agreement does not exist. A direct test of Key's and Dahl's statements about the distribution of democratic agreements and of other of their speculations about the differences between various groups in the population thus constitutes an indirect test of their dynamic hypotheses.

The present chapter aims at breaking down the generalized Dahl-Key theory into its separate hypotheses and assumptions about differences between the various sections of the population of a stable democracy. In the course of the discussion some extensions of the theory will be introduced particularly in regard to political issues. Some of these extensions are not logically implied by the theory, but they are

---

[4] R. A. Dahl, *Who Governs?* (New Haven, Conn.: Yale University Press, 1961), p. 316.

[5] A further reason for examining relationships between the three groups applies particularly to some of the extensions of Dahl's and Key's arguments put forward later in the present chapter. Most if not all hypotheses rest on the assumption that the politicians form an interacting and self-conscious group. Comparisons with the electors of the general population, a selection of persons who do not interact to the same extent and are not conscious of themselves as forming a political entity, can form a good test of this assumption.

suggested by it and appear congenial to the line of argument it pursues. Such extensions will however be clearly noted as such.

Political Effectiveness

The theory assumes that politicians are more politically effective than the general population. It is only this assumption which makes it important that politicians do agree more specifically and intensely on democratic procedures. In numbers alone the politicians, even with the addition of the political stratum, could hardly outweigh the "a-democratic" citizenry. Only in terms of their superior political weight and influence can the importance of their more consistent adherence to democratic principles be understood.

Dahl and Key also regard the political stratum as more politically effective than the general population. So much so, in fact, that they both tend to think of the political stratum as "those more highly involved in political thought, discussion and action than the rest of the population," to quote Dahl.[6] The higher political effectiveness of the political stratum when compared with that of the general population must therefore be taken as its defining characteristic. The relationship is not one which can properly be subjected to empirical test, but, rather, must be taken as a (definitional) given.

General Democratic Principles

No suggestion is made in the generalized Dahl-Key theory that politicians or political stratum agree on abstract norms of political behavior to any greater extent than the general population. But it is assumed that the general population does not agree on such abstract principles to any greater extent than politicians or political stratum. On the premises of the Dahl-Key theory, therefore, no significant differences are anticipated among the three groups in the extent to which they agree that general democratic norms should be upheld. If any significant differences do occur it will be because the politicians are more highly agreed than electors.

Specific Applications of Democratic Principles

It is with respect to agreement on specific applications of general democratic norms that the generalized Dahl-Key theory anticipates considerable differences among the groups. Politicians and members

---

[6] Dahl, *op. cit.*, p. 90, and Key, *op. cit.*, p. 550.

of the political stratum are expected to agree more on actual applications of democratic principles than the general population. This statement over-simplifies, however, in anticipating that the contrast will hold in every case. For Key at least thinks that on some specific applications the general population will be widely agreed, and that as a result of their agreement no significant difference will appear between them and the other two groups in such cases. Key's assertion that the general population will be widely agreed on some democratic courses of action is supported both by his own survey evidence and by the findings produced by McClosky.

But although no difference in agreement on specific courses of action may appear in certain situations it is anticipated that politicians and the political stratum will generally be more agreed and more consistent in applying general democratic principles to actual situations. And it is also assumed that this tendency will never be reversed; that is, it is assumed that the general population will never be more agreed than politicians or political stratum in these specific cases, although they may agree to the same extent.

The extent of agreement among politicians and the extent of agreement among political stratum on actual courses of democratic action is not specifically discussed by Dahl or Key. One would expect to find that in one or two cases the politicians were more agreed than the political stratum, but it would not be surprising to find little contrast.

Agreement on Factual Appraisals about Democracy

Another set of relationships among the three political groups is both logically and empirically implied in the Dahl-Key theory, although it is not specifically mentioned by either of its exponents. Agreement can exist either on preferences or on facts. The theories of consensus which have been discussed almost exclusively emphasize agreements on preferences. The Dahl-Key theory, however, assumes that agreement also exists on certain facts. For unless the politicians are aware of a certain agreement among themselves on their preference for democratic procedures (and thus are widely agreed on the fact of agreement among themselves), they would be totally unable to close ranks in the manner hypothesized by Dahl, against challenges to the democratic order. They would not be aware that there was any basis of common preferences on which they could combine.

It is obviously important also that some electors agree on their appraisals—for example, that their general preferences are respected by their leaders and that democracy exists in their political system.[7] Thus the authors of *Voting* mention "consensus on the focus of debate, on some of the criteria by which issues and candidates should be judged, on certain expectations about future events . . . on the effect of . . . votes, on some issues, and on the rules by which the election is carried out.[8] At least half of these agreements are on matters of fact. Similarly *The American Voter* stresses the importance to political action of "consensus on issue positions of the parties." It reasons that the absence of such consensus on the facts of the situation would prevent the translation of clear-cut preferences into "clear issue outcome."[9]

This last point can be applied to general democratic preferences as well as to issue preferences. A group could be extremely attached to democratic procedures, but it would be unlikely to take action to defend democratic institutions unless its members also agreed on the fact that these institutions were themselves democratic. If the politicians and political stratum are more likely than other members of the population to take decisive action in defense of democracy, therefore, they must agree to a greater extent upon the fact that democratic practices are followed in the political system. Accordingly Dahl does refer to certain factual as well as preferential "axioms" shared by New Haven politicians.[10] Most persons in these two groups are likely also to agree that general agreement exists on the established democratic political processes. For if the previous hypotheses are correct, the majority in each group will have strong preferences for democratic processes. We know from general psychological studies that strong preferences produce supportive appraisals.[11] Strong pro-democratic preferences are likely, therefore, to produce a certain amount of wishful thinking about the extent of support for democracy. Thus their own democratic enthusiasms will incline activists to the belief that their preferences are shared by the majority of the population. This is particularly likely in that the ideas of democracy which politicians and political stratum share lay great stress on the full consent of the governed to the political system under which they live.

---

[7] Dahl, *op. cit.*, p. 316.

[8] B. Berelson, P. F. Lazarsfeld, and W. McPhee, *Voting* (Chicago: University of Chicago Press, 1955), p. 192.

[9] A. Campbell, P. Converse, W. E. Miller, and D. E. Stokes, *The American Voter* (New York: Wiley, 1960), pp. 183ff.

[10] Dahl, *op. cit.*, pp. 94–95.

[11] On this point see L. Festinger, *A Theory of Cognitive Dissonance* (Stanford, Calif.: Stanford University Press, 1957), pp. 4–6, and Chap. 3.

Agreement about Which Topics Are Agreed Upon

Agreement on another set of factual appraisals might distinguish politicians from the general population. Professional politicians are more likely to be agreed not only on the fact that they agree but also on the question of what specific topics they agree about.

It should be made clear that this hypothesis is not an implicit assumption of the Dahl-Key theory, but rather an extension which it is proposed to make to that theory. It is however a very plausible extension. The politicians, it is implied, are people who come into frequent contact with each other. They are also, according to Dahl's statement of the theory, able to recognize challenges to established procedures relatively rapidly and to work together efficiently to overcome them. This implies that most politicians recognize their own agreement on democratic procedures and on the fact that democracy exists, as well as on some of the 'axioms' discussed by Dahl and cited above.[12] There are thus reasonable theoretical grounds for surmising that politicians share this additional agreement about the topics on which shared appraisals and preferences exist.[13]

One would not expect the political stratum to show a much wider agreement than the general population here. As McClosky points out: "although (the political stratum) can be distinguished from other citizens by their activity and concerns, they are in no sense a community, they do not act as a body. . . ."[14] Since they are not distinguished by a high level of social mixing and personal contact, they do not have the same opportunity as politicians to form a consensus on such a general appraisal of politics as what exactly they agree about. Such a consensus represents a type of agreement that seems much more an implicit understanding dependent on extensive group intermingling than the types of agreement previously discussed.

---

[12] Dahl, *op. cit.*, pp. 94–95.

[13] Supporting empirical evidence for the likelihood of such agreement among politicians is available for the United States. Rose's and McClosky's surveys showed that community leaders and political activists agreed on a considerable number of factual appraisals of the political system. They agreed considerably more than electors that they were not manipulated by a power elite. They had more knowledge of (and hence agreed more on) the workings of the social system and were more likely to concur on the fact that American government was responsive to the wishes of the people. See A. M. Rose, "Alienation and Participation," *American Sociological Review*, 27 (1962), 836–38 *passim.*, and H. McClosky, "Consensus and Ideology in American Politics," *APSR*, 58 (1964), 370.

[14] *Ibid.*, p. 363.

Agreement on Evaluations of the Political
Parties and Party Leaders

If politicians' ability to work together in emergencies depends upon the existence of a body of shared understandings, such understandings are likely to extend beyond the general appraisals just discussed to evaluations of the parties and party leaders. These evaluations need not necessarily be related only to the democratic beliefs of the parties, but could cover such practical matters as the basis of their electoral support, their relative efficiency, and the personal qualities of their leaders. Agreement on these more specific matters could equally well arise from politicians' closer interaction. Though not so essential to cooperation as is agreement on the appraisals mentioned above, these agreements on practical matters can smooth the workings of a coalition by preventing protagonists treading on each others' toes and by enabling them to recognize the limitations under which their allies work. It is, of course, true that the parties and party leaders are involved in interminable controversies and that both indeed serve as permanent symbols of division to the nation at large.[15] Thus it is to be expected that, to some extent, opinions about parties and leaders will be fluctuating and colored by the passions of the moment. But politicians are not only involved in conflicts, they also have to manage and exploit conflicts for their own benefit and for that of the causes they have at heart. Thus one can anticipate that they may show some capacity for stepping aside from controversies of the moment viewing them with detachment, and discovering their functional possibilities. Factual agreements thus established would indicate that party loyalties are not so exclusive that they foreclose cooperation on some occasions.

Agreement about Preferences on Political Issues

It is highly unlikely that politicians will have different preferences on all the decisions they have to take on substantive topics such as foreign affairs, education, the economy, and so on. At any rate, they would not disagree on all their issue-preferences in a stable democracy; otherwise it would soon cease to be stable. Procedural rules regulate

---

[15] One finding from the survey on which later discussion will be based shows that in naming topics of disagreement in Britain, the second highest proportion of electors mentioned party politics.

political conflicts, but such conflicts would soon bring the rules into dispute if they were sufficiently intense, widespread and bitter.[16] Certainly, as McClosky and his associates discovered, the general population may agree among themselves more than the politicians on some issue-preferences. But such a distribution of agreement is not to be expected on all issues because the agreements already attributed to the politicians must be buttressed to a large extent by agreement on the substantive courses of action which they must undertake. Moreover politicians are likely to be more homogeneous than electors in social background,[17] which in turn should bring about a marked congruence of opinion on many of these courses of action.

Agreement on Factual Appraisals of Political Issues

As with democracy, so with political issues: it is possible to argue that agreement on preferences is facilitated and supported by agreement on factual appraisals of the issue. The most important of these are the considerations that must be taken into account when decisions about appropriate action are made, namely:
1. The question of whether a political issue exists or not
2. What courses of action are "open" or "available" to pursuit on the issue
3. What effects the issue will have
4. What stands are taken by the political parties in relation to the issue.[18]

---

[16] Dahl (*op. cit.*, p. 94) speaks of the general reformist ideology of the politicians in New Haven, Connecticut. See also R. A. Dahl, *Preface to Democratic Theory* (Chicago: University of Chicago Press, 1956), p. 77.

[17] J. Blondel, *Voters, Parties, and Leaders* (Harmondsworth, England: Penguin, 1963), Chap. 5 *passim.*, and D. Matthews, *The Social Background of Political Decision-Makers* (New York: Random House, 1954), *passim.*

[18] Dahl has also argued for the key part of purely factual appraisals in the decision-making process, explicitly pointing out that a "factor that helps determine the quality of one's appraisals [is] the amount and validity of one's factual information. Two of the five kinds of appraisal . . . consist of evaluations of factual or empirical knowledge. These are . . . likely consequences of pursuing each of the alternative courses of action . . . the probability that the various consequences will actually occur." "Consideration of the alternative courses of action 'open' or 'available' " also seems to depend on the state of one's factual knowledge. R. A. Dahl, *Modern Political Analysis* (Englewood Cliffs, N.J.: Prentice-Hall, 1963), pp. 95–97. See also H. D. Lasswell, *The Future of Political Science* (New York: Atherton, 1963), pp. 1–2, 133, 196, 221, 231ff. Lasswell, like Dahl, stresses the purely factual appraisals ("expectations") involved in decision-making. His Stages 3, 4 and 5 at least involve purely factual considerations.

These appraisals of facts *about* an issue are the only facts referred to in the whole of the following discussion and analysis. They should not be confused with facts *bearing* on an issue (*e.g.*, in the British debate over capital punishment the factual question of whether or not the death penalty does deter). Appraisals of facts bearing on an issue are likely to be much more controverted, even among politicians, since they form the ammunition that the opposing sides fire at each other in debate. On the other hand politicians' greater experience and realism should promote agreement on facts about the issue (*e.g.*, whether or not it actually exists as an issue).

The significance for political action of these issue-appraisals is stressed by a discussion in *The American Voter* of the conditions that strengthen or diminish the influence of specific issues on the individual's voting-decision.[19] One of these conditions is that the individual must have heard about the issue. This is by no means a formal or empty requirement. It has been repeatedly demonstrated by survey evidence that many electors do not hear about issues that for the politically involved are everyday topics of discussion.[20] For the link between such specific issues and voting to become effective it is also necessary that the voter know what policy the different parties endorse. If he lacks such knowledge, then his vote is really being cast at random with no relation to his position on the issue. Yet many electors have hazy conceptions of exact party policies.[21] The same discussion in *The American Voter* also stresses that voters must feel affected by an issue before it can influence their vote. Most public issues probably do carry some effects for the majority of the population in some way or another. At times, however, the majority of electors do not feel affected.[22]

The full-time decision-makers, too, have to form judgments about the courses of action "open" on an issue and the effects it will have. In a democracy these judgments are shaped primarily by discussion and negotiation in the legislature and in a multiplicity of committees. This situation makes for considerable identity in the views of politicians who are constantly exchanging appraisals of issues. Such agreement will not be found among persons outside that close, interacting

---

[19] Campbell, *et al.*, *op. cit.*, Chap. 8.

[20] For example the survey upon which the present study is based showed that one-third of the sample of London electors had not heard about the current reorganization of Greater London government. Three-quarters had not heard about the Transport Bill, which was being discussed in Parliament as interviewing proceeded, and 16 percent had not heard about the Wage Pause. See Chapter 6, Table 6.1.

[21] See Chapter 5.

[22] See Chapter 6.

group at the center of discussion.[23] The process is circular: discussion fosters wider agreement on issue-appraisals, but this agreement must be present for constructive discussion and negotiation to take place. Where "the partisans disagree not only on the stands they take on various issues but also on *what* political issues are relevant to take stands on" they "hardly join issue at all—they argue past one another— and the political debate languishes."[24] What has been said about the importance of agreement on issue-appraisals among electors applies, then, with greater force to its importance for politicians, since their dependence upon discussion is greater. The extent to which political debate in stable democracies must involve electors is limited. Detailed discussion of important but specific issues is confined largely to the politicians. For effective debate and bargaining—*i.e.*, for the proper functioning of stable democracy—it is therefore necessary that the politicians' factual appraisals of most issues agree very much more than do those of the general population.

The political stratum also may be more widely agreed than the general population on these facts about an issue because its capacity for political debate is no doubt greater, because its members tend to read more political news in similar newspapers, because they tend to view the same television and political programs, and so on. As a more cohesive group, however, the politicians can be expected to show more

---

[23] A major finding from the New Haven study, the study that prompted Dahl to develop his consensual theory, might seem to go against the argument that politicians are more agreed on factual issue appraisals than electors. Leaders were found to specialize in particular issue areas. In New Haven only the mayor was equally involved in the fields of political nominations, education, and urban redevelopment. See Dahl, *Who Governs?, op. cit.*, p. 175. Matthews also refers to the norm of "specialization" in the Senate whereby a legislator makes himself known as a master of a particular subject matter on which his colleagues listen with respect to his views. He extends the same courtesy to them. See D. Matthews, *U.S. Senators and Their World* (Chapel Hill: University of North Carolina Press, 1960), pp. 95–97, and J. Wahlke, H. Eulau, C. Buchanan, and L. Ferguson, *The Legislative System* (New York: Wiley, 1962), Chap. 9. However far from leading to a diversity of factual views on issues, such specialization seems much more likely to produce uniformity. The specialists' views on their particular subject command attention. Even if the policy recommendations they make are rejected as partisan, most of the purely factual elements are likely to be accepted. Thus the specialists' appraisals are liable to be repeated even by those not highly involved in the issue, and in an interacting group greater uniformity will thus prevail. For further evidence that politicians are likely to agree more than electors in their issue appraisals, see J. N. Rosenau, *National Leadership and Foreign Policy* (Princeton, N.J.: Princeton University Press, 1963), pp. 165, 191. See also Dahl, *Who Governs?, op. cit.*, pp. 262–63, and S. Stouffer, *Communism, Conformity and Civil Liberties* (Garden City, N.Y.: Doubleday, 1955), Chap. 3.

[24] Berelson, *et al., op. cit.*, p. 192.

agreement on these points than the political stratum. In fact it is necessary for democratic stability that they should do so because their capacity for negotiation must be more highly developed. Thus the comparison that has most relevance in light of the general discussion is that between politicians and general population.

Summary of Preceding Predictions

The preceding discussion has produced a number of specific hypotheses that are either derivations from or extensions of the generalized Dahl-Key theory. It will clarify matters to set them out in a list which states quite clearly what the relationship of these hypotheses to the theory is—that is, whether they are explicit assertions, implicit assumptions upon tests of which its validity also depends to some extent, or extensions which are relevant but not essential parts of the central reasoning. The entries in parentheses after each hypothesis refer forward to the chapter in which it is discussed and checked against the survey data.

A. Predictions which are based upon Explicit Statements of the Generalized Dahl-Key Theory
In stable democracies:
1. The political effectiveness of politicians is higher than the political effectiveness of the general population (Chapter 10).
2. The general population does not agree on any of the general or abstract principles of democracy to a greater extent than politicians (Chapter 8).
3. The general population does not agree on any of the general or abstract principles of democracy to a greater extent than the political stratum (Chapter 11).
4. In a majority of cases the politicians agree on the application of democratic principles in specific situations to a greater extent than the general population (Chapter 8).
5. In a majority of cases the political stratum agrees on the application of democratic principles in specific situations to a greater extent than the general population (Chapter 11).

B. Predictions which are based upon Implicit Assumptions of the Generalized Dahl-Key Theory
In stable democracies:
6. The politicians agree on factual appraisals about democracy—namely, that democracy exists in their country, that widespread agreement on democratic procedures exists, that their agree-

ments are more important than their disagreements—to a greater extent than the general population (Chapter 9).

7. The political stratum agrees upon these same factual appraisals about democracy to a greater extent than the general population (Chapter 11).

C. Predictions which are based upon Extensions to the
Generalized Dahl-Key theory

In stable democracies:

8. The politicians agree about the topics on which there is general agreement in the country to a greater extent than the general population. And by extension they are also likely to agree about the topics upon which there is not general agreement to a greater extent than electors (Chapter 4).

9. The politicians agree in their evaluations of the political parties and party leaders to a greater extent than the general population (Chapter 5).

10. Politicians tend to agree to a greater extent than the general population in their preferences on a substantial number of political issues (Chapter 7).

11. Politicians tend to agree to a greater extent than the general population in their factual appraisals of a majority of political issues (Chapters 5 and 6).

After some necessary clarifications of terms, the following chapters will assess the extent to which these predictions succeed in anticipating the actual replies of the two London samples.

3 | VARIETIES OF AGREEMENT

In the preceding discussion new terms such as "political issues" and, notably, "agreement" and " disagreement" have had a prominent place. Although these words have acquired an implicit definition from the way in which they have been employed, it is well to spell out their meanings in full. Otherwise certain ambiguities may appear only at the stage of testing the hypotheses in which the concepts are embodied; this would, in turn, lead to doubts as to whether the hypotheses had been upheld or disconfirmed.[1]

POLITICAL ISSUES

Political issues are fully discussed in Appendix C and are taken as any topic in regard to which a course of action is currently being urged by the government or upon it by representative bodies, pressure groups or the mass media. Thus they are not regarded exclusively as matters at dispute between the political parties. The definition also helps to ensure that the investigator does not create his own issues, so to speak. This precaution is important because politicians sometimes stifle potentially divisive issues. If the investigator were free to ask questions about any matter he took to be an issue, he might tap disagreements which would never be widely debated because the politicians would never allow them to assume this prominence. Such disagreements would be significant, but not as political issues.

GENERAL DEFINITIONS OF AGREEMENT
AND DISAGREEMENT

The definition and operationalization of "agreement" and "disagreement" and their synonyms "consensus" and "dissensus" pose a

---

[1] H. M. Blalock, *Social Statistics* (New York: McGraw-Hill, 1960), p. 91.

much more difficult problem to which the rest of this chapter will be devoted. Dahl equates consensus with agreement,[2] and Key defines consensus as an "overwhelming public agreement" upon a question of public policy.[3] "Agreement" in both Dahl's and Key's cases refers to agreement on preferences. But a detailed argument has already been advanced to show that some agreements on facts have to be assumed if their theory is to hold true. The possibility of "consensus" referring to both preferences and factual appraisals is recognized by Lasswell and Kaplan who define consensus as: "a demand (preference) or expectation (factual appraisal) noncontrovertible in the group."[4]

Like democracy and stability, consensus or agreement can be regarded as a scale. There can be 100 percent or 75 percent support for a policy or there can be a 50–50 split. Thus Key's "overwhelming public agreement" can be operationalized for purposes of research as over 75 percent agreement.[5] It is well to note that such an operational definition ignores the dimension of intensity, that is, the question of whether an alternative is supported more or less strongly than another alternative.[6] Fortunately, however, certain aspects of the London data presented in Table 3.1 enable discussion to avoid this additional complication.

This table shows the strength of feeling of politicians and electors in regard to the nine political issues that will be discussed in later chapters and that are described in detail in Appendix C.

On five issues we will compare distributions of numerical agreement on preferences or appraisals among one group which feels strongly and among another many of whose members have no strong

---

[2] R. A. Dahl, *Preface to Democratic Theory* (Chicago: University of Chicago Press, 1956), pp. 78, 87.

[3] V. O. Key, Jr., *Public Opinion and American Democracy* (New York: Knopf, 1961), p. 28.

[4] H. D. Lasswell and A. Kaplan, *Power and Society* (New Haven, Conn.: Yale University Press, 1950), p. 39. Synonyms in brackets are inserted.

[5] J. N. Rosenau, *National Leadership and Foreign Policy* (Princeton, N.J.: Princeton University Press, 1963), p. 26. The reasoning is that of J. W. Prothro and C. M. Grigg in "Societal Co-ordination by the Educated Minority," *Prod*, 3 (January 1960), 7. This operational definition is also used by H. McClosky in his article, "Consensus and Ideology in American Politics," *APSR*, 58 (1964), 363.

[6] This element is given due weight in Key's use of "J" and "U" curves to summarize numerical distributions of agreement and disagreement along a continuum from "agree strongly" to "disagree strongly." See Key, *op. cit.*, pp. 29, 34. A limitation on such curves is the fact that they summarize reactions to only one concrete alternative on the issue, ignoring the other (often numerous) alternatives that might be advanced. For similar curves and a full discussion of the influence of intense feelings on agreement, see Dahl, *op. cit.*, pp. 92–105.

Table 3.1: Strength of Feeling of Politicans and Electors
on Nine British Political Issues February–July 1962

	POLITICIANS (percent)				ELECTORS (percent)			
	Very Strong	Moderate	Don't care partic-ularly	None	Very Strong	Moderate	Don't care partic-ularly	None
Wage Pause	80	18	0	2	63	17	4	17
Transport Bill	67	32	0	2	48	20	3	29
Greater London government	58	34	6	2	26	16	7	51
Monopolies	70	24	4	2	41	20	7	32
Immigration Bill	74	22	4	0	71	17	3	8
Common Market	78	21	0	2	50	16	4	30
Berlin negotiations	77	19	2	2	49	18	3	29
Housing shortage	87	11	0	2	73	16	1	9
Education shortages	75	16	5	3	57	26	3	13

feelings. In four cases the comparison will involve distributions of numerical agreement among two groups which feel equally strongly.

On the basis of these data it can be assumed throughout analysis that politicians' issue preferences and appraisals are always strong to moderate. Among electors, on the other hand, there is likely to be a considerable body of people who have very little feeling about the issue. This state of affairs seems, according to the table, to exist on all issues except immigration, housing, education and possibly the wage pause. A decision to ignore intensity in testing predictions that politicians are more agreed than electors thus constitutes a conservative assumption in the analysis, since any enhancement in consensus resulting from considerations of intensity would accrue to the politicians.

Although the figures in the table apply only to political issues, they provide some grounds on which to extrapolate to the other aspects of politics with which discussion will be concerned. It is plausible to assume on all the other topics where comparative agreement will be estimated that politicians feel at least as strongly as electors and possibly more strongly. Hence our concern will be solely with the problem of finding a satisfactory definition of agreement in the numerical sense. The question narrows to what proportion of a group must agree on a topic before we can say that there is consensus in that group about that topic.

Figure 3.1. An Example of 50 Percent
Agreement on a Policy-Alternative

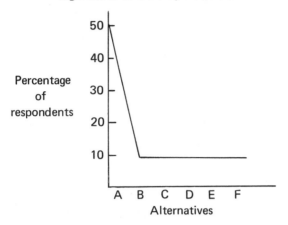

Seventy-five percent is universally accepted as an arbitrary cut-off point adopted because it is half way between 100 percent agreement and a 50–50 split. The argument here is simply that it is necessary to have a cut-off point somewhere, and that 75 percent is the most convenient. Yet the selection of such a point is not based on any conception of what level of agreement is required to maintain the stability of a group or, indeed, to carry a policy through.

These are not the only objections that one can make to this measure. The selection of this figure has been strongly conditioned by the type of survey question—the "YES-NO" type—with which it has been associated. Certainly in such a case of dichotomous choice complete dissensus would be marked by a 50–50 split. But suppose the range of alternatives open to endorsement extended to five or six. A 50 percent choice of one alternative might represent a significantly high degree of consensus on the question if no other alternative was chosen by more than 10 percent. It seems likely in this case that alternative A, with "only" 50 percent support, will be chosen, assuming that the proponents of alternatives B, C, D, E and F are unable to produce a compromise agreed among themselves. And 50 percent may be an even more overwhelming figure if another 25 percent show no support for any alternative.

On the other hand 50 percent agreement on an alternative could mark the existence of a profound cleavage in a situation where six alternatives were open to choice but only two were chosen. If alternatives

Figure 3.2. A Second Example of 50 Percent
Agreement on a Policy-Alternative

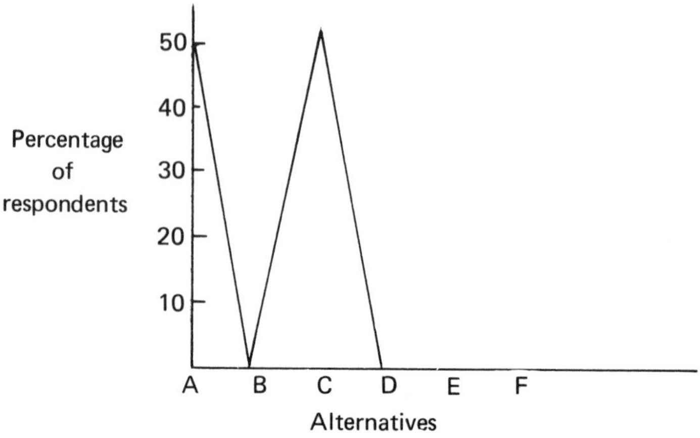

A and C were incompatible with each other, a profound difference of opinion would divide the group.

The sense in which the term "agreement" has been used in the hypotheses put forward in Chapter 2 is essentially comparative. For example, one leading hypothesis states that agreement to specific democratic procedures is higher among politicians than among the general population, and is higher among politically oriented citizens than among those not politically oriented. In other words if a substantial body of agreement exists among politicians and not among the general population, then the politicians will be regarded as being more agreed than the general population, and the hypothesis will be regarded as confirmed. It does not matter whether the proportion of politicians who agree is 75 percent or less. This situation is represented in Figure 3.3.

The superiority of the method of defining agreement in comparative terms consists in the information it provides on the greater likelihood of one group rather than the other taking a specific course of action on the question, other things being equal. If we insisted on 75 percent agreement before we could regard any group as exhibiting a significant level of consensus, we should have to regard the difference between the groups in the figure as trivial and uninteresting. But this difference could have definite results in action—*e.g.*, the adoption of alternative A by the politicians and its imposition on the whole political system. Therefore the relative definition of consensus seems superior to the one which would define it in terms of a 75 percent cut-off point.

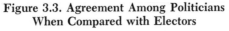

Figure 3.3. Agreement Among Politicians
When Compared with Electors

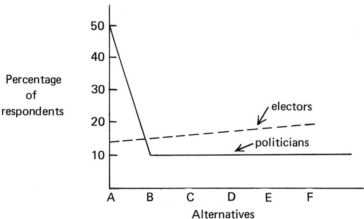

The problem of defining agreement now reduces itself to the question of when one group can be said to share an alternative to a greater extent than the other. Operationally and in terms of the distributions shown in Figure 3.3, this is the problem of deciding whether politicians' or electors' replies cluster more on a single alternative. In the case of this Figure we are in no doubt that politicians' replies cluster to a greater extent, but we cannot assume that the situation will always be as clear-cut as this. One point of general importance that emerges from Figure 3.3 is that in assessing comparative agreement, we are focusing on the most popular alternatives on each side. We say that politicians are more in agreement because the number of politicians endorsing alternative A, most popular alternative on their side, is very much greater than the number of electors endorsing alternative F, most popular choice on their side. It emerges further that on this view of agreement the substantive preferences or appraisals which are being compared need not be the same for both groups. On each side alternatives are marked out for comparison by the simple fact that they attract the largest cluster of replies.

In order to decide on agreement in situations where the main clusters on each side are not so obviously disproportionate as in Figure 3.3, we can add to the comparison a further requirement. One group will not be regarded as more agreed than another unless the number endorsing its most popular alternative is significantly greater than the number in the other group endorsing the alternative most popular

Figure 3.4. Disagreement Among Both Politicians and Electors

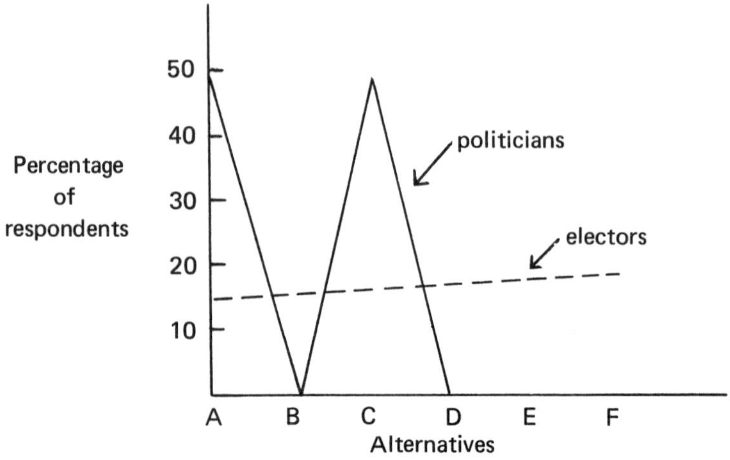

among its members. Whether this requirement has been met can be determined by means of a simple statistical test such as the chi-square.

We seem, therefore, to have arrived at an operational definition of consensus or agreement couched in some such terms as the following: One group is regarded as exhibiting more consensus than another group in relation to a given topic if the preference or factual appraisal that is most often mentioned in each group is shared by a (statistically) higher proportion of the members of the one group than of the other.

However, one awkward case must be provided for. The definition given above provides for the case shown by Figure 3.3 in which alternatives other than A are each supported by small numbers of politicians. But if we stick to this definition, we must also contend that the politicians show more agreement than electors in the case shown in Figure 3.4. Here we have a deep cleavage in the ranks of politicians, contrasted with an almost even distribution of opinion among electors. In a sense, of course, the politicians may be said to be more agreed than electors, since they have reduced the preferred or perceived alternatives to two, instead of to six.[7] But the consequences may equally well be inability to undertake action.

In order to avoid having to accept a 50–50 split as indicating greater agreement, one has to ensure that the group taken as more agreed never splits equally, or almost equally, between two leading alternatives. Politicians will be taken as equally disagreed as electors in

---

[7] See Appendix B for a fuller discussion of this point and alternative definitions of "consensus" and "agreement."

the case illustrated in Figure 3.4 if we add to the previous requirements a stipulation that the proportion endorsing the most popular
alternative must always exceed by some fixed percentage the proportion endorsing the next most popular alternative. This percentage must
be sufficient to ensure acceptance of the most popular alternative—and
thus avoidance of stalemate—by the group taken as more agreed. The
fixed percentage is set at 20 percent for the ensuing analysis. This percentage gap is arbitrary in that it is based on what only speculatively
seems a sufficient superiority in proportions to make the most popular
alternative the choice of the whole group. Others might make the
figure 30 or 40 percent.

But although an arbitrary element has been introduced into the
definition, it still seems better than the 75 percent cut-off point, since it
deals with the real-world situation of multiple alternatives, rather than
with the survey-created situation of dichotomous choice.

Thus our operational definition of consensus or agreement in the
case of mutually exclusive alternatives takes this final form:

*A group (A) is regarded as exhibiting more consensus than an-
other group (B) in relation to a given topic if the preference or factual
appraisal most often mentioned in each group is shared by a (statistically) higher number of the members of group (A), and if the proportion endorsing the preference or appraisal most often mentioned in
group (A) is at least 20 per cent greater than the proportion endorsing
the next most often mentioned preference or appraisal in group (A).*

"Disagreement" or "dissensus" are taken as any situation other than
those just defined as states of "agreement" or "consensus."

Agreement in Multiple-Choice Situations

This definition for "agreement" or "consensus" was reached with
reference solely to cases where one response precluded another, *i.e.*,
where choice of only one preference or appraisal was possible because
the choices were mutually exclusive. The more common case in situations of political choice[8] is however one where preferences or appraisals
do not necessarily preclude each other, *i.e.*, where a simultaneous
choice of two or more preferences or appraisals can be made by the
same person.

In this case, a group must be regarded as exhibiting more consensus than another group in relation to a given topic if the *preferences* or

---

[8] See the discovery reported in Chapter 7 that most policy alternatives mentioned in regard to political issues can perfectly well be pursued in conjunction
with each other.

factual appraisals most often mentioned in each group are shared by (statistically) higher numbers of the members of the former.

The reason for the modification rests on the fact that we are no longer dealing with a case in which the support of a substantial proportion of a group for one preference or appraisal invariably implies that less support is offered for other preferences or appraisals. For a number of preferences or appraisals can now be supported simultaneously by members of the group. Thus a number of preferences or appraisals may in this case (other things being equal) be held simultaneously by considerable proportions of the group and simultaneously become policies or views of the group. Thus all such preferences or perceptions would seem more likely than others to affect the group's actions. For again there is a greater probability of the most popular preferences' being accepted as the (joint) policies of the whole group[9] or, in the case of factual appraisals, of becoming accepted as "facts" by the whole group. And again there is a greater probability of the group whose most popular preferences or appraisals were mentioned by higher proportions of its members being more capable than the other groups of accepting the most popular preferences or appraisals as premises for group action.[10]

In estimating the comparative agreement of politicians and electors, therefore, it seems necessary to compare the numbers sharing the most often mentioned preferences or factual appraisals, in each case. To illustrate this point Figure 3.5 presents distributions based on survey data that will be discussed in the next chapter. The distributions summarize politicians' and electors' replies to a question on what people in Britain agree about. Here it is clear from comparing the largest clusters of responses on each side that more politicians name the same topics than do electors.

But just as in the case of mutually exclusive preferences or appraisals it was necessary to allow for the case where a deep and concentrated cleavage in the ranks of politicians contrasted with a near even distribution of electors (Figure 3.4), so in the case of multiple responses it will be necessary to check that different preferences or appraisals are not held by nearly equal groups of politicians.

---

[9] Again the implicit qualification to these suppositions is that intensity (in the case of preferences) and certainty (in the case of factual appraisals) can be eliminated for purpose of analysis.

[10] This is apart from the operation of such factors as greater political knowledge and information, which might promote both a wider choice of multiple alternatives and greater agreement upon them. For a discussion of these effects, see Chapter 12 and Appendix B. Here we are assuming that, all other factors being equal, a greater clustering of replies on the part of one group will enhance its ability to take joint action.

**Figure 3.5. Replies of Politicians and Electors on
Topics of Consensus in Britain**

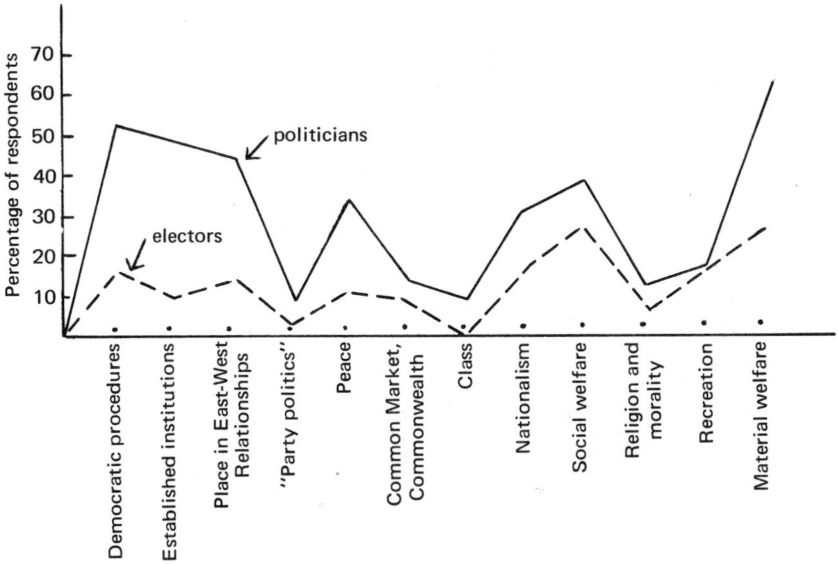

It is possible that the distribution of responses on the graph in
Figure 3.5 masks a profound cleavage in the ranks of politicians. Given
the information presently available, it is quite possible that the politicians who perceive a general agreement in Britain over nationalism
are generally the same persons who name social welfare, and that these
persons, in turn, overlap extensively into the group that mentions
material welfare. On the other hand one can suppose that those who
refer to peace, East-West relations, established institutions and democratic procedures are also generally the same people. But suppose also
that there is very little overlap between these relatively equal groups,
that most of those who mention material welfare do not mention democratic procedures and vice versa. Such a (as yet hypothetical) situation is presented in Figure 3.6.

In such a case as that illustrated in Figure 3.6 it would be true
only in a very circumscribed sense to say that politicians were more
agreed than electors. For purposes of combination and action they
would be in a condition of equal dissensus. For if very few electors
concur in naming any one topic, the lack of any common ground between the two roughly equal groups of politicians makes it just as difficult to conceive of the whole body's accepting joint preferences or
appraisals.

To ensure that this type of division among politicians is not accepted as representing a state of consensus superior to that among

**Fig. 3.6. Disagreement Among Politicians on Topics of
Consensus in Britain: Hypothetical Distribution**

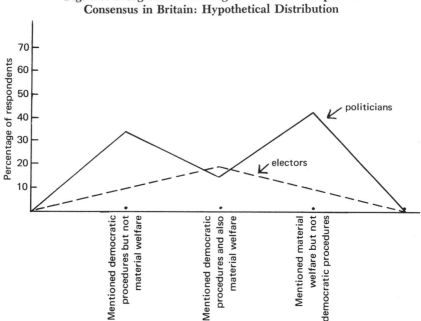

electors, *it is necessary not only to show the distribution of the replies
given by both samples over the various topics as reported in Figure 3.5,
but also to give some indication of the lack of overlap between the replies of members of each sample.* At least some indication of the lack
of overlap among the members giving the most popular responses on
either side must be given, since it is on a comparison of the numbers
giving the most popular responses on each side that the estimate is
formed of which sample is in greater agreement.

An example of the degree of overlap among the members of the
two samples is given in the distributions illustrated in Figure 3.7.
These distributions can be obtained by first noting the proportion of
respondents who mentioned the most popular topic on each side, elim-
inating these respondents, and then obtaining the numbers of those
who mentioned the topic that was most popular among those who did
not mention the most popular topic. The information we get from this
maneuver is minimal but vital. We can now estimate from the distributions shown in Figure 3.7 the percentage difference between the two
largest proportions in each sample who endorse mutually exclusive
alternatives, *i.e.,* who do not overlap in their replies. If the proportion
of politicians who did not mention the overall most popular alternative

Figure 3.7. Agreement Among Politicians on
Topics of Consensus in Britain: Actual Distribution

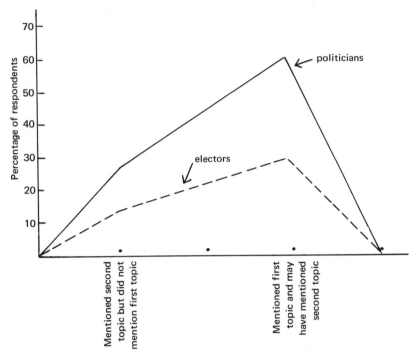

approaches equality with the proportion who did, then the condition
of dissensus shown in Figure 3.6 is present in the sample which is
seemingly more agreed. By putting Figure 3.7 together with Figure 3.5
we can estimate whether the sample of politicians is more agreed than
the sample of electors on what topics of consensus exist in Britain. We
have the general knowledge that more politicians than electors name
the same topics (Figure 3.5). We also know that politicians do not
split into two more or less equal groups with different perceptions
(Figure 3.7), for the largest single cluster of politicians who do not
mention the most popular topic on their own side is 26 percent. We do
not need to know how many of the 61 percent who mention the most
popular topic also mention this second topic. Even if we assume the
worst possible situation for the prediction that politicians are more
agreed—*i.e.*, if we assume that of the 61 percent who mention the first
topic none also mentions the second—the one body of agreement still
outweighs the other in terms of numbers.

It is true that the information given by Figure 3.7 is incomplete,
for some of those mentioning the overall most popular topic, and some

of those mentioning the topic that is most popular among those who did not mention the overall most popular topic, may both have mentioned a third topic. In such a case their perceptions would overlap in a way ignored by the procedure which produced Figure 3.7, since it concentrates only on lack of overlap between the most popular alternatives. Consideration of this additional form of overlap however could only work to favor politicians' greater agreement. As it stands the procedure implicitly assumes that the two main groups of politicians diverge completely on all topics: any change to take account of other topics held in common would increase the overlap revealed in politicians' opinions. If the present study aims at showing politicians to be generally more agreed than electors, the present procedure is conservative. It is also the easiest to apply to the data. For both of these reasons it will be employed in the subsequent analysis.

With these operationalizations we end the initial discussion of theory and turn in the next chapters to seeing how far the predictions made in Chapter 2 anticipated the actual patterns of agreement discovered in the British survey data.

4

POLITICIANS AND ELECTORS: AGREEMENT ON GENERAL APPRAISALS OF CONSENSUS AND DISSENSUS IN BRITAIN

Clearly the greater the mutual understanding among politicians, the more easily they can work together. And on the premises of the generalized Dahl-Key theory it is necessary for Government and Opposition and otherwise opposing cliques to work together at least on some occasions in order to maintain democratic procedures. One would therefore expect to find a great number of understandings among British politicians. These understandings may relate to support for certain rules and obligations, but the discussion has also emphasized that they may be purely factual in nature. Dahl, in fact, speculates on certain 'axioms' shared by the high-powered sections of the political stratum in New Haven.[1] In the following chapters such 'understandings' among politicians will be examined with regard to political issues and procedures. Here they will be analyzed in their more general form, as they apply to the whole field of agreements and disagreements in Britain.

The topic derives importance from the fact that management and exploitation of conflict (and consensus) is a major concern of democratic politicians. The individual politician's success may in fact depend largely on his ability to judge correctly which are the topics where he can play off one side against another, and which are those where he is faced by an unbreakable unanimity. These judgments have an important effect on the degree of agreement that will prevail among politicians, and the extent of agreement or disagreement will either stimulate or hinder cooperative action by the whole group. A politician is naturally hesitant to risk his political future by cooperating with a person

---

[1] R. A. Dahl, *Who Governs?* (New Haven, Conn.: Yale University Press, 1961), pp. 94–95.

whom he regards as a political incompetent, *i.e.*, one who does not agree with him on what the political conflicts and agreements are. The leading prediction that emerges from this line of thought is that politicians will be more agreed than electors in their appraisals of what specific topics are subjects of consensus and dissensus in Britain.

AGREEMENT ON TOPICS OF CONSENSUS AND DISSENSUS AMONG POLITICIANS AND ELECTORS

Table 4.1 presents replies to two questions about topics of agreement which were asked at different points in the survey interviews. The first question asked was: "Do you think there are any things people in Britain agree about?" (*If yes*) "What are the things they agree about?" The second question, asked later, was worded as follows: "Could you please write down any problems facing the country at the moment on which, in your view, there is general agreement?" Answers to the two questions were coded together into the same categories.[2]

The overall distribution of replies—Distribution A of Table 4.1—is the distribution graphically presented in Figure 3.5. It gives us information about the proportions endorsing the most popular alternatives on each side, which is one element in the operational definition adopted for comparative agreement in multiple-choice cases such as this. We limit comparisons to the three most popular choices on each side, since the proportions endorsing further choices are usually much smaller, especially among electors. This is not very evident in the present case but will become so later. We apply a two-by-two chi-square test to assess the significance of the difference between the numbers endorsing the most popular alternative on each side (in Table 4.1 the 61 percent of politicians and the 33 percent of electors mentioning material welfare); a similar test for the significance of the difference between the numbers endorsing the next most popular alternative on each side (in Table 4.1, the 51 percent of politicians mentioning democratic procedures and the 30 percent of electors mentioning social welfare); and a similar test for the significance of the difference between the numbers endorsing the third most popular alternatives on each side (in Table 4.1, the 44 percent of politicians mentioning established institutions and the 20 percent of electors mentioning nationalism). These three

---

[2] Full distributions for all summary tables in this book and detailed instructions used to code original responses into those distributions may be found in the Appendices to I. Budge, *Patterns of Democratic Agreement* (Ph.D. dissertation, Yale University Library; also published by University Micro Films, Ann Arbor, Mich., 1967).

Table 4.1: Agreement of Politicians and Electors on Topics
About Which There is Consensus in Britain

| | OVERALL MULTIPLE CHOICE: DISTRIBUTION A | |
	POLITICIANS (percent)	ELECTORS (percent)
Democratic procedures	51	19
Established institutions	44	10
Place in East-West relations	40	16
"Party" politics	7	5
Peace	32	14
Common Market Commonwealth	12	10
Social class	7	1
Nationalism	32	20
Social welfare	37	30
Religion and morality	11	8
Recreation	16	16
Material welfare	61	33
	PROPORTIONS ENDORSING MOST POPULAR TOPICS: DISTRIBUTION B	
First proportion: endorsing topic most popular on each side	61	33
Second proportion: endorsing topic most popular on each side among those not endorsing overall most popular	26	11
Other	13	56

Politicians N = 57; Electors N = 147

final chi-square values really tell us all we want to know about the overall multiple-choice distributions on each side: if they are significant and in the expected direction, we know that more politicians choose the most popular alternatives on their side than electors do on their side. In comparisons of subsequent multiple-choice distributions we shall, therefore, report only these final chi-square statistics, which are given in Table 4.2 for the comparisons just carried out on the overall multiple-choice distribution (A) of Table 4.1. These show that the proportions of politicians endorsing the most popular topics of agreement on their side are significantly greater than the proportions of electors endorsing the most popular topics of agreement on their side.

In terms of the operational definition of agreement adopted in Chapter 3 for such multiple-choice situations, we still cannot finally decide whether politicians are more agreed than electors until we have some idea of the lack of overlap between the proportions endorsing the

Table 4.2: Statistics Summarizing Relative Agreement
on Distributions Presented in Table 4.1 and on
Topics about Which There Is Dissensus in Britain

Topics of Consensus:

Politicians' Consensus Gap (B distribution)   35 percent

Comparison on A distribution involving:

Most popular topics	$\chi^2 = 10.724 \ p < .0005$
Second most popular topics	$\chi^2 = 5.984 \ p < .01$
Third most popular topics	$\chi^2 = 10.022 \ p < .0005$

Topics of Dissensus:

Politicians' Consensus Gap (B distribution)   46 percent

Comparison on A distribution involving:

Most popular topics	$\chi^2 = 9.926 \ p < .0005$
Second most popular topics	$\chi^2 = 4.218 \ p < .025$
Third most popular topics	$\chi^2 = 5.756 \ p < .001$

NOTE: The chi-square test of departure from statistical independence as employed throughout this book incorporates Yates' Correction for continuity with small numbers and takes advantage of the hypotheses outlined in Chapter 2 in order to predict the direction of differences between groups—that is, that in every case the politicians will be more agreed than electors.

various most popular alternatives on the politicians' side. Otherwise we cannot be sure that there are not two independent and roughly equal groups of politicians making quite different choices, a state, actually, of dissensus rather than consensus.

To assess this probability we turn to the reworked Distribution B in Table 4.1. Distribution B in Table 4.1 is identical with the distribution graphically presented in Figure 3.7. In other words it is derived from Distribution A in Table 4.1 by the procedures described in the last section of Chapter 3. The procedure is, first, to note the proportion of respondents who mentioned the most popular topic on each side (the 61 percent of politicians and 33 percent of electors who mentioned material welfare); then, to eliminate these respondents, and, finally, to obtain the proportion of those who mentioned the topic that was most popular among those who did not mention the most popular topic.

As previously mentioned, the percentage difference (which we shall term the "consensus gap") between these two proportions gives the maximum estimate for lack of overlap in each sample. It is, of course, the politicians' lack of overlap in which we are mainly interested, since they have already been shown by the chi-square values to cluster more markedly on their most popular alternatives. Their consensus gap is in fact 35 percent, which is substantially over the 20 percent that we have laid down as the minimum acceptable difference between the leading mutually exclusive proportions in the group which is taken as more agreed. Had the consensus gap been under 20 percent, it would have pointed to a situation where relatively equal numbers of politicians endorsed different alternatives and, hence, were in disagreement. If the consensus gap is under 20 percent for politicians, we already have all the evidence of internal dissensus we need to say that they cannot be more agreed than electors; hence we need not report the chi-square values obtained from the comparison of the leading proportions in the overall multiple choice distributions.

The four summary statistics reported under the heading of "Topics of Consensus" in Table 4.2 are, therefore, sufficient to measure relative agreement on this appraisal. Because the politicians' consensus gap is over 20 percent and all the chi-square values are significant under the .05 level of probability, we can conclude that politicians agree more than electors about topics of consensus in Britain.

Two further questions were asked at different points in the survey about topics of disagreement. The first asked: "Generally, do you think there are any things people in Britain disagree about?" (*If yes*) "In your opinion, what are the things they disagree about?" The later question asked: "Could you please write down any problems facing the country at the moment on which, in your view, a strong minority disagrees with the majority?" Answers were coded together into the same categories as those used to code replies to the questions on topics of agreement. They thus form an overall multiple-choice distribution of the same type as Distribution A in Table 4.1, which can, in turn, be used to generate a distribution similar to Distribution B in Table 4.1. From the latter the maximum lack of overlap on this topic among politicians can be estimated through the consensus gap reported under the heading of "Topics of Dissensus" in Table 4.2. At 46 percent this is well over the 20 percent which we have taken as the minimum acceptable difference between the leading mutually exclusive groups of politicians.

The chi-square values listed under the same heading in Table 4.2 are obtained from the comparison of the numbers of politicians and electors endorsing the topics most popular on each side as such topics emerge on the overall multiple-choice distribution. Since all these values attain significance in the expected direction (*i.e.*, all proportions of politicians are greater than the proportions of electors with whom they are compared), we can conclude that politicians also agree more than electors on topics of dissensus in Britain.

Overall, therefore, politicians do share to a greater extent than electors a common "map" of the British political terrain.

AGREEMENT ON TOPICS OF CONSENSUS AND DISSENSUS AMONG PARTY GROUPINGS OF POLITICIANS AND ELECTORS

In the context of the overall discussion of Chapter 2 parties are important groups to examine because given the British political situation, it is as natural to order political participants in terms of their party allegiances as in terms of their status as politicians or electors. Party loyalties and party unity might in many, if not all, situations outweigh feelings of solidarity with other politicians. It could be argued that in concentrating the comparison upon the agreement of politicians and electors as such,[3] the discussion is ignoring the really significant political bodies. The relative distribution of agreement inside the party groups must, therefore, be carefully examined.

Table 4.3: Agreement of Conservative Politicians and Electors on Topics of Consensus and Dissensus in Britain

Topics of Consensus:	
Politicians' Consensus Gap (B distribution)	24 percent
Comparison on A distribution involving:	
Most popular topics	$\chi^2 = 4.463 \; p < .025$
Second most popular topics	$\chi^2 = 5.553 \; p < .01$
Third most popular topics	$\chi^2 = 4.306 \; p < .025$
Topics of Dissensus:	
Politicians' Consensus Gap (B distribution)	32 percent
Comparison on A distribution involving:	
Most popular topics	$\chi^2 = 0.003 \; p > .50$
Second most popular topics	$\chi^2 = 0.001 \; p > .50$
Third most popular topics	$\chi^2 = 0.006 \; p > .50$

Politicians N = 34; Electors N = 58

Table 4.3 presents statistics for Conservative politicians and electors derived from their comments on consensus and dissensus in Britain. In neither case do the consensus gaps for Conservative politicians fall below 20 percent; thus Conservative politicians are not disqualified by their internal disagreement from being regarded as more agreed than Conservative electors. Thus on topics of consensus the Conservative politicians agree more than Conservative electors, as can be seen from

---

[3] It should be noted that this comparison does not test any of the predictions put forward in Chapter 2 since those all refer to the *body* of politicians compared to the *body* of electors, not to Conservative politicians compared with Conservative electors, or Labour politicians compared with Labour electors.

**Table 4.4: Agreement of Labour Politicians and Electors
on Topics of Consensus and Dissensus in Britain**

Topics of Consensus:

Politicians' Consensus Gap (B distribution)	48 percent
Comparison on A distribution involving:	
Most popular topics	$\chi^2 = 6.852 \; p < .005$
Second most popular topics	$\chi^2 = 1.878 \; p < .10$
Third most popular topics	$\chi^2 = 3.452 \; p < .05$

Topics of Dissensus:

Politicians' Consensus Gap (B distribution)	80 percent
Comparison on A distribution involving:	
Most popular topics	$\chi^2 = 11.640 \; p < .0005$
Second most popular topics	$\chi^2 = 9.358 \; p < .005$
Third most popular topics	$\chi^2 = 4.970 \; p < .025$

Politicians $N = 25$; Electors $N = 58$

the chi-square values. But on the question of dissensus the numbers of Conservative politicians mentioning the most popular topics on their side are not significantly greater than the numbers of Conservative electors endorsing the most popular topics on theirs. An obvious explanation would hypothesize an increased sharing of the same appraisals by both electors and politicians as a result of their common party tie. In fact it does not appear that this negative finding results from any increased identity of views between Conservative politicians and electors. The most popular topics on the electoral side do not appear from the original distributions to be the same as the most popular topics among politicians. The internal disagreement of Conservative politicians appears as a recurrent phenomenon in this analysis, and is discussed further below.

Labour politicians seem from Table 4.4 to be more agreed than Labour electors on both sets of appraisals. Their "consensus gap" and, hence, their internal agreement is very high in both cases. On appraisals of dissensus all chi-square values are significant. The chi-square values for the first and third topics of consensus are significant, but the value for the second topic is not. This result seems to support the conclusion that the politicians are more agreed.

Thus in terms of agreement on what constitute topics of consensus and dissensus in Britain a reasonably consistent difference opens up between politicians and electors as such, regardless of party ties. The division of politicians themselves according to party does not necessarily increase their internal agreement. Agreement among Labour politicians and Conservative politicians can be compared with agreement among the body of politicians, both in regard to the proportions in each group making the most popular responses in the "A" distribution,[4] and in regard to the difference between the proportions falling into the first and second categories in the "B" distribution. On both of these comparisons the Labour politicians emerge as the most agreed of the three groupings, and the Conservative politicians as the least agreed. The whole body of politicians is less agreed than Labour politicians but more agreed than Conservative politicians. This is an interesting point, for if party divisions as such had constituted the main line of cleavage in the politicians' opinions, agreement would have increased in both cases when they divided by party.

CONCLUSIONS

The data analyzed in this chapter have therefore:

1. Upheld the expectation that politicians agree to a greater extent than electors about the topics on which there is general agreement and disagreement in Britain (Chapter 2, Prediction 8).
2. Shown that in three out of four comparisons politicians agree more on these topics than electors of their own party.

---

[4] The full "A" distributions for these groups are not reported here, but they are given in full in Tables 5.1, 5.2, 6.1 and 6.2 of Budge, *op. cit.*

POLITICIANS AND ELECTORS:
AGREEMENT ON GENERAL APPRAISALS
INVOLVING THE POLITICAL PARTIES

This chapter narrows and intensifies the analysis of the way conflict is regarded by examining appraisals of the most widespread and
permanent cleavage in British politics—the division between the two
British political parties. The topic relates sufficiently closely to that
discussed in the last chapter for the same prediction to be advanced:
that politicians will be more agreed than electors in the majority of
their appraisals of parties and party leaders. For these appraisals, too,
will constitute part of the body of understandings which politicians in
a stable democracy must necessarily share if they are to cooperate on
any occasions.

The main set of data against which the prediction will be tested
consists of the answers given by politicians and electors to a standard
series of "open" questions derived from the surveys carried out by the
Survey Research Center, University of Michigan. The question asked
what the respondent liked and disliked about the two major parties and
their leaders. Apart from such direct reactions the survey also enables
us to assess agreement on where the parties stood on nine issues current
in early 1962. Responses here are of considerable interest in showing
how far party loyalties can affect what appear at first to be strictly
factual appraisals.

INCIDENCE OF POSITIVE AND NEGATIVE APPRAISALS
OF THE PARTIES AMONG POLITICIANS AND ELECTORS

A prior step to comparing the actual likes and dislikes mentioned
by politicians and electors is to contrast the proportions of those in each
sample who made definite appraisals of parties and party leaders with

the proportions of those who forcefully replied that they either liked or disliked nothing at all about them. For if the supporters of each party disliked nothing about their own party and liked nothing about the opposing party, a substantial dissensus in British politics would already stand revealed.

Table 5.1 shows that such verbal hostility between supporters of the two parties is widespread among electors and very limited among politicians. In almost every case about half the electors say that they like (or dislike) nothing about the parties and their leaders. Further analysis shows that the composition of this group of electors changes with the appraisal. Those denying that they like anything about the Conservatives or Macmillan or that they dislike anything about Labour or Gaitskell, are overwhelmingly Labour supporters. Those who react in an entirely negative fashion to the Labour Party and Gaitskell but make favorable appraisals of Macmillan and the Conservative Party are largely Conservative. Among electors, therefore, can be discerned two sets of partisans with mutually exclusive opinions.

The situation among politicians is quite different. The numbers of those who are consistently unable to see anything wrong with their own party or party leader or anything right about their political opponents are very limited—never more than 15 percent of the whole sample. This is natural enough, for one would expect that the complex political experiences of the politicians—their bargaining, negotiating, compromising procedures—would weigh against the adoption of a simplistic black and white view of politics according to which one party

Table 5.1: Incidence of Definite and Negative Appraisals
of Parties and Party Leaders by Politicians and Electors

	POLITICIANS (percent)		ELECTORS (percent)	
	Made some definite appraisal	"Nothing"	Made some definite appraisal	"Nothing"
Like About Conservatives	92	8	46	54
Dislike About Conservatives	92	8	74	26
Like About Labour	88	12	57	43
Dislike About Labour	93	7	82	18
Like About Macmillan	86	14	51	49
Dislike About Macmillan	85	15	57	43
Like About Gaitskell	95	5	52	48
Dislike About Gaitskell	95	5	48	52

Politicians N = 59; Electors N varies between 134 and 143

is all that is good and another all that is bad. On the other hand the electors' limited knowledge and experience of politics predisposes them to think in stereotyped terms.

AGREEMENT OF POLITICIANS AND ELECTORS IN THEIR DEFINITE APPRAISALS OF PARTIES AND PARTY LEADERS

Comparison of the incidence of definite and entirely negative appraisals on each side is, however, only the first stage in estimating the relative agreement among each sample in their opinions of parties and party leaders. Agreement on the definite appraisals actually made must be compared before the prediction that politicians will be more agreed in their opinions of the parties and party leaders can be said to have been upheld.

Table 5.2 presents the results obtained from comparisons of the eight sets of definite appraisals of parties and party leaders made by politicians and electors in answer to the questions reported above. The table summarizes results which are based on distributions similar to those presented in full in Table 4.1. Each row presents the four summary statistics necessary to decide whether politicians agree more than electors on the like or dislike under consideration. First the consensus gap reveals the presence or absence of two different and roughly equal groups of politicians with different likes or dislikes. If such groups are absent (*i.e.*, if the consensus gap is over 20 percent), the chi-square values show whether the numbers of politicians endorsing the likes or dislikes most popular on their side are substantially greater than the numbers of electors endorsing the likes or dislikes most popular on their side.

From Table 5.2 it can be seen that politicians appear equally as disagreed as electors on four of the appraisals under consideration. This conclusion was reached because on all these appraisals, except their likes about Gaitskell (and very nearly these as well), there was relatively little overlap between the opinions of two relatively equal and mutually exclusive groups in the politicians' ranks. This can be seen from the fact that consensus gaps fall below 20 percent in each of these cases. As will appear from the discussion of Conservative and Labour replies, these divergences among politicians are not solely due to a party division, since considerable dissensus exists among the politicians within each party group.

On the other hand the prediction that politicians would agree more than electors in their judgments of the parties and party leaders is up-

Table 5.2: Agreement of Politicians and Electors on Definite Appraisals of the Two Major Parties and Party Leaders

Appraisals on which politicians were more agreed than electors:	Politicians' Consensus Gap B distribution (percent)	COMPARISON ON A DISTRIBUTION INVOLVING:		
		Most popular topics	Second most popular topics	Third most popular topics
Likes Conservative Party	23	$\chi^2 = 18.830$ p $< .0005$	$\chi^2 = 5.909$ p $< .01$	$\chi^2 = 2.202$ p $< .10$
Dislikes Conservative Party	37	$\chi^2 = 9.191$ p $< .005$	prediction of difference reversed	
Dislikes Labour Party	24	$\chi^2 = 7.346$ p $< .005$	$\chi^2 = 1.659$ p $< .10$	$\chi^2 = 2.925$ p $< .05$
Dislikes Gaitskell	26	$\chi^2 = 6.630$ p $< .01$	$\chi^2 = 8.582$ p $< .005$	$\chi^2 = 6.280$ p $< .01$
Appraisals on which politicians were not more agreed than electors:				
Likes Labour Party	17			
Likes Gaitskell	20	$\chi^2 = 1.676$ p $< .10$	$\chi^2 = 11.053$ p $< .0005$	$\chi^2 = 8.931$ p $< .005$
Likes Macmillan	5			
Dislikes Macmillan	17			

Politicians N = 59; Electors N varies between 134 and 143

held on a number of cases equal to those on which it is disconfirmed.[1] This finding makes it rather difficult to judge whether the prediction should be regarded as false or valid (it is valid at any rate to a limited extent). But it should be borne in mind that the topics about which the appraisals were made were highly controversial—no less than the principal symbols and realities of cleavage among the politicians. Given the highly contentious nature of the appraisals and the supporting evidence of Table 5.1, it is perhaps more surprising that the politicians should be in relative agreement on so many as half than that they should not agree more than electors on half.

A striking feature of Table 5.2 is the fact that appraisals on which politicians agree less than electors relate in three out of four cases to the party leaders rather than to the political parties. This finding might indicate that politicians tend to agree more on the enduring and long-term political objects by which they are confronted, (*i.e.*, the parties themselves), rather than on the less enduring and, in recent years, rapidly changing objects, *i.e.*, the party leaders.

AGREEMENT AMONG PARTY GROUPS OF POLITICIANS AND ELECTORS IN THEIR APPRAISALS OF PARTIES AND PARTY LEADERS

The imposition of a control for party does not increase the contrast between the agreement of politicians and that of electors in their appraisals of parties and party leaders—quite the reverse, in fact, as will be seen from Tables 5.3 and 5.4.

These tables present the results of comparisons between electors and politicians of the same parties. As in the case of Table 5.2 they present a "consensus gap" which is actually a maximum estimate of the extent to which two groups exist among politicians who are roughly equal in numbers and make completely different appraisals of the parties and party leaders. Where the consensus gap is over 20 percent and is thus large enough to discount the possibility that an internal dissensus exists among politicians, the tables further present chi-square values for the comparison of the numbers endorsing the three most popular appraisals on each side in the overall multiple-choice distribu-

---

[1] It will be observed that the statistics are somewhat inconsistent on three appraisals where politicians are judged to be more agreed. In each case the evidence that politicians do agree seems weightier. But there can be no doubt that the inconsistency results from a lower level of agreement generally among politicians than was encountered on appraisals of topics about which there is consensus and dissensus. The same inconsistency, giving rise to the same conclusion, will be found in Tables 5.3 and 5.4.

Table 5.3: Agreement of Conservative Politicians and Electors on
Definite Appraisals of the Two Major Parties and Party Leaders

Appraisals on which politicians were more agreed than electors:	Politicians' Consensus Gap B distribution (percent)	COMPARISON ON A DISTRIBUTION INVOLVING:		
		Most popular topics	Second most popular topics	Third most popular topics
Dislikes Labour Party	30	$\chi^2 = 3.758$ p $< .05$	$\chi^2 = 3.414$ p $< .05$	$\chi^2 = 0.375$ p $< .35$
Appraisals on which politicians were not more agreed than electors:				
Likes Labour Party	6	. . . .	. . . .	. . . .
Likes Conservative Party	18	. . . .	. . . .	. . . .
Dislikes Conservative Party	30	$\chi^2 = 2.000$ p $< .10$	$\chi^2 = 0.033$ p $< .45$	*
Likes Gaitskell	17	. . . .	. . . .	. . . .
Dislikes Gaitskell	9	. . . .	. . . .	. . . .
Likes Macmillan	21	$\chi^2 = 0.485$ p $< .25$	$\chi^2 = 5.188$ p $< .025$	*
Dislikes Macmillan	14	. . . .	. . . .	. . . .

Politicians N = 34; Electors N = 58
* denotes that numbers are too small for further comparison

Table 5.4: Agreement of Labour Politicians and Electors on
Definite Appraisals of the Two Major Parties and Party Leaders

Appraisals on which politicians were more agreed than electors:	Politicians' Consensus Gap B distribution (percent)	COMPARISON ON A DISTRIBUTION INVOLVING:		
		Most popular topics	Second most popular topics	Third most popular topics
Dislikes Labour Party Dislikes Conservative Party	52	$\chi^2 = 5.711\ p < .01$	$\chi^2 = 0.224\ p < .35$	*
Likes Gaitskell	44	$\chi^2 = 2.731\ p < .05$	$\chi^2 = 1.506\ p < .15$	*
Dislikes Gaitskell	36	$\chi^2 = 6.520\ p < .01$	$\chi^2 = 9.384\ p < .005$	*
	46	$\chi^2 = 9.692\ p < .005$	$\chi^2 = 11.871\ p < .0005$	*
Appraisals on which politicians were not more agreed than electors:				
Likes Conservative Party	12			
Likes Labour Party	24	$\chi^2 = 0.046\ p < .45$	*	
Likes Macmillan	16			*
Dislikes Macmillan	8			

Politicians N = 25; Electors N = 58
* denotes that numbers are too small for further comparison

tion. If the consensus gap is over 20 percent and the chi-square values are significant in the expected direction (of showing that politicians cluster more on the most popular choices), then the politicians can be regarded as agreeing more than electors.

When Conservative politicians are compared with Conservative electors, dislikes about the Labour Party form the only appraisal upon which politicians agree more. This end result of the comparison might merely mark an increase in agreement among both politicians and electors. What is surprising is that the pattern of relative agreement does not take the shape summarized in Table 5.3 because Conservatives, whether politicians or electors, agree more with each other. It takes the shape it does because of an extensive dissensus among the Conservative politicians in their appraisals of the parties and party leaders. On three appraisals only—their dislikes about the Conservative Party, likes about Macmillan, and dislikes about Labour—does a condition of dissensus not exist among Conservative politicians. On the other five appraisals roughly equal and mutually exclusive groups advance different judgments. In the case of the Conservatives the cohesion of the politicians has not been advanced by confining the analysis to the opinions of one party group.

Labour politicians, in contrast, tend to exhibit a higher degree of consensus on these appraisals than Labour electors. Again they differ from Conservative politicians in that an internal dissensus exists among them only in regard to likes about the Conservative Party, likes about Macmillan, and dislikes about Macmillan. On the other appraisals Labour politicians are in considerable agreement, although they do not agree to a greater extent than electors about the qualities they admire in the Labour Party.

As in the comparison of appraisals about general agreements and disagreements carried out in the last chapter, there seems a tendency for Labour politicians to agree to a greater extent than Conservative politicians. Party ties of themselves, however, do not appear to increase agreement among politicians; otherwise Conservative and Labour politicians would be more agreed than the general body of politicians.[2]

---

[2] This finding is of particular interest because of the light it casts upon one explanation for the absence of relative agreement among the body of politicians on four appraisals. It could be said that in evaluating their own parties and party leaders, Labour and Conservative politicians were naturally prone to make quite different appraisals under the influence of their strong partisan feelings. But since a common party identification did not increase agreement on the appraisals among party sub-groups of politicians, party hardly seems capable of causing disagreement among the whole body of politicians.

AGREEMENT OF POLITICIANS AND ELECTORS
IN THEIR APPRAISALS OF PARTY STANDS

Table 5.5 presents a summary comparison of agreement in replies to questions on where the parties and the Trades Union Congress stood on nine current issues—for, against or neutral? (The Trades Union Congress is strongly linked with politics by reason of its intimate relations with the Labour Party.) Since respondents could place the party in one position only, responses are mutually exclusive, and, hence, one chi-square value suffices for each comparison.

In 22 out of the 36 cases in the table politicians are more agreed than electors—a proportion of 61 percent successes for the hypothesis compared to 39 percent failures. In eight cases an internal dissensus existed among politicians, although six of these cases involved the Liberals and T.U.C. positions which were not so highly visible as the policies of the two major parties.

Taking Table 5.5 as a whole, the prediction that politicians will be more agreed than electors is upheld in the majority of appraisals. Particularly since agreement was here estimated on a different type of data by a different method from those previously employed, the finding forms valuable confirmation of the trend to superior agreement among politicians on this kind of judgment.

However disagreement is obviously present on a substantial minority of the appraisals. If the divergent pull of party loyalties is responsible for this, one would expect to find relative agreement increasing when politicians and electors of the same party were compared. It is conceivable, of course, that agreement among politicians might not increase relative to that among electors because electors, too, were induced by their common party loyalties to agree more, although this eventuality has not arisen on previous appraisals. However the possibility can be checked once the overall pattern of relative agreement among politicians and electors has been examined.

Not a relative increase but a relative diminution in the agreement of Conservative politicians takes place when their appraisals are compared with those of Conservative electors. Politicians are more agreed than electors on only half the total number of cases. In seven of the cases where politicians appear as no more agreed than electors they are adjudged no more agreed because an internal dissensus appears in their own ranks (as compared to eight such cases of dissensus among all politicians). The decrease in appraisals where politicians are more agreed seems due in part to an increase in the agreement of electors,

Table 5.5: Agreement of Politicians and Electors on Appraisals of Party and T.U.C. Stands on Issues

	Conservative Party Stand		Labour Party Stand		Liberal Party Stand		T.U.C. Stand	
	Politicians' Consensus Gap (percent)	Chi-square	Politicians' Consensus Gap (percent)	Chi-square	Politicians' Consensus Gap (percent)	Chi-square	Politicians' Consensus Gap (percent)	Chi-square
Common Market	38	1.043 $p < .25$	81	25.28 $p < .0005$	88	42.84 $p < .0005$	55	29.936 $p < .0005$
Berlin negotiations	3	....	54	1.735 $p < .10$	34	0.775 $p < .25$	15	....
Transport Bill	84	33.433 $p < .0005$	90	43.808 $p < .0005$	13	....	84	32.872 $p < .0005$
Education shortages	27	4.556 $p < .025$	94	12.855 $p < .0005$	94	16.315 $p < .0005$	79	8.034 $p < .005$
Monopolies	4	....	72	20.602 $p < .0005$	52	21.222 $p < .0005$	45	11.134 $p < .0005$
Immigration Bill	68	9.628 $p < .005$	32	9.196 $p < .005$	32	10.410 $p < .005$	0	....
Housing shortage	23	0.769 $p < .25$	32	prediction of difference reversed	29	1.9333 $p < .10$	19	....
Greater London government	88	18.214 $p < .0005$	62	23.265 $p < .0005$	1	....	52	7.191 $p < .005$
Wage Pause	96	7.593 $p < .005$	64	7.437 $p < .005$	7	....	58	6.107 $p < .01$

Politicians N varies from 45 to 48; Electors N varies from 129 to 131

Table 5.6: Agreement of Conservative Politicians and Electors on Appraisals of Party and T.U.C. Stands on Issues

	Conservative Party Stand		Labour Party Stand		Liberal Party Stand		T.U.C. Stand	
	Politicians' Consensus Gap (percent)	Chi-square	Politicians' Consensus Gap (percent)	Chi-square	Politicians' Consensus Gap (percent)	Chi-square	Politicians' Consensus Gap (percent)	Chi-square
Common Market	12	······	66	4.980 $p < .025$	76	15.830 $p < .0005$	54	7.630 $p < .005$
Berlin negotiations	5	······	29	0.020 $p < .45$	21	0.002 $p < .50$	8	······
Transport Bill	92	23.220 $p < .0005$	92	26.902 $p < .0005$	33	5.588 $p < .01$	80	11.623 $p < .0005$
Education shortages	25	0.006 $p < .50$	88	5.010 $p < .025$	88	5.850 $p < .01$	62	2.312 $p < .10$
Monopolies	34	4.758 $p < .025$	62	9.410 $p < .005$	50	9.051 $p < .005$	33	1.878 $p < .10$
Immigration Bill	58	5.629 $p < .01$	8	······	30	6.296 $p < .01$	38	5.494 $p < .01$
Housing shortage	25	prediction of difference reversed	9	······	29	0.053 $p < .45$	4	······
Greater London government	100	23.265 $p < .0005$	70	18.199 $p < .0005$	8	······	40	13.127 $p < .0005$
Wage Pause	100	2.421 $p < .10$	58	1.551 $p < .15$	24	3.847 $p < .025$	56	2.580 $p < .10$

Politicians N varies between 24 and 25; Electors N varies between 52 and 54.

Table 5.7: Agreement of Labour Politicians and Electors on Appraisals of Party and T.U.C. Stands on Issues

	Conservative Party Stand		Labour Party Stand		Liberal Party Stand		T.U.C. Stand	
	Politicians' Consensus Gap (percent)	Chi-square	Politicians' Consensus Gap (percent)	Chi-square	Politicians' Consensus Gap (percent)	Chi-square	Politicians' Consensus Gap (percent)	Chi-square
Common Market	66	2.702 $p < .10$	92	24.660 $p < .0005$	100	18.840 $p < .0005$	57	6.490 $p < .01$
Berlin negotiations	0	. . . .	82	3.661 $p < .05$	48	2.296 $p < .10$	39	0.297 $p < .35$
Transport Bill	77	9.501 $p < .005$	82	14.117 $p < .0005$	13	. . . .	83	17.635 $p < .0005$
Education shortages	66	5.211 $p < .025$	100	8.240 $p < .005$	100	13.326 $p < .0005$	92	6.100 $p < .01$
Monopolies	18	. . . .	82	11.168 $p < .0005$	50	11.777 $p < .0005$	57	7.035 $p < .005$
Immigration Bill	78	8.562 $p < .005$	57	9.554 $p < .005$	35	1.360 $p < .15$	57	4.965 $p < .025$
Housing shortage	56	8.207 $p < .005$	57	1.521 $p < .15$	19	. . . .	46	1.848 $p < .10$
Greater London government	74	7.115 $p < .005$	52	6.636 $p < .005$	27	7.452 $p < .005$	65	9.908 $p < .005$
Wage Pause	92	4.521 $p < .025$	69	7.429 $p < .005$	26	0.810 $p < .25$	61	2.701 $p < .10$

Politicians N varies between 21 and 23; Electors N varies between 54 and 57

but it is clear that Conservative politicians are hardly more agreed internally than the body of all politicians. Had the party tie of itself been the cause of disagreement on appraisals of party and T.U.C. policies among politicians, Conservative politicians would have been noticeably more agreed themselves than the body of all politicians.

No diminution in the incidence of politicians' agreement relative to that of electors is observed for Labour. In fact the number of these cases increases slightly from 22 to 24. There are only four cases in which an internal dissensus appears among Labour politicians. Thus some increase in the agreement of both Labour politicians and of Labour electors seems to have taken place. The greater agreement of Labour politicians compared with Conservative politicians on party stands is in line with their tendency to greater agreement on appraisals of the parties and party leaders and on appraisals of topics about which there is consensus and dissensus in Britain.

CONCLUSIONS

The findings of this chapter have therefore:

1. shown that politicians are more inclined than electors to mention favourable points about the party to which they do not belong and unfavourable points about their own party
2. upheld on four out of eight comparisons the expectation that politicians would agree to a greater extent than electors on their appraisals of the parties and party leaders (Chapter Two, Prediction 9)
3. shown that Labour politicians agree on appraisals of parties and party leaders to a greater extent than Labour electors and Conservative politicians
4. upheld on 22 out of 36 comparisons the expectation that politicians agree more than electors in their appraisals of where the parties stand on issues (Chapter Two, Predictions 9 and 11)
5. shown that on approximately half the comparisons politicians agree more on appraisals of party stands than electors when both come from the same party.

6

POLITICIANS AND ELECTORS: AGREEMENT ON ISSUE APPRAISALS

In comparing agreement among British politicians with that among electors in areas of controversy, it is obviously not possible to restrict the discussion to such general appraisals of conflict and the parties as those already examined. It is also desirable to consider agreement on preferences and on appraisals formed in relation to specific matters under dispute which have to be handled in some manner by the democratic political processes. These matters are in fact political issues. Since the strong feelings and hostilities engendered by such substantive topics form the shifting and unpredictable elements that constantly threaten to bring democratic procedures down, it is of obvious interest to see whether such feelings are counterbalanced in any way by understandings such as have been shown to exist on appraisals of the general political conflicts in British society.

The particular issues discussed in this and the next chapter are fully described in Appendix C, and the criteria for their selection given in detail. They are all current issues in the sense of topics on which a course of action was being urged by or upon the government through representative bodies, pressure groups or the mass media during the period of the survey. The issues vary: some of these topics were subjects of straight party conflict; others divided one or both parties internally; and one united the parties. Other differences relate to subject matter and coverage by the mass media.

The labels given to each issue in the tables are necessarily brief and uninformative; a fuller description follows: British negotiations to enter the Common Market; the question of opening new negotiations with the Russians over Berlin; the Bill to split up the British Transport Commission (being considered by Parliament during the first half of 1962); the problem of shortages in education; the problem of private monopolies in Britain; the Bill to limit the entry of Commonwealth

immigrants to Britain (which became law in the middle of the interviewing period); the fact that the supply of housing in Britain was not
meeting the demand; the Bill to reorganize the government of the
Greater London conurbation (being considered by Parliament in the
first half of 1962); the government's action in refusing to grant pay increases to its employees until March, 1962, and the imposition of re-
straint in its pay awards after that date.

We are interested here in the degree of agreement on the factual
appraisals of the issues. In situations where opportunities for bargaining and compromise exist at all, mutual understandings on appraisals
of disputed points may play a large part in making negotiations easier
and in speeding an agreed settlement. The issue appraisals upon which
agreement is to be estimated are judgments about the existence of a
political issue, the range of alternative policies seen as open to pursuit
on an issue, and the consequences anticipated from an issue. Greater
agreement on these points should narrow the area of controversy with
which negotiations have to deal in the first place and by the promotion
of arguments acceptable to all sides should at least avail to narrow any
gap between participants' initial issue preferences.[1] It should be repeated that the three facts *about* issues mentioned above are the only
factual appraisals to which discussion and analysis refer. They should
not be confused with facts *bearing* on the issues (*e.g.*, whether the
Common Market would actually benefit Britain), a question on which
no prediction is either advanced or tested.

EXISTENCE OF ISSUES

The data presented in Table 6.1 show that politicians agree more
than electors on a substantial majority of issues (six out of nine). Even
in the cases where no difference appears, it is because electors, like
politicians, agree nearly unanimously about the existence of the issue.

The interest in the findings of Table 6.1 lies less in the unsensa-
tional unanimity of politicians than in the considerable numbers of

---

[1] One can, of course, see that the opposite situation could conceivably make
for compromise. Where one set of politicians does not feel affected by a problem
and another set does, it is then easier for the first group to yield to the others' demands since they do not feel their interests affected. But given that most political
policies involve a diversion of resources from still other areas of use, compromise
might not after all be easier in such a situation. As always in speculating on these
topics, it is necessary to argue in regard to what seem the most common cases and
on the basis of the most weighty actual consequences of the situation that is envisaged. On these grounds the consequences mentioned in the text seem the most
likely to ensue.

Table 6.1: Agreement of Politicians and Electors
on the Existence of Issues

	POLITICIANS (percent)		ELECTORS (percent)	
	Yes	No	Yes	No
Have you heard anything about:				
Common Market	100	0	91	9
Berlin negotiations	96	4	77	23
Transport Bill	89	11	24	76
Education shortages	100	0	90	10
Monopolies	100	0	70	30
Immigration Bill	100	0	85	15
Housing shortage	100	0	97	3
Greater London government	100	0	70	30
Wage Pause	100	0	84	16

Politicians N varies between 53 and 58; Electors N varies between 139 and 147.

electors who did not recognize some issues. In entering into any discussion, hardly any politicians would need to be persuaded of the political relevance of the issue at hand, whereas many electors would have to be convinced that political action was really necessary. Under such circumstances the issue may very easily be settled among the politicians without external intervention.

A comparison of Labour electors with Labour politicians produces exactly the same pattern of agreement as does the comparison of all politicians with all electors. Conservative politicians, however, are not more agreed than Conservative electors on Berlin and the Wage Pause.

AGREEMENT ON ALTERNATIVE POLICIES PERCEIVED AS OPEN TO PURSUIT

Consider the consequences if the policies advanced by one political group broke like thunderbolts out of the blue upon other politicians. The result would be a marked intensification of the uncertainty in which politicians already live to a considerable extent. Such uncertainty has been stressed in Chapter 1 as a threat to politicians' adherence to any very specific democratic procedures. Intensified uncertainty seems very likely to undermine these attachments still further. Politicians, subject to even more sudden and multiple pressures from their environment than they seem likely to endure now could afford even less than at present to commit themselves to a specific and detailed procedural code. In the stable democracy of Britain we do not expect to encounter such extreme uncertainty; hence we anticipate considerable agreement among politicians on the practicable policies open to pursuit on each issue. Table 6.2 summarizes the survey data bearing on this point.

The issues on which politicians agree more than electors in their appraisals of viable alternatives substantially outnumber those on which they do not. Thus the leading hypothesis must be regarded as upheld by the survey data. Two exceptions to the general pattern do however emerge: on immigration and education. On neither issue does a dissensus exist among politicians, but on both politicians fail to appear as more agreed than electors because the latter exhibit a high degree of internal consensus.

An examination of agreement among Conservative politicians and electors reveals that the general pattern is the same as that which appears when the body of politicians is compared with the body of electors. On education both politicians and electors are highly agreed and for this reason no difference appears between them. On immigration, however, two relatively equal and non-overlapping groups appear among the politicians, with the result that they display much more dissensus than electors.[2]

The case of the Labour Party is more interesting than that of the Conservatives, for here the pattern of agreement shifts. Politicians are still more agreed than electors in seven out of nine cases. One of the cases in which they are more agreed is, however, education, and one of those in which they are not more agreed is wages. In the case of wages the proportion of Labour electors mentioning the possibility of a more generous wages policy approached the proportion of Labour politicians mentioning government policy or a total incomes policy (which tied for the most popular responses among their group). The almost unanimous mention by Labour politicians of the possibility of increasing education expenditure helped to make them more agreed on this appraisal than Labour electors, 67 percent of whom also mentioned such an increase.

On immigration Labour politicians did not display a dissensus of the same sort as the Conservative politicians, but the numbers men-

---

[2] Again some inconsistent results appear in the table. Where the consensus gap is relatively large and the comparison of the most popular alternatives produces a significant result in the predicted direction, the politicians have been taken as more agreed. While the appearance of inconsistency may be taken as evidence that Conservative politicians are less agreed relative to Conservative electors, it should also be remembered that the reduction of the base number in the table makes it more difficult to obtain significance with the chi-square statistic.

Table 6.2: Agreement of Politicians and Electors on Alternatives Open to Pursuit on Issues

	Politicians' Consensus Gap B distribution (percent)	COMPARISONS ON A DISTRIBUTION INVOLVING:		
		Most popular alternatives	Second most popular alternatives	Third most popular alternatives
Common Market	31	$x^2 = 8.939$ p $< .005$	$x^2 = 11.554$ p $< .0005$	$x^2 = 7.972$ p $< .005$
Berlin negotiations	61	$x^2 = 14.709$ p $< .0005$	$x^2 = 7.148$ p $< .005$	$x^2 = 9.519$ p $< .005$
Transport Bill	40	$x^2 = 17.312$ p $< .0005$	$x^2 = 22.783$ p $< .0005$	$x^2 = 14.300$ p $< .0005$
Education shortages	70	$x^2 = 2.421$ p $< .10$	$x^2 = 6.666$ p $< .01$	$x^2 = 8.303$ p $< .005$
Monopolies	25	$x^2 = 21.168$ p $< .005$	$x^2 = 26.466$ p $< .0005$	$x^2 = 14.757$ p $< .0005$
Immigration Bill	24	$x^2 = 0.010$ p $< .50$	$x^2 = 0.005$ p $< .50$	$x^2 = 0.189$ p $< .35$
Housing shortage	59	$x^2 = 29.340$ p $< .0005$	$x^2 = 8.909$ p $< .005$	$x^2 = 6.935$ p $< .005$
Greater London government	23	$x^2 = 11.907$ p $< .0005$	$x^2 = 12.727$ p $< .0005$	$x^2 = 26.248$ p $< .0005$
Wage Pause	59	$x^2 = 22.076$ p $< .0005$	$x^2 = 22.855$ p $< .0005$	$x^2 = 6.096$ p $< .01$

Politicians N varies between 53 and 58; Electors N varies between 138 and 146

Table 6.3: Agreement of Conservative Politicians and Electors on Alternatives Open to Pursuit on Issues

	Politicians' Consensus Gap B distribution (percent)	COMPARISONS ON A DISTRIBUTION INVOLVING:		
		Most popular alternatives	Second most popular alternatives	Third most popular alternatives
Common Market	48	$x^2 = 8.152$ $p < .005$	$x^2 = 6.935$ $p < .005$	$x^2 = 0.483$ $p < .25$
Berlin negotiations	44	$x^2 = 3.207$ $p < .05$	$x^2 = 2.386$ $p < .10$	*
Transport Bill	39	$x^2 = 8.316$ $p < .005$	$x^2 = 8.316$ $p < .005$	$x^2 = 2.627$ $p < .10$
Education shortages	53	$x^2 = 0.001$ $p < .60$	$x^2 = 6.461$ $p < .01$	$x^2 = 0.737$ $p < .25$
Monopolies	29	$x^2 = 6.633$ $p < .01$	$x^2 = 3.171$ $p < .05$	$x^2 = 4.806$ $p < .025$
Immigration Bill	17	....	....	....
Housing shortage	61	$x^2 = 10.765$ $p < .005$	$x^2 = 1.598$ $p < .15$	$x^2 = 0.187$ $p < .35$
Greater London government	23	$x^2 = 3.480$ $p < .05$	$x^2 = 4.148$ $p < .025$	*
Wage Pause	59	$x^2 = 15.308$ $p < .0005$	$x^2 = 16.855$ $p < .0005$	$x^2 = 3.888$ $p < .025$

Politicians N varies between 29 and 33; Electors N varies between 52 and 58
* denotes that numbers are too small for further comparison

Table 6.4: Agreement of Labour Politicians and Electors on Alternatives Open to Pursuit on Issues

	Politicians' Consensus Gap B distribution (percent)	COMPARISONS ON A DISTRIBUTION INVOLVING:		
		Most popular alternatives	Second most popular alternatives	Third most popular alternatives
Common Market	20	$x^2 = 3.178$ p < .05	$x^2 = 2.611$ p < .10	✻
Berlin negotiations	72	$x^2 = 13.165$ p < .0005	$x^2 = 10.798$ p < .005	✻
Transport Bill	88	$x^2 = 22.437$ p < .0005	$x^2 = 8.778$ p < .005	$x^2 = 11.130$ p < .0005
Education shortages	84	$x^2 = 3.647$ p < .05	$x^2 = 11.769$ p < .0005	$x^2 = 3.882$ p < .025
Monopolies	52	$x^2 = 23.532$ p < .0005	✻	✻
Immigration Bill	36	$x^2 = 0.027$ p < .45	$x^2 = 1.208$ p < .15	$x^2 = 0.837$ p < .25
Housing shortage	76	$x^2 = 5.597$ p < .01	$x^2 = 15.213$ p < .0005	$x^2 = 8.453$ p < .005
Greater London government	20	$x^2 = 3.955$ p < .025	$x^2 = 6.662$ p < .005	✻
Wage Pause	48	$x^2 = 2.637$ p < .10	$x^2 = 11.465$ p < .0005	$x^2 = 9.315$ p < .005

Politicians N varies between 24 and 25; Electors N varies between 56 and 58
✻ denotes that numbers are too small for further comparison

tioning the most popular policies were not significantly greater than the numbers of Labour electors who named the most often mentioned alternatives on their side.

AGREEMENT ON THE EFFECTS OF POLITICAL ISSUES

If one set of politicians sees a movement to end a colonial war in purely economic terms while another group views it solely as a matter of national honor, the chances of compromise between them seem much less favorable than if they all viewed it in economic or in national terms or in both. Of course this might not always be the case. Suppose some politicians thought in one set of moral terms—e.g., that colonial revolts must be repressed as a matter of national honor—and others thought in quite contrary moral terms—e.g., that colonial peoples should be helped to attain national independence as soon as possible. In such a situation an agreed solution might be harder to attain than if the two camps viewed the effects of the issue in entirely different frames of reference.

Granted that such situations could and do occur, it still seems plausible to argue that negotiating procedures are generally better served if politicians are in agreement on what the effects of issues are. If one side uses economic arguments and the other uses moral, they are not really in a negotiating situation at all, they are talking past each other without employing common terms of reference. Even if two opposed moral positions are taken up on the basis of agreed appraisals of the effects, at least a common language is being employed, and this seems a first prerequisite for effective discussion.[3] The reasons for expecting a link between democratic stability and agreement on the specific effects of issues apply with even greater force to agreement on the prior question of whether any effect is felt from the issue at all. Where some politicians felt themselves unaffected by an issue, even remotely, they would tend to see no reason for doing anything about it. And this

---

[3] This argument seems to make some of the same points in terms of the "effects" of issues, as does D. E. Stokes when he discusses the different "dimensions" along which different participants in a political situation may view events. In any one political system or political culture people may interpret an issue in terms of diverse and even opposed criteria or in terms of the same criteria. Variations in the extent to which politicians and populations view political situations along the same "dimensions" may affect the functioning of the party system (may help produce a multi-party system, for example). Stokes does not discuss the influence of such variations on democratic stability, but inferences similar to those presented in the preceding paragraphs can be drawn from his argument. See D. E. Stokes, "Spatial Models of Party Competition," *APSR*, 57 (1963), 368–77. Note especially here "The Axiom of Unidimensionality" and "The Axiom of Fixed Structure."

could lead to extreme tension in a case where another group who felt themselves affected were pressing for immediate action. The democratic crises associated with the emergence of working-class political movements can be traced partly to the fact that the politicians who opposed them felt no personal or political effects from unemployment or from the lack of social welfare services.[4]

A. Agreement on Being Affected or Not Affected by Issues

Table 6.5 shows quite clearly that politicians are more agreed than electors on every issue and that the politicians generally feel affected by the issue. Agreement among politicians is high by any standard— relative or absolute. The only two issues on which electors are in considerable agreement are the Common Market and the housing problem.

Table 6.5: Agreement of Politicians and Electors on Being Affected or Not Affected by Issues

	POLITICIANS (percent)		ELECTORS (percent)	
	Yes	No	Yes	No
Do you feel that you (or anyone/anything in which you take an interest) are affected by:				
Common Market	100	0	85	15
Berlin negotiations	96	4	72	28
Transport Bill	88	12	66	34
Education shortages	91	9	65	35
Monopolies	89	11	67	33
Immigration Bill	91	9	56	44
Housing shortage	98	2	82	18
Greater London government	98	2	50	50
Wage Pause	100	0	61	39

Politicians N varies between 53 and 57; Electors N varies between 138 and 147.

B. Agreement on the Substantive Effects Expected from Issues

Turning now to the actual effects anticipated from the issue by members of the two samples (as distinct from the initial appraisals considered in Table 6.5 of whether or not one is affected at all), it can

---

[4] S. M. Lipset, *Political Man* (Garden City, N.Y.: Doubleday, 1960), p. 85.

Table 6.6: Agreement of Politicians and Electors on the Substantive Effects Expected from Issues

	Politicians' Consensus Gap B distribution (percent)	COMPARISONS ON A DISTRIBUTION INVOLVING:		
		Most popular effects	Second most popular effects	Third most popular effects
Common Market	72	$\chi^2 = 4.833\ p < .025$	$\chi^2 = 13.826\ p < .0005$	$\chi^2 = 0.638\ p < .25$
Berlin negotiations	66	$\chi^2 = 8.804\ p < .005$	$\chi^2 = 3.466\ p < .05$	$\chi^2 = 3.420\ p < .05$
Transport Bill	37	$\chi^2 = 0.346\ p < .35$	$\chi^2 = 5.206\ p < .025$	$\chi^2 = 3.226\ p < .05$
Education shortages	40	$\chi^2 = 1.802\ p < .10$	$\chi^2 = 0.008\ p < .50$	$\chi^2 = 9.379\ p < .005$
Monopolies	71	$\chi^2 = 6.458\ p < .01$	$\chi^2 = 6.458\ p < .01$	$\chi^2 = 7.367\ p < .005$
Immigration Bill	38	$\chi^2 = 3.990\ p < .025$	$\chi^2 = 6.182\ p < .01$	$\chi^2 = 6.262\ p < .01$
Housing shortage	23	$\chi^2 = 2.773\ p < .05$	$\chi^2 = 0.859\ p < .25$	$\chi^2 = 3.087\ p < .05$
Greater London government	74	$\chi^2 = 49.182\ p < .0005$	$\chi^2 = 7.645\ p < .005$	$\chi^2 = 3.532\ p < .05$
Wage Pause	50	$\chi^2 = 4.782\ p < .025$	$^2\chi = 34.931\ p < .0005$	$\chi^2 = 0.947\ p < .25$

Politicians N varies between 53 and 58; Electors N varies between 138 and 146

NOTE: The question responsible for data in this table is a follow-up to that reported in Table 6.5: "*How* does it (the issue in question) affect you?" (or person/thing in which you take an interest?).

Table 6.7: Agreement of Conservative Politicians and Electors on the Substantive Effects Expected from Issues

	Politicians' Consensus Gap B distribution (percent)	Comparisons on a distribution involving:		
		Most popular effects	Second most popular effects	Third most popular effects
Common Market	73	$\chi^2 = 0.138$ p $< .40$	$\chi^2 = 1.949$ p $< .10$	*
Berlin negotiations	35	$\chi^2 = 0.075$ p $< .40$	$\chi^2 = 0.739$ p $< .25$	*
Transport Bill	35	$\chi^2 = 0.153$ p $< .35$	$\chi^2 = 0.027$ p $< .45$	*
Education shortages	44	$\chi^2 = 2.545$ p $< .10$	$\chi^2 = 0.129$ p $< .40$	*
Monopolies	41	$\chi^2 = 0.581$ p $< .25$	*	*
Immigration Bill	47	$\chi^2 = 7.700$ p $< .005$	$\chi^2 = 1.649$ p $< .10$	*
Housing shortage	21	$\chi^2 = 1.101$ p $< .15$	$\chi^2 = 2.400$ p $< .10$	$\chi^2 = 0.313$ p $< .35$
Greater London government	67	$\chi^2 = 18.472$ p $< .0005$	*	*
Wage Pause	36	$\chi^2 = 0.063$ p $< .45$	*	*

Politicians N varies between 29 and 33; Electors N varies between 53 and 58
* denotes that numbers are too small for further comparison

be seen from Table 6.6 that there are six issues in regard to which politicians agree more than electors on anticipated effects. On the majority of cases, therefore, the initial prediction that politicians would tend to agree more than electors is convincingly upheld. The minority, where politicians do not agree more than electors, are transport, education and housing. On none of these does an internal dissensus exist among politicians; rather, they appear as failing to agree more than electors on substantive effects because the numbers naming the most popular effects on their side were not greater than the number of electors mentioning the most popular effects on their side. In fact on their appraisals of effects from the housing problem (not shown in Table 6.6) electors were for the first time in this analysis found to be in greater agreement than politicians.

The imposition of a control for parties upon the comparison of politicians and electors produces extensive changes in the pattern of agreement. In the case of both parties the issues on which politicians within each party are *not* more agreed than electors within the same party outnumber those on which they are more agreed. This is particularly true of the Conservatives, but also applies to Labour.

On none of the issues in Table 6.7 does the conclusion that Conservative politicians are not more agreed than Conservative electors rest upon the existence in the "B" distributions of two roughly equal and mutually exclusive groups of politicians with different appraisals of effects. The decision is reached because the numbers of politicians naming the most popular responses on their side are not significantly greater (on seven out of the nine issues) than the numbers of electors making the most popular replies on theirs. And the most popular responses on these seven issues are the same for both sides. On London government and immigration the most popular responses on each side differ owing to the politicians' preoccupation with political effects.

It could well be maintained as the result of these findings that the ties of party are here bringing the appraisals of politicians closer to those of electors, and that this influence shows in the table by a reduction in the number of cases in which politicians show themselves more agreed than electors. But a similar identity of views on the effects anticipated from most issues was revealed when all politicians were compared with all electors. On the same seven issues as emerged on the Conservative comparison, the most popular responses were the same for both politicians and electors.[5]

---

[5] These observations are made on the basis of the original overall multiple-response distributions reported in full in I. Budge, *Patterns of Democratic Agreement* (Ph.D. dissertation, Yale University Library; also published by University Micro Films, Ann Arbor, Mich., 1967).

Table 6.8: Agreement of Labour Politicians and Electors on the Substantive Effects Expected from Issues

	Politicians' Consensus Gap B distribution (percent)	Comparisons on a distribution involving:		
		Most popular effects	Second most popular effects	Third most popular effects
Common Market	68	$\chi^2 = 4.388\ p < .025$	$\chi^2 = 14.834\ p < .0005$	*
Berlin negotiations	76	$\chi^2 = 13.165\ p < .0005$	*	*
Transport Bill	36	$\chi^2 = 0.088\ p < .40$	$\chi^2 = 5.826\ p < .01$	*
Education shortages	36	$\chi^2 = 0.022\ p < .45$	$\chi^2 = 1.337\ p < .15$	*
Monopolies	80	$\chi^2 = 2.410\ p < .10$	*	*
Immigration Bill	20	$\chi^2 = 0.005\ p < .50$	$\chi^2 = 2.501\ p < .10$	*
Housing shortage	20	$\chi^2 = 1.093\ p < .15$	$\chi^2 = 0.375\ p < .35$	$\chi^2 = 0.256\ p < .35$
Greater London government	64	$\chi^2 = 27.255\ p < .0005$	*	*
Wage Pause	60	$\chi^2 = 4.236\ p < .025$	$\chi^2 = 10.940\ p < .0005$	$\chi^2 = 0.832\ p < .025$

Politicians N varies between 24 and 25; Electors N varies between 56 and 58
* denotes that numbers are too small for further comparison

Labour politicians prove again to be more agreed when compared with Labour electors than Conservative politicians are when compared with Conservative electors. However the issues on which they are not more agreed than electors do barely outnumber the issues on which they are more agreed. As with Conservative politicians no dissensus exists among Labour politicians on distribution "B" for any issue. The question of whether politicians were more agreed than electors was decided by reference to the difference between the numbers making the most popular responses on each side. The most popular responses were the same except for immigration and London government (as with the Conservatives). On those issues on which Labour politicians were more agreed than electors, the tendency was for them to be more agreed than Conservative politicians, and for Labour electors to be less agreed than Conservative electors.

The difference in the extent of relative agreement among politicians of the two parties seems in fact to lie in this tendency for Labour politicians to focus to a greater extent upon the same effects and for Labour electors to be more dispersed in their answers. Thus with these findings the difference in relative agreement between Conservative and Labour politicians, (discovered on topics of consensus and dissensus and appraisals of party stands but not on appraisals of viable alternatives) emerges once again.

CONCLUSIONS

The findings of this chapter:

1. Uphold the expectation that politicians agree more than electors in their appraisals of whether they are affected by political issues, of the specific effects arising from issues, of the policies open to pursuit on issues, and of the existence of issues (Chapter 2, Prediction 11).
2. Show that politicians agree more on appraisals of policies open to pursuit than electors of their own party.
3. Show that in most cases politicians do not agree more than electors of their own party in their appraisals of the specific effects arising from issues, but that Labour politicians tend to agree more among themselves than Conservative politicians.

POLITICIANS AND ELECTORS:
AGREEMENT ON ISSUE PREFERENCES

The prediction that politicians will agree more than electors has been upheld so far as issue appraisals go. The more important hypothesis relating to politicians' superior agreement on issue preferences has still to be tested however. Obviously agreement or disagreement on issue preferences will exert a more decisive influence upon negotiation and bargaining than the sharing of perceptions. It would be unrealistic to expect politicians to agree more than electors on all the topics of controversy into which they are plunged, but in terms of previous arguments they can be expected to agree more on at least a substantial minority.

The survey findings, however, have a somewhat chilling effect upon this expectation of superior consensus among politicians. Table 7.1 reveals that on seven out of nine issues examined politicians do not agree more than electors so far as their preferences are concerned. Moreover on six of these seven issues there exist relatively equal and mutually exclusive groups of politicians holding different preferences. Only on education, Berlin and housing does this dissensus not appear among politicians; and only on the latter two issues can they be said to agree more than electors in the sense that larger numbers of their group endorse the most popular alternatives.

A further examination of the preferences held by electors reveals that on only two issues—on education and (barely) on immigration—does a dissensus similar to that encountered among politicians not appear among electors. Neither on education nor immigration is there a significant difference between the numbers of politicians and electors choosing the most popular preferences for each sample. Thus electors are not found to be more agreed than politicians on any issue.

If the expectation that politicians would agree to a noticeably greater extent than electors has not been upheld by the data, neither,

Table 7.1: Agreement of Politicians and Electors on Issue Preferences

	Politicians' Consensus Gap B distribution (percent)	COMPARISONS ON A DISTRIBUTION INVOLVING:		
		Most popular preferences	Second most popular preferences	Third most popular preferences
Common Market	12	. . . .	. . . .	. . . .
Berlin negotiations	40	$\chi^2 = 10.990 \ p < .0005$	$\chi^2 = 6.406 \ p < .01$	$\chi^2 = 3.570 \ p < .05$
Transport Bill	9	. . . .	. . . .	. . . .
Education shortages	31	$\chi^2 = 1.985 \ p < .10$	$\chi^2 = 1.034 \ p < .25$	$\chi^2 = 4.294 \ p < .025$
Monopolies	4	. . . .	. . . .	. . . .
Immigration Bill	6	. . . .	. . . .	. . . .
Housing shortage	45	$\chi^2 = 27.107 \ p < .0005$	$\chi^2 = 6.054 \ p < .01$	$\chi^2 = 8.458 \ p < .005$
Greater London government	0	. . . .	. . . .	. . . .
Wage Pause	13	. . . .	. . . .	. . . .

Politicians N varies between 53 and 57; Electors N varies between 138 and 145

therefore, has the rival hypothesis that electors agree more than politicians. What is upheld is mainly the null hypothesis that there is no significant difference in agreement on substantive issue preferences between electors and politicians.

THE SIGNIFICANCE OF WIDESPREAD DISSENSUS
ON ISSUE PREFERENCES FOR THE ATTACHMENT
OF POLITICIANS TO BARGAINING AND COMPROMISE

The fact that politicians are only slightly more agreed than electors over all their issue preferences has been established by Table 7.1. If politicians do possess a greater capacity than electors for settling their disagreements through debate and compromise, it must, therefore, be sought in other factors than in their superior consensus on issue preferences. (Such other factors may, of course, be their superior consensus on factual appraisals of general political conflicts and issues and any of their agreements on democracy which appear from the subsequent analysis.)

Turning aside for the moment from comparisons of politicians and electors, however, it still has to be asked how the marked dissensus in preferences on six out of the nine issues examined can co-exist with any procedural agreements at all among politicians. For the whole discussion has stressed that conflicts over substantive policies will in the end tend to involve any procedural agreements that exist. If feelings on both sides of a dispute are sufficiently strong, the losing side will not be content to adhere to the rules which have brought about its defeat but rather will tend to question their validity.

As has been shown politicians do feel strongly about most of the issues under analysis (Table 3.1). Therefore struggles over any of these issues are quite likely to change into procedural struggles. Even in the event that agreement is discovered among politicians over procedures, how can such a delicate web of understandings restrain the brute passions aroused by clashes of strongly held substantive preferences?

There is, however, an implicit assumption in this line of argument which should be examined here. The assumption is that the existence of two roughly equal and non-overlapping groups of politicians holding different preferences denotes the presence of a zero-sum situation in which one group can get its preferences accepted only by preventing the other group from carrying through its preferences. Such a direct opposition of preferences would indeed be calculated to arouse bitterness and hostility between the two opposed groups. The end result could only be either stalemate or the triumph of one and utter defeat of the other. With this prospect facing them the minority might well query the rules of the game.

The assumption that such zero-sum situations do prevail on the issues upon which a dissensus exists among politicians can, however, be checked against the survey evidence. To test the assertion it is only necessary to identify the anonymous preferences held in common by the roughly equal and mutually exclusive groups of politicians on the "B" distributions of policies that they endorsed on the Wage Pause, Transport Bill, reorganization of London government, monopolies, Immigration Bill and the Common Market. If the majority of these preferences do in fact turn out to be directly opposed so that the adoption of one precludes the adoption of the other, then indeed it does seem likely that clashes on these issues will be bitter enough to involve democratic procedures. If, however, the majority of preferences are not directly opposed, it would seem that negotiation and bargaining could go a long way toward producing a compromise outcome in which the demands of both groups of politicians could be to some extent reconciled.

On examining the policies listed in Table 7.2, it is obvious that in the case of only two issues can they be said to be conflicting in the sense that adoption of one preference as a policy would preclude adop-

Table 7.2: Preferences Held on Six Issues by Roughly Equal and Mutually Exclusive Groups of Politicians

	PREFERENCE HELD BY SLIGHTLY LARGER GROUP	PREFERENCE HELD BY SLIGHTLY SMALLER GROUP
Wage Pause	Improve industrial relations.	Expand economy.
Transport Bill	Technical proposals for improving transport services.	Coordination and central direction of transport services.
Greater London government	Status quo.	Larger area of administration for education than that of new boroughs.
Monopolies	More vigorous action within existing framework of laws and regulations.	Anti-monopoly action along socialist lines.
Immigration Bill	More racial integration within Britain.	Regulation of immigration so as to keep the unhealthy and criminal out.
Common Market	Join unconditionally.	Join if E.F.T.A. and Commonwealth safeguarded.

tion of the other. The two cases are those of monopolies and the Common Market. On monopolies more vigorous action within the existing framework would have to be replaced by Socialist anti-monopoly action, a plan which would change the existing framework. On the Common Market a desire for Britain to join unconditionally does, of course, preclude getting guarantees for E.F.T.A. and Commonwealth. Otherwise, however, no necessary opposition can be seen between the preferences listed in Table 7.2. On the Wage Pause both the policies are technical and non-partisan. On the Transport Bill the coordination and central direction of services was indeed a policy strongly advocated by the Labour Party, but the most popular preference was for various technical methods of improving transport service: the two policies thus are quite compatible. On London government the full retention of the status quo is quite compatible with partial retention of the status quo in the shape of keeping the educational services of the old London County Council together. And greater racial integration inside Britain could well proceed in spite of—perhaps because of—refusal of entry to the physically or morally unfit.

Thus the disagreements discovered among politicians seem on the whole to take the negative form of a lack of support for a preference which is central for another group rather than that of a head-on collision between two directly opposing policies. And such a non-zero sum situation, far from being one which is likely to implicate procedural agreements in substantive disputes of preference, seems much rather likely to encourage bargaining and compromising tactics which are facilitated by debate and discussion. In light of these findings even the pattern of disagreement among politicians seems on the whole to encourage their attachment to democratic procedures. This is especially true when all the other issue agreements that have been discovered among politicians are considered.[1]

The discovery that on most issues on which they disagree politicians espouse compatible rather than competing preferences is important for the whole of the subsequent argument. It is worthwhile pausing at this point, therefore, to consider a central criticism that might be levelled at the finding and one interesting modification of our view of agreement which emerges from it.

The criticism is that our selection of issues may be suspect precisely because most preferential disagreements are not zero-sum. Ac-

---

[1] A similar examination of opposed issue preferences among electors on issues where a dissensus existed among them showed that on three out of the six issues the preferences supported by roughly equal and mutually exclusive groups of electors were diametrically opposed (on the Wage Pause, Reorganization of London Government and the Common Market).

cording to this view a matter can only be regarded as an issue if there is a strong clash of opinion about it. Basically this objection is definitional and was considered in Chapter 3. There we made the point that if issues were defined purely in terms of party (or other) controversy, then, of course, we should discover only disagreement among politicians: we should have made sure of this by our method of selection. But it seemed more relevant to define issues as all the topics that are being debated politically at a given moment, since it is the substantive agreement or disagreement engendered by such topics that strengthens or strains procedural agreements. The framing of issues in this way leaves open the question of whether politicians agree or disagree and the precise form their disagreement may take.

The nine issues selected for study in the present case were selected on these grounds because they were being debated in the first half of 1962, when interviews were taken. Thus the form which disagreement might take was not definitionally prejudged and seems likely to reflect the normal political situation in a stable democracy. Indeed the finding that only a minority of disagreements are head-on clashes seems eminently plausible, since one reason why essential procedures survive is merely that they have not suffered undue strain from bitter substantive disagreements.

The discovery that non-zero-sum disagreements exist on the majority of issues suggests a modification in the previous sharp contrast drawn between states of agreement and disagreement. Before examining the actual compatibility of the preferences held by roughly equal and mutually exclusive groups of politicians, the situation which seemed to emerge was one of utter dissensus on six sets of policies and relative agreement on two. By introducing the additional consideration of whether the preferences held by the roughly equal and opposing groups are compatible or incompatible, a greater variety of states between complete agreement and complete disagreement can be seen to exist. The agreement-disagreement question in the numerical sense can always be regarded as a continuum in that the consensus gap between the proportions endorsing the most popular and the second most popular alternative can vary from 0 percent to 100 percent.

Still taking the relative size of clusters on the two leading alternatives into account, but also having regard to the substantive content of these alternatives, we can spread the nine issues along a two-dimensional continuum from more or less complete consensus to complete dissensus among politicians. Complete dissensus is now regarded not only as a situation where the two main clusters differ by less than 20 percent, but also as being marked by the fact that the alternatives on which they cluster are inherently incompatible. A second kind of dis-

Table 7.3: Distribution of Political Issues Between Complete Consensus and Dissensus among Politicians

Complete Dissensus

Roughly equal and mutually exclusive groups with opposing preferences	Monopolies Common Market
Roughly equal and mutually exclusive groups with compatible preferences	Wage Pause Transport Bill Greater London government Immigration Bill
Group which supports most popular preference 20% greater than any other group but includes less than 50% of all politicians	Education shortages
Group which supports most popular preference 20% greater than any other group and includes more than 50% of all politicians	Berlin negotiations Housing shortage

Complete Consensus

sensus that is in purely numerical terms indistinguishable from the first can now be regarded as less serious than the first because its leading alternatives are compatible. Both types of dissensus can be distinguished from states of consensus in numerical terms, of course. Additionally there seems to be some ground for distinguishing between a situation where the cluster on the leading alternative includes the majority of the group and one where it does not, although in both cases the major cluster leads any other by more than 20 percent.

It will be observed that little connection appears between agreement on factual appraisals of a particular issue and preferential agreement upon that issue. For example politicians did not agree more than electors in appraising the effects of the housing problem, but they did agree more on appraisals of effects and of alternatives open to pursuit for monopolies and the Common Market. This anomaly must cause some misgivings about the argument that considers the effects of factual agreement upon negotiation and bargaining beneficial. On the other hand it could be maintained that the impact of current issues upon procedural agreement is collective. All topics being discussed at any one time have to be handled together, as a complete nexus, by politicians. Action taken on one current issue will have repercussions upon the others: agreement on one issue—or one aspect of one issue—will affect agreement on other aspects of other issues. Thus the important fact remains that considerable factual consensus exists about the body of current issues and that the number of zero-sum disagreements is limited. The view that the impact of current issues upon procedural agreement is collective seems plausible, and in this analysis issue agreements will continue to be evaluated contextually, although with necessary caution.

AGREEMENT ON ISSUE PREFERENCES AMONG PARTY SUB-GROUPS OF POLITICIANS AND ELECTORS

Looking now at the parties, it appears that the overall pattern of agreement remains the same for Conservative politicians compared with Conservative electors, as it was for the body of politicians compared with the body of electors. The fact that the politicians now share the same party affiliation does not notably increase their agreement, for on six of the issues—the Wage Pause, Transport Bill, London government, monopolies, immigration and education—relatively equal and mutually exclusive groups shared different preferences. Only one of these disagreements—on education shortages—can be judged zero-sum, however. Moreover the common party affiliation does not decrease the number of issues on which politicians are more agreed than electors, although it does change the actual issues themselves. Agreement on the Common Market increased, and agreement on Berlin decreased. Conservative electors seem neither more nor less agreed than electors as a whole.

The situation with Labour is very different from the situation among Conservatives. The fact that politicians have a similar party identification here greatly increases their agreement. They show greater consensus than electors over Berlin and housing—as was the case in the general comparison—but they also show more agreement over education, monopolies, transport and (barely, owing to the high agreement of Labour electors) over wages.

The contrast between the relatively more unified preferences of Labour politicians and the less unified preferences of Conservative politicians is quite striking. It is the opposite of what would be expected from the history of the two parties and from the socio-economic backgrounds of their politicians, for both show Labour to be the less united party.[2] Conflicts of opinion have, however, also been revealed among

---

[2] See particularly S. E. Finer, H. B. Berrington, and D. J. Bartholomew, *Backbench Opinion in the House of Commons 1955–59* (London: Pergamon, 1961), pp. 22–23, 80–81.

Table 7.4: Agreement of Conservative Politicians and Electors on Issue Preferences

	Politicians' Consensus Gap B distribution (percent)	COMPARISONS ON A DISTRIBUTION INVOLVING:		
		Most popular preferences	Second most popular preferences	Third most popular preferences
Common Market	26	$\chi^2 = 3.838$ p $< .05$	$\chi^2 = 1.915$ p $< .10$	*
Berlin negotiations	23	$\chi^2 = 1.431$ p $< .15$	*	*
Transport Bill	18	. . . .	. . . .	. . . .
Education shortages	9	. . . .	. . . .	. . . .
Monopolies	14	. . . .	. . . .	. . . .
Immigration Bill	3	. . . .	. . . .	. . . .
Housing shortage	59	$\chi^2 = 22.360$ p $< .0005$	$\chi^2 = 1.601$ p $< .15$	*
Greater London government	6	. . . .	. . . .	. . . .
Wage Pause	17	. . . .	. . . .	. . . .

Politicians N varies between 29 and 33; Electors N varies between 53 and 58
* denotes that numbers are too small for further comparison

Table 7.5: Agreement of Labour Politicians and Electors on Issue Preferences

	Politicians' Consensus Gap B distribution (percent)	COMPARISONS ON A DISTRIBUTION INVOLVING:		
		Most popular preferences	Second most popular preferences	Third most popular preferences
Common Market	8	....	....	....
Berlin negotiations	48	$\chi^2 = 14.834$ p $< .0005$	*	*
Transport Bill	64	$\chi^2 = 22.955$ p $< .0005$	$\chi^2 = 2.395$ p $< .10$	*
Education shortages	60	$\chi^2 = 8.620$ p $< .005$	*	*
Monopolies	36	$\chi^2 = 23.523$ p $< .0005$	*	*
Immigration Bill	12	....	....	....
Housing shortage	40	$\chi^2 = 8.301$ p $< .005$	$\chi^2 = 8.550$ p $< .005$	....
Greater London government	8	....		
Wage Pause	40	$\chi^2 = 2.942$ p $< .05$	$\chi^2 = 1.754$ p $< .10$	$\chi^2 = 2.637$ p $< .10$

Politicians N varies between 24 and 25; Electors N varies between 56 and 58
* denotes that numbers are too small for further comparison

the Conservative ranks. Such conflicts may be less enduring than those among Labour politicians, but this finding points to the possibility that they may be as extensive while they exist.[3]

Part of the contrast between the parties may simply be due to the peculiarities of the specific historical period during which interviews were taken. It so happened that a substantial number of the issues then being debated related to traditional rallying-points of the Labour Party. Socialists since Karl Marx have advocated state intervention as a way of dealing with monopolies. The Labour Party has consistently identified itself with working class aspirations in the fields of housing, education and wages. On transport Labour politicians were at least sure that pure cutting of financial losses was suspect.

However this may be, the contrast between the agreement of the two groups of party politicians is striking. For the moment it is enough to conclude that party is neither a factor that reduces the contrast between politicians and electors nor one that necessarily increases the agreement of politicians inside the party. For Conservative politicians are no more agreed in their preferences than the whole body of politicians.

CONCLUSIONS

The findings of this chapter:

1. Do not uphold the expectation that politicians are more agreed than electors on a substantial number of issue preferences (Chapter 2, Prediction 10).
2. Show that most disagreements among politicians on issue preferences are not irreconcilable (*i.e.*, of a zero-sum nature).
3. Show that Labour politicians agree on issue preferences to a much greater extent than Labour electors, and that Conservative politicians do not agree on issue preferences to a much greater extent than Conservative electors.

---

[3] *Ibid.*, pp. 85–100 *et passim.*

8

POLITICIANS AND ELECTORS: SUPPORT FOR DEMOCRATIC PROCEDURES

The reversal inflicted upon initial expectations by the findings discussed in the last chapter lends additional interest to the analysis of agreement on democratic procedures themselves. For the prediction that politicians will be more agreed than electors on the specific application of such procedures is not an extension, but a central assumption of the Dahl-Key theory. A test of this assumption will show whether it is correct to generalize the theory *in toto* from American politics to those of other stable democracies, or whether some such systems (Britain being the case in point) rely to a greater extent upon the direct attachment of the whole population to democratic procedures.

GENERAL PRINCIPLES OF DEMOCRACY

Table 8.1 reports the survey data relevant to the prediction that the population as a whole does not agree on any of the general principles of democracy to a greater extent than politicians. The prediction is cast in this rather negative form because it is expected that agreement on the abstract principles of democracy will be rather great among all sections of the population. There is, therefore, no reason to anticipate any greater agreement among politicians than among electors on these abstract statements. But if on the whole the attachment of politicians to general democratic principles is no greater than that of electors, it is at least in keeping with the generalized Dahl-Key theory to predict that electors will not be more agreed than politicians on abstract procedures. If there is any difference between the groups, all the forces mentioned previously—the politicians' longer education and greater political interest—should work to make the politicians' attachment to abstract democracy even greater than that of electors.

Table 8.1: Support of Politicians and Electors
for General Principles of Democracy

	POLITICIANS		ELECTORS	
	Demo-cratic (per-cent)	Non-demo-cratic (per-cent)	Demo-cratic (per-cent)	Non-demo-cratic (per-cent)
Democracy is the best form of government (Agree)	98	2	82	18
Public representatives should be chosen by majority vote (Agree)	98	2	96	4
Every citizen should have an equal chance to influence government policy (Agree)	72	28	93	7
The minority should be free to criticize majority decisions (Agree)	100	0	93	7
People in the minority should be free to try to win majority support for their opinions (Agree)	100	0	96	4

Politicians N varies between 46 and 47; Electors N varies between 135 and 139

NOTE: Democratic replies to statements are in parentheses after each statement. The statements are Prothro's and Grigg's original set, adapted in some cases to British conditions.

The prediction that electors will not prove more attached to these abstract democratic principles than politicians is upheld by every set of responses reported in Table 8.1 except those related to the statement "Every citizen should have an equal chance to influence government policy." Here the direction of the difference between electors and politicians is quite decisively reversed: only 7 percent of electors but 28 percent of politicians disagree with this general statement upholding majority rule. The reason for this reversal is perhaps the dislike of some politicians in such a traditionally hierarchical political system as the British system for the implication that all and sundry should be able to approach the arcana of government. In fact proportionately double the number of established politicians—M.Ps.—as of office-seeking politicians disagree with the statement.

An alternative explanation is, of course, that the 28 percent of politicians who dissent are not interpreting the statement as directly related to majority rule. It is a recurrent difficulty in this type of survey work to know if questions are actually tapping the dimension they are meant to, and one must qualify any assertions based on the findings with the warning that such findings may reflect error in measurement. Nevertheless there do seem convincing reasons for assuming that the dissenting responses arise from suspicion of majority rule rather than from a misunderstanding of the question's intent. In the first place the statement has been accepted previously—*e.g.*, in the prototype survey carried out by Prothro and Grigg—as one that accurately elicits attitudes toward the abstract principle of majority rule. Second, the 72 percent of politicians who agree to the statement presumably interpreted it in terms of the principle of majority rule; why would the dissenting 28 percent not so interpret it? And third, the percentage dissenting varies systematically between candidates and MPs (as we have already noted) and between Conservatives and Labour in a way that suggests that those more attached to hierarchical values tend to dissent more from the statement. Had there been misunderstanding of its implications, we should have expected the misunderstanding to be shared equally by all groups.

The real center of opposition to the idea of an equal chance for all citizens to influence policy seems to be found among Conservative politicians. Two out of twenty-three Labour politicians oppose the statement, but eleven out of twenty-four Conservatives oppose it. The latter, who, as will be seen, regard the ideal of equality of opportunity in any sphere of life with some suspicion, oppose it also when they sense its presence in a political statement. We certainly should not interpret such dissent as a rejection of regular elections, an idea which is not implied in the statement; but it does seem to reflect suspicion of any stronger form of participatory democracy than that. It is interesting, however, that only half the Conservative politicians adopt this position, while the other half endorse an opposite point of view. Here again one encounters the finding—a finding repeatedly encountered in the analysis of politicians' agreement over issues—that the dissensus does not occur *between* Labour and Conservative politicians but *among* Conservative politicians.

However politicians do assent significantly more than electors to the statement that democracy is the best form of government, and if the two statements about minority rights are formed into a scale (where each pro-democratic answer counts one and any other answer, nothing), politicians score significantly higher than electors. But on the equivalent scale for the principles of majority rule, which includes the statement about citizens' equal right to influence government policy, electors score higher than politicians. The initial prediction is again falsified when the answers to all five statements on the table are combined into a scale of "Agreement with the General Principles of Democracy" with scores ranging from nothing to five.[1]

All this is to say that over the whole group of answers reported in Table 8.1 politicians show a less consistent support than electors for democratic procedures considered in the abstract. This conclusion must not be overstressed. It rests upon the non-democratic response of slightly over a quarter of the politicians to one out of a set of five statements. Even in reply to this statement 72 percent took the democratic position—a great enough number for one to conclude that politicians show substantial agreement by any definition. And again there must be measurement qualifications. Although the five statements cover two main aspects of democratic procedures, they by no means exhaust the whole list of democratic principles. Possibly if another five had been employed, they would have produced a different set of replies.[2]

Perhaps the important point to note about the support accorded to abstract democratic principles—in spite of minor discrepancies—is the widespread agreement of politicians and general population alike on the democratic answers to all statements.[3]

The pattern of replies on the electoral side reflects the findings of Prothro and Grigg about the extent of support for these general principles among the American population.[4] Agreement is almost equally high among British and American electors on the four statements about abstract procedures. Widespread agreement on these general points seems to exist among the whole population of both countries.

-----

[1] The statistical test used throughout this chapter is the 2×2 Chi-square test of departure from statistical independence with Yate's correction for continuity where this is appropriate. In the case of tables with very small numbers Fishers' Exact Test has been employed. For statistical comparisons scales have been dichotomized between "high" and "low" scores. The distribution of the samples on these scales and the exact way in which scores have been grouped into "high" and "low" are given in Appendix G of I. Budge, *Patterns of Democratic Agreement* (Ph.D. dissertation, Yale University Library; also published by University Microfilms, Ann Arbor, Mich., 1967).

[2] This argument, however, has to be treated with caution. No survey can ask all possible questions on a given topic; therefore the results of every survey analysis could be described as incomplete. What has been done here, in accordance with usual practice, is to analyze replies to a set of central and strategic questions and to generalize results to the whole area of abstract democratic values. Failing direct evidence to the contrary, we take the generalized results as valid for the whole area.

[3] It is worthwhile noting that the difference between politicians and electors remains under very few controls. With reference to the discussion of Chapter 10 it is especially noteworthy that no difference occurs between politicians who pay a great deal of attention to issues and the corresponding group of electors.

[4] J. W. Prothro and C. M. Grigg, "Fundamental Principles of Democracy: Bases of Agreement and Disagreement," *Journal of Politics*, 22 (1960), 284–86.

SPECIFIC APPLICATIONS OF THE
PRINCIPLES OF DEMOCRACY

The prediction relating to the support of politicians and electors for democratic courses of action in concrete situations is much more positive in form than the previous hypothesis. In a majority of cases, politicians are expected to agree on specific applications of democratic procedures to a greater extent than the general population. Table 8.2 presents the replies of both groups to statements embodying specific applications of the principles of majority rule, whose derivation from the abstractions reported in Table 8.1 should be clear.

It is obvious from the table that politicians agree overwhelmingly on democratic procedures in the majority of specific situations listed in the table, and to a significantly greater extent than do electors. One

**Table 8.2: Support of Politicians and Electors
for Principle of Majority Rule in Specific Terms**

	POLITICIANS		ELECTORS	
	Demo-cratic (per-cent)	Non-demo-cratic (per-cent)	Demo-cratic (per-cent)	Non-demo-cratic (per-cent)
In a borough election only people who are well-informed about the problems being voted on should be allowed to vote. (Dissent)	100	0	72	28
Only rate-payers should be allowed to vote (Dissent)	100	0	69	31
The people should not allow a legally elected West Indian to be mayor (Dissent)	100	0	74	26
The people should not allow a legally elected Communist to be mayor (Dissent)	94	6	55	45
The B.M.A. has a right to try to increase the influence of doctors by getting them to vote as a bloc in elections (Agree)	11	89	34	66

Politicians N = 47; Electors N varies from 132 to 134

NOTE: Democratic replies to statements are in parentheses after each statement. The statements are Prothro's and Grigg's original set, adapted in some cases to British conditions.

statement on which, to be sure, they agree overwhelmingly stands, however, on the non-democratic side. This is the case of the hypothetical attempt of a pressure-group (the British Medical Association) to influence policy through democratic elections. If one of the essential elements of the general principle of majority rule—*i.e.*, the idea that every citizen should have an equal chance to influence government policy—is to be upheld, such an attempt must be allowed. If all citizens should have an equal opportunity to exercise influence on government policy, then some should have the right to organize themselves as a voting bloc. There are several possible rationales lying behind the politicians' dissent in this hypothetical case.

On the one hand we must remember that the idea that all citizens should have an equal opportunity to influence government policy was an idea to which a quarter of the politicians previously objected. This group of politicians could reasonably be expected to dissent in the hypothetical B.M.A. case. Yet *more* than a quarter of the politicians dissented in this case. We can plausibly conclude that those politicians who do endorse the equal influence concept, but who dissent on certain specific applications of the concept either fail to see any connection between the specific application and the general concept or interpret the specific application in an unusual way.

Despite the widespread dissent in the B.M.A. case, no politician wished to restrict the local franchise to ratepayers or to the well-informed; their positions on these two statements are supportive of the principle of the equal opportunity of all to influence government. From this we can infer that there is some confusion among politicians when it comes to specific applications of this principle. On the one hand it is possible that the right of the B.M.A. to organize doctors as a voting bloc is not seen as a deduction from the general principle in the sense that the other statements have been. Certainly it is obvious that most politicians fail to see a connection here. On the other hand it is possible that some of these politicians interpret B.M.A. participation as a *violation* of the equal influence principle on the grounds that the Association's greater resources would ensure that some voters had greater weight than others. However we are not bound to accept the politicians' reasoning on this point, and remain free to interpret their reluctance to accord the right of organization to the B.M.A. as detracting from their overall support of majority rule.

Whatever rationale lies behind the negative responses, opposition to the B.M.A.'s right to organize doctors in an election may also in part result from the politicians' natural distaste for any procedure that might make elections more difficult for them. The opposition of some Conservative politicians perhaps follows from the suspicion that many of them have of general equality of political influence. The Labour politicians' position in this situation may stem from the general hostility of the British Medical Association to the Labour Party's proposals for the National Health Service that were made in the immediate post-War period and from B.M.A.'s the continuing critical attitude towards the Service.

On the first three out of the five statements in Table 8.2 electors also display a considerable measure of agreement on the democratic side. Their support of specific majority applications is less marked than that of politicians, but on the statements involving restriction of the local franchise it is much greater than that displayed by Prothro's and Grigg's American interviewees.[5] On the questions involving the Communist and the Medical Association dissensus is almost as prevalent as in the United States.

It is clear from Table 8.2—and confirmed by scores on the scale formed when answers to the five statements are combined—that politicians agree more than electors on the courses of action to be followed in these cases and that generally they support the democratic course of action. This difference between politicians and electors holds under all controls.

The discussion now turns to the replies of both samples to the questions on minority rights in specific situations. In the majority of cases there can be no doubt that the politicians are substantially more agreed than are electors in their support for the rights of specified minorities; there is no need for any summary scale to confirm the trend. The exceptional case where politicians are not significantly more agreed than electors occurs because electors are equally agreed, not because politicians waver in their enthusiasm for the democratic posture. Only one politician in a single instance gives a non-democratic answer.

In three cases the electors also exhibit a substantial amount of agreement. Two of these cases involve freedom of speech about religion and for Communists. A third relates to the right of West Indians to run for political office. It is curious that so many of the electors who were prepared to allow a Communist to speak were not prepared to allow him to seek office. Perhaps, however, this is due to an impression that speaking is a more innocuous form of political activity than office-seeking. On the other hand opinions are sharply divided in another case of freedom of speech: advocacy of wholesale government ownership.

---

[5] *Ibid.*, p. 285.

Table 8.3: Support of Politicians and Electors for
Principle of Minority Rights in Specific Terms

	POLITICIANS		ELECTORS	
	Democratic (percent)	Nondemocratic (percent)	Democratic (percent)	Nondemocratic (percent)
A person should be allowed to speak against churches and religion (Agree)	100	0	84	16
A person should be allowed to speak for government ownership of the whole economy (Agree)	98	2	55	45
An admitted Communist should be allowed to speak (Agree)	100	0	92	8
A West Indian should not be allowed to stand for borough council (Dissent)	100	0	81	19
An admitted Communist should not be allowed to stand for borough Council (Dissent)	100	0	64	36

Politicians N = 47; Electors N varies from 131 to 135

NOTE: Democratic replies to statements are in parentheses after each statement. The statements are Prothro's and Grigg's original set, adapted in some cases to British conditions.

Replies here were perhaps tinged by current political controversies in Britain over the question of Nationalization.

The pattern of agreement and disagreement among this sample of British electors provides an interesting contrast with the responses of Prothro and Grigg's American sample. The Americans overwhelmingly agreed—as did the British—that no one should be debarred from political candidacy on racial grounds. However the Americans also agreed that speeches in favor of extending government ownership should be permitted. In contrast with the British they disagreed on the question of allowing Communist or anti-religious speeches. They split more markedly than the British on allowing a Communist candidacy.[6]

Comparisons on the summary scale of Specific Minority Rights were instituted between sub-groups of politicians and electors. From

---

[6] *Ibid.*, p. 285.

these comparisons it emerged that electors who paid considerable attention to issues showed as extensive support for specific minority rights as the corresponding politicians. In all other comparisons politicians showed greater support.

The threads of our discussion can best be drawn together by comparing the scores of the two samples on a summary scale of "Agreement with the Procedural Principles of Democracy." This scale merely sums up the overall tendencies that have been apparent in the three tables previously examined. A score of one is given to each democratic answer on the fifteen statements set out in the previous tables of this chapter, and the final position on the range, which extends from 0 to 15, indicates the respondent's general tendency to give democratic or non-democratic answers to the questions. The merit of the scale lies in its emphasis on the general tendencies at work in each group. Thus interesting but exceptional responses such as the unexpected reaction of the politicians to the statements on equal opportunities for influence and on the election activities of the B.M.A. are put in the context of the generally greater support of politicians for democratic courses of action.

Table 8.4: Agreement of Politicians and
Electors with Democratic Procedures

	POLITICIANS (percent)	ELECTORS (percent)
Low		
Score Six or Under	0	8
Score Seven–Eight	0	12
Score Nine–Ten	0	24
Score Eleven–Twelve	28	36
Score Thirteen–Fourteen	72	21
High		

Politicians N = 47; Electors N = 136

When this synoptic view of their responses is taken, there can be no doubt that politicians are somewhat more highly agreed than electors on democratic procedures. While the latter spread over the various categories of the table, the former cluster in the high scoring cells. And this situation remains when the comparison is carried out under controls for age, party and television exposure. Only the sub-groups of politicians and electors distinguished by high issue orientation do not differ significantly.

This last finding serves to stress the fact that substantial numbers of electors support democratic procedures to a considerable extent. A majority support eleven or more pro-democratic courses of action, and this must include support for at least seven out of ten specific applications of democratic norms. It is true, of course, that there are inconsistencies between their overwhelming support of abstract democratic principles and some of the positions they endorse in specific situations, inconsistencies that are evident in their attitudes to Communists and the B.M.A. on specific cases of majority rule and to proponents of wholesale nationalization and Communists in cases of specific minority rights. But on the other hand many politicians may also be inconsistent in maintaining that every citizen should have an equal chance to influence government policy at the same time that they deny the B.M.A. the right to organize its supporters. Here the politicians may also have lost sight of general democratic principles in their immediate reaction to the specific group involved.

EQUALITY OF OPPORTUNITY

The coolness shown by politicians toward the statements involving the B.M.A. and the equal chance of citizens to influence policy would be more easily interpretable if it could be regarded simply as hostility to purely egalitarian doctrines. Such doctrines certainly involve support for equality of opportunity, but also include a belief in equal capabilities and the right to equal rewards. Outside Utopia this trust in equal capabilities is rejected by all social and political systems including Communist systems, since it is obvious that people do differ in their capabilities. Normally, too, it is accepted that different capabilities should command different rewards. Thus Herbert McClosky encountered considerable anti-egalitarianism among his samples of American politicians and electors when he examined their beliefs about social, political and economic equality.[7]

However the statements put to politicians and electors in the present survey did not imply that all persons are equally capable of governing, a belief that would have no relevance to democratic procedures as we have defined them. What the statements do uphold is equality in the opportunity afforded to exercise political influence; and this is central to the view of democracy which we have adopted. Moreover it is probably true that the principle of equality of opportunity commands much more support than the idea of equal rewards or the belief in equal capabilities. So the politicians' ambivalence towards equality of political opportunities cannot be explained simply in terms of general hostility to vulgar egalitarianism.

---

[7] H. McClosky, "Consensus and Ideology in American Politics," *APSR*, 58 (1964), 369.

It is interesting to compare the responses of politicians and those of electors on a further set of statements about equality of opportunity —this time in regard to education and jobs—with their previous replies to the questions on democratic procedures. The comparison is especially relevant because the questions on education and job opportunities were modelled very closely on the statements about democratic procedures. Table 8.5 shows that the responses of politicians and electors vary rather differently over the second group of statements. Electors endorse equality of opportunity in general terms almost to a man. On the specific applications they agree substantially only on the question of public schools. There is thus little consistency between their general views and their feelings about specific lines of action in particular cases. The politicians' replies reveal considerable agreement on equality of educational opportunity. They are unanimous in support

Table 8.5: Support of Politicians and
Electors for Equality of Opportunity

	POLITICIANS		ELECTORS	
	Pro-equality (percent)	Non-equality (percent)	Pro-equality (percent)	Non-equality (percent)
All public posts should be awarded by equal and open competition (Agree)	66	34	96	4
Everyone should be given an equal opportunity to get the education necessary for the career he wants to pursue (Agree)	100	0	99	1
Certain people are better qualified to run this country (Dissent)	63	37	56	44
Native British people ought not to have the first chance of government jobs before strangers like the Southern Irish and West Indians (Agree)	43	57	29	71
It's no use giving some children an expensive education (Dissent)	67	33	46	54
Don't open public schools to all and sundry (Dissent)	89	11	76	24

Politicians N varies from 44 to 47; Electors N varies from 118 to 134

NOTE: Responses signifying support for equality of opportunity are in parentheses after each statement.

of the general principle and support it (with modified enthusiasm) when it is applied to specific situations. On the question of equality of opportunity for government jobs dissensus is evident on both general principle and specific cases. Thus the politicians' consensus on a general principle is followed, by and large, by consensus on specific applications of the general principle; and dissensus on a general principle, by dissensus on its specific applications. The politicians display greater *consistency* than electors, but no greater *support* for equality of opportunity.

The center of opposition to general and specific equality of opportunity, as in the case previously examined of the equal chance of all to influence government policy, is found among Conservative politicians. Table 8.6 shows the disproportionate extent, when compared with Labour politicians, to which this sub-group opposes the principle of equality of opportunity.

As on the political issues a marked dissensus among Conservative politicians appears, according to Table 8.6, to exist on equality of opportunity. While many more Conservative than Labour politicians tend to oppose equality of opportunity in its various forms, a substantial number varying from roughly one-third to one-half support it. Labour politicians are overwhelmingly for equality except on the one case of

Table 8.6: Politicians' Support for Equality of Opportunity by Party

	CONSERVATIVE		LABOUR	
	Pro-equality (percent)	Non-equality (percent)	Pro-equality (percent)	Non-equality (percent)
All public posts should be awarded by equal and open competition (Agree)	48	52	86	14
Certain people are better qualified to run this country (Dissent)	30	70	96	4
Native British people ought not to have the first chance of government jobs. (Agree)	30	70	57	43
It's no use giving some children an expensive education. (Dissent)	46	54	91	9

Conservative Politicians N varies from 23 to 24; Labour Politicians N varies from 21 to 23

NOTE: Responses signifying support for equality of opportunity are in parentheses after each statement.

preferences on government jobs. Again, therefore, Table 8.6 seems to demonstrate the existence of more dissensus in Conservative ranks than in those of Labour. Equally there can be no doubt that the consistent opposition to equality of opportunity came from one group of Conservatives.

A tendency to division in their views on equal opportunity is discernible among electors, but not to the same extent as among politicians. However if Labour electors are compared with Conservative electors on a general scale of "Agreement with Equality of Opportunity," a significant difference does appear between them. Labour electors tend to display more enthusiasm for equality both generally and in its specific applications. No difference shows between the scores of Conservative politicians and electors on the scale, but the scores of Labour politicians are even higher than the scores of Labour electors.

The probable explanation for the shape that this set of results takes is indicated by the differences just discussed between politicians and electors of the two parties. The official ideology of the Conservative Party stresses the values of order and hierarchy. Indeed views on equality of opportunity are probably a fundamental "Liberal-Conservative" difference in most countries. Conservative ideology is buttressed by a certain self-interest on the part of its adherents in that both politicians and electors of that party tend disproportionately to come from the more privileged sections of society. By the same token, both the ideology and self-interest of Labour militates against social hierarchy and for the principle of equal opportunity. And the Labour politicians spearhead the attack—possibly because they feel even more keenly than their supporters that they and their like are kept down by the prevalence of inequality.

It is, however, rather more difficult to account for the body of Conservative support for equality of opportunity which is also a finding of the analysis. Possibly the existing two-party structure of British politics forces non-Socialist radicals into the Conservative Party, where they find themselves uneasy about many of the established opinions of the party and where they form a body of consistent dissent. This explanation, however, is entirely speculative.

When politicians as a group are compared with the body of electors on a general scale of "Agreement with Equality of Opportunity" (formed by scoring one for any answer supporting equal opportunities on the statements under consideration), no significant difference is found to exist between their scores. This finding contrasts with the somewhat greater support given by politicians as compared with electors to the procedures of democracy. It is worth noting that the disagreement among politicians over the question of equality of opportunity is paralleled by a similar disagreement among electors. What consensus does exist in the British political system has so far been found in almost all cases among politicians. When it is absent among them it tends also to be absent elsewhere.

The disagreement over educational and job opportunities has not been regarded as involving democratic beliefs on one side or the other, since equality of opportunity aside from the question of influencing government policy is no part of the definition of democracy adopted in Chapter 3. In part this distinction may constitute formalistic evasion of a difficulty, but, on the other hand, the definition of democracy purely in terms of political procedures seems perfectly satisfactory. There is no need to regard a Conservative supporter of the public schools as an opponent of democracy because of his position on that issue. Thus none of the results just discussed can be considered a test of any predictions derived from the initial discussion.[8]

If this distinction between democracy and equality of opportunity is accepted, one can, however, point to the effect of current political controversies on agreement with democratic procedures. The general democratic procedure least accepted by the politicians was that related to equal opportunities for influencing government policy. Obviously here the partisan feelings engendered by controversy over equality of opportunity in other spheres have affected support of this principle. Labour hostility to the B.M.A. seems to overwhelm other considerations in Labour politicians' response to the question of whether the B.M.A. should indulge in unrestricted electoral activity.

In the question of equality of opportunity we have, therefore, encountered a problem that combines substantive issues of current policy with certain aspects of democratic procedures. One possible explanation points to the possibility that the politicians' disagreement here may be supported by a unique attitude that does not exist on any other question directly involving procedures.[9]

Most politicians are where they are politically because of inherited (social or political) advantages.[10] This fact may militate against the belief that everyone has or should have equal opportunities, since such

---

8 This is in contrast to the position taken by McClosky who regards a belief in equality of opportunity as constituting just as essential a portion of democratic ideology as procedural rules. Such an inclusive definition seems to reflect American rather than general conditions, however. See McClosky, *op. cit., passim.*

9 Such as that of the position of immigrants. See Chapter 12.

10 See D. Matthews, *The Social Background of Political Decision-Makers* (New York: Random House, 1954), *passim*, for evidence on the disproportionate wealth and education of politicians.

a belief may either represent a threat to their present position or reflect upon the way they attained it.

Even those politicians who have worked their way up to their present status may, for the same reasons, feel doubtful about full equality of political opportunity. Their previous experience has demonstrated that in politics at any rate, they are more capable than most people. They may, therefore, feel considerable skepticism about any suggestion that incapable people should have a chance to exercise responsibility and, thus, possibly to wreck the system.

What we are suggesting therefore is that the very established nature of the politicians' position—which on other procedural matters should make them more attached to the rules which safeguard their status—may here cause a tension, a tension that seems to be reflected in ambivalence about the idea of giving everyone a potential equality of political influence.

These possible explanations for the unique procedural controversy involved in the principle of equality finds support from two empirical findings. There is the finding from the present survey that on all other aspects of democratic procedures politicians shared a wide and consistent agreement; and there is similar evidence from the American survey conducted by McClosky.

Thus there seem good grounds for regarding this particular procedural-substantive ambivalence among politicians as exceptional. Even if exceptional, however, the strong effect exerted by substantive conflicts over equality on politicians' adherence to democratic principles lends empirical support to McClosky's assertion that "democratic ideas and rules of the game are ordinarily encountered not in pure form or in isolation but in substantive contexts that are bound to influence the ways in which we react to them."[11] The connection also emphasizes the strong relevance to any consensual theory of democracy of the agreements on issues and conflicts investigated previously. For all the issues and all the conflicts studied earlier have the latent power to drag democratic procedures into dispute. That they do not do so may be due in part to the agreements discovered upon them.

CONCLUSIONS

1. Analysis of responses to various statements directly involving democratic procedures:
   A. Upholds the expectation that politicians are more agreed than

---

[11] McClosky, *op. cit.*, p. 376.

electors in their attachment to democratic procedures (Chapter 2; Predictions 2 and 4).

    B. Shows that both politicians and electors are strongly (although somewhat inconsistently) attached to democratic procedures.

2. The findings of this chapter also show that roughly half the Conservative politicians in the sample oppose equality of opportunity in social as well as political spheres.

9

POLITICIANS AND ELECTORS: AGREEMENT ON FACTUAL APPRAISALS OF DEMOCRACY

In spite of detailed qualifications, two points of major importance emerge from the analysis of agreement on democratic procedures. British politicians and British electors are both widely agreed in their pro-democratic preferences. The virtual unanimity of both groups is an astonishing phenomenon which goes a long way in itself toward explaining British democratic stability.

Precisely because British electors are not far behind politicians in their support for democratic procedures, the survey results cast some doubt on an assertion that is central to the generalized Dahl-Key theory—that in a stable democracy the politicians have a key part to play in maintaining and defending procedures. For if electors' support for these procedures is only somewhat less (numerically) than that given by politicians, there seems, on the face of it, no reason for claiming that the politicians' support is more vital to democratic stability than the electors'.

Of course it has already been shown that politicians are more agreed than electors on many factual appraisals of political issues and general political conflicts, and this raises the possibility that they are better able to stick to democratic procedures in settling political problems. These previous empirical findings do provide one body of evidence which acts to uphold the hypotheses that politicians have a special part to play in maintaining democratic stability.

The agreements on issues can also be used as an analogy in the present discussion of agreements on procedures. In their issue preferences politicians were not very much more agreed than electors. It was argued, however, that so long as their preferences did not directly oppose each other and thus did not set them at loggerheads among themselves, superior agreements on factual appraisals could allow them to act as a unified group and could serve in a special way to maintain democratic procedures of negotiation and discussion.

By analogy it could be said that the study of democratic preferences has shown that politicians are not markedly more attached to democratic procedures than are electors. But they still are very much attached and reasonably consistent in their application. The similarity between politicians' and electors' preferences on democracy does not, therefore, foreclose the possibility that other agreements may distinguish politicians from electors and enable them to play a special role in maintaining and defending democratic procedures.

What other agreements are necessary for such a role? Concerted pro-democratic action on the part of any group would seem impossible in the absence of any of the following conditions:

1. Members must be relatively highly agreed that the existing system is democratic.
2. Members must realize that their own preference for democracy is shared by a considerable number of other members.
3. Members must realize that their common agreements are more important than their disagreements.

The first of these conditions is clearly prerequisite to any action in support of the status quo that is prompted by pro-democratic sentiments. The existing system must not only be democratic in fact, it must also be widely perceived to be democratic. The second and third conditions are necessary for joint democratic action. If members do not realize that their democratic preferences are shared, they are unlikely to conceive of the possibility of uniting the group in support of such preferences; instead they are more likely to indulge in uncoordinated individual actions or in soliciting outside intervention. The third condition—the perception that agreements common to members of the group outweigh their disagreements—may, of course, relate not only to democratic preferences but to the body of other agreements discovered on issues. Such a realization would encourage coalition-building, for there would then seem to be much common ground which members could unite in defending. Absence of the realization that agreements are more important than disagreements would profoundly discourage attempts at combination, since any alliance would be thought more likely to founder under the weight of disagreement than to lead to a successful defense of democracy.

If, then, politicians share these appraisals to a more marked degree than do electors, they are more likely to be the group whose support is vital to the maintenance of democratic procedures. Such support need not be thought of as necessary only in the event of severe crises, such as a military coup or mass uprising: both are unlikely in contemporary Britain (although one should recognize that their improbability stems in part from the strong pro-democratic orientations of politicians). The politicians' ability to close ranks in defense of democracy can also be seen as operative in less dramatic directions, perhaps most notably during the 'sixties in suppressing the various initiatives aimed at reducing the resident colored population to permanent second-class status. Politicians as a whole have been able to combine across party in ignoring the popular support given to figures who incited racial feeling without seeming doubtful about the response they could expect from most of their colleagues. The most plausible explanation for their unity in this routine but vital defense of democratic rights seems to be the existence of some such agreements as those mentioned above.[1]

AGREEMENT THAT BRITAIN IS A DEMOCRACY

The definition of democracy adopted in Chapter 3 laid down various conditions designed to ensure that the political system was broadly responsive to the wishes of its citizens. It is appraisals of this responsiveness of government to the desires of its citizenry that are examined in this section. The questions that prompted the appraisals are widely used survey questions which have the advantage of comparability and which are broadly related to the definition of democracy given in the Introduction. By asking whether British political institutions meet the needs of individual citizens, the questions seek to estimate the extent to which the conditions laid down in the definition of "polyarchy" are actually seen to exist.

From the United States, Arnold Rose reports that his sample of community leaders were satisfied that the government did pay some attention to their preferences.[2] Similarly McClosky notes that the trust of his politicians in the integrity of government and of politicians, and

---

[1] The main initiatives against the colored population have come from the Birmingham area, where they have concentrated heavily. In 1964 the Conservative Alderman Griffiths won the heavily Labour seat of Smethwick on a racial platform. He was subsequently cold-shouldered by *both parties* in the House of Commons and defeated by Labour in 1966. In 1968 the hard-line speeches of Enoch Powell, a former Conservative Minister, on the racial question brought his dismissal from the Conservative Shadow Cabinet and attacks from both Conservatives and Labour.

[2] A. M. Rose, "Alienation and Participation," *American Sociological Review*, 27 (1962), 836–38.

Table 9.1: Agreement of Politicians and Electors that Britain is Democratic

	POLITICIANS		ELECTORS	
	Respon-sive (percent)	Not respon-sive (percent)	Respon-sive (percent)	Not respon-sive (percent)
Do you think you can trust local councillors or that they become tools of special interests? (Trust)	98	2	40	60
I don't think local councillors care much about what people like me think (Disagree)	82	18	39	61
People who go into public office usually think of the good of the people more than of their own good. (Agree)	85	15	60	40
If people really knew what was going on in high places in the government it would blow the lid off things (Disagree)	81	19	33	67
It doesn't matter which party wins elections, the interests of the little man don't count (Disagree)	100	0	69	31

Politicians N varies from 45 to 47; Electors N varies from 129 to 131

NOTE: Replies indicating a view of government as responsive are in parentheses after each statement.

in the responsiveness of political agencies to the people's preferences, was greater than that of electors.[3] The replies of the present samples of British politicians and electors to various questions on the responsiveness of local and national government are given in Table 9.1.

It is quite obvious that politicians take a much more optimistic view of the democratic character of the British political system than do electors. Large numbers of the latter take a consistent but largely pessimistic view of its operations. On two statements about local government and one about national government the majority of electors feel that the system is corrupt and that office-holders are selfish and uncon-

---

[3] H. McClosky, "Consensus and Ideology in American Politics," *APSR*, 58 (1964), 370.

Table 9.2: Sense of Political Efficacy and
Political Alienation of Politicians and Electors

| | SENSE OF POLITICAL EFFICACY | | POLITICAL ALIENATION | |
| | Politicians | Electors | Politicians | Electors |
	(percent)		(percent)	
Low				
Score 0	0	20	66	15
Score 1	0	32	21	18
Score 2	4	24	9	23
Score 3	34	20	2	18
4 or More	62	4	2	26
High				

Politicians N = 47; Electors N varies from 134 to 136

cerned. On the other two statements one-third of electors do not think
any concern is displayed for their interests.

It is hardly surprising that politicians should have a high regard
for local councillors, people in public office and those in high places—
they are radiating self-esteem. Many of them are local councillors, and
most occupy public office of some kind. On the other hand it is quite
conceivable that politicians in some systems would have a very low
regard for their own morality and would display complete cynicism
about their colleagues. By the same token it is likely that such systems
are unstable.[4] Whatever the origins of the politicians' belief that democracy exists in Britain, the existence of the belief does make it possible for their preferences to get into action in defense of established
democratic procedures.

Another table reinforces the findings contained in Table 9.1. It reports the distribution of the two samples on two scales: a scale of political efficacy and a scale of political alienation. The scale of political
efficacy measures the strength of the feeling that one is able to get
things done through politics, that the political system is responsive to
one's relevant preferences if one has any. The scale of political alienation measures, in a sense, the opposite belief, the feeling that the political system is unresponsive and undemocratic. The separate questions
reported in Table 9.1 are combined with others in each of these scales,[5]
and together they sum up the tendency of each sample to take an opti-

---

[4] See G. A. Almond and S. Verba, *The Civic Culture* (Princeton, N.J.: Princeton University Press, 1963), pp. 108, 109, 267, for variations in trust and cynicism
between the populations of different political systems.

[5] For details of the construction of these scales and of the questions of which
they are composed, see Appendix D.

mistic or pessimistic view of the extent to which the political system reacts to popular demands.

The politicians are overwhelmingly confident that political activity brings results and overwhelmingly reject the idea that politicians ignore the needs of ordinary people. The electors spread more widely with a bias to the opposite ends of both scales, tendencies that point to their serious doubts about the effectiveness of British democratic procedures.

Thus politicians satisfy the first condition for united pro-democratic action to a markedly greater extent than electors: they do overwhelmingly believe in the responsiveness and representativeness of British government. While substantial numbers of electors share these opinions, large numbers do not. Thus a marked dissensus among electors must be contrasted with an overwhelming agreement among politicians.

AGREEMENT ON THE EXTENT TO WHICH DEMOCRATIC PREFERENCES ARE SHARED

The politicians' greater trust in the representative character of British government makes them more likely defenders of British political institutions in situations where electors might hesitate, but the form that would be taken by their defense is still uncertain. Would it consist of unconcerted individual action or attempts to form a coalition of most politicians against the threat to democracy? The generalized Dahl-Key theory assumes that politicians would tend to act as a unified group. If politicians would naturally think of combining with other politicians to defend democratic procedures, it is probable, first, that most would feel that they shared agreements which formed the basis for an alliance and, second, that these agreements included a common belief in democracy. Such agreements would act as even more powerful cement for a grouping that had as its object the defense of democracy.

Table 9.3: Agreement of Politicians and Electors
on the Existence of Agreements in Britain

	POLITICIANS (percent)	ELECTORS (percent)
Agreement in Britain:		
Exists	96	77
Does not exist	4	23

Politicians N = 57; Electors N = 144

NOTE: The question which prompted replies is: "So far we've been talking about things people in Britain disagree about. Do you think there are any things people in Britain agree about?"

The survey allows a check to be made on both of these predictions. On the broad question of whether agreements do exist in Britain politicians are somewhat more agreed than electors. But consensus among electors is nevertheless very great.

The contrast between politicians and electors is not very marked in Table 9.3. However the point raised by the survey question that produced the data is very general: merely whether interviewees thought people in Britain agreed about any matters. Probably the vital question from the point of view of investigating agreement that might give rise to combined pro-democratic action is the question of what agreements in Britain are about. After people were asked whether they thought people in Britain agreed about anything, they were asked to name the topics people agreed about. Answers to this query are reported in Table 9.4.

**Table 9.4: Agreement of Politicians and Electors
on the Nature of Agreements in Britain**

	POLITICIANS (percent)	ELECTORS (percent)
Agreement exists on:		
Democracy	51	20
Established institutions	16	5
Neither of above	33	76

Politicians N = 57; Electors N = 143

Half the politicians consider democracy to be a subject of agreement as compared to one-fifth of the electors. But to those politicians who perceived an agreement on democracy can be added those who mentioned agreement on established institutions in Britain. For not only are these established institutions democratic in fact, but as Tables 9.1 and 9.2 demonstrate they are seen by politicians themselves to be democratic. Two-thirds of the politicians, therefore, show themselves aware of general agreement on democratic procedures compared with a quarter of electors. Nor, since Table 9.4 reports answers to a quite non-directive question, can the other third of the politicians be regarded as positively denying that such agreement exists. Of course this point applies to the remaining electors as well. But the contrast between the proportions of politicians and of electors who believe that agreement on democracy and established institutions exists in Britain means that initial expectations are convincingly upheld on this point.

Both politicians and electors agree overwhelmingly that disagreements exist in Britain. This is a realistic view of British politics and has been confirmed by the survey findings in relation to issue preferences and equality of opportunity. However only two politicians and three electors think that democracy itself is a topic of disagreement.

Electors, therefore, seem to regard democracy not as a positively agreed, but rather as a non-disputed topic in Britain. They are not spontaneously conscious of the existence of agreement on this subject as politicians are shown to be in Table 9.4.

AGREEMENT ON THE IMPORTANCE OF AGREEMENTS

Even after the foregoing analysis it remains a possibility that politicians may still regard the topics on which they disagree as more important than their democratic agreements even when the latter are strengthened by other agreements. Such a situation would also hinder group cooperation in working within and protecting democratic institutions, for it would obviously be of little use to build a coalition of people who constantly put their divergent interests ahead of their common interests.

Table 9.4 has shown that politicians regard democracy and its institutions as one of the points upon which they are agreed. Survey data elicited by a general question on the importance of agreements in Britain compared with disagreements is, therefore, quite suitable for testing the assertion that the politicians regard their agreements—including those on democratic procedures—as more important than their disagreements on other matters.

Obviously a large number of politicians do regard their agreements as being more important than their disagreements; substantially more politicians than electors share this view. The difficulty is that the opinion that agreements are as important as disagreements would also tend to encourage attempts at coalition-building, and if the electors who share this appraisal are added to those who think agreements more important, their numbers are much nearer those of the politicians

Table 9.5: Agreement of Politicians and Electors on Importance of Agreements and Disagreements in Britain

	POLITICIANS (percent)	ELECTORS (percent)
Agreements are:		
More important	63	48
As important	18	25
Less important	19	27

Politicians N = 57; Electors N = 142

who share these appraisals. Thus a significant difference exists between politicians and electors on the dichotomized appraisal as to whether or not agreements are more important than disagreements in Britain, but no significant difference appears on the trichotomized appraisal as to whether agreements are more important, as important, less important than disagreements.

It could be argued that the essential comparison between the two groups relates to the dichotomized appraisal, that is, whether more politicians regard their agreements as more important than their disagreements. Thinking that agreements are as important as disagreements is obviously not so much of a spur to concerted group action as the more confident perception that agreements are more important. This, however, is a fine point, and it is best to conclude that while the majority of politicians are somewhat more confident than electors that their agreements outweigh their disagreements, the difference between the samples on this condition for concerted pro-democratic action is much less than it was on the previous two.

Considered as a whole, however, the analysis undertaken in this chapter has shown that British politicians share factual appraisals to a noticeably greater extent than do British electors. These make it possible for them to combine in support of democratic procedures, whether the threat arises from a major crisis or whether a small erosion of minority rights is involved. Thus the agreements on factual appraisals uphold the central assertion of the generalized Dahl-Key theory that politicians play a vital role in spearheading the defense of democratic procedures and in adhering to them in the handling of political conflicts and issues.

CONCLUSION:

1. The findings of this chapter uphold the expectation that politicians on the whole agree more than electors in their appraisals of British democracy (Chapter 2, Prediction 6).

10

POLITICIANS AND ELECTORS: POTENTIAL EFFECTIVENESS

The findings of the last chapter indicated that politicians were probably more capable than electors of acting as a cohesive group in support of democratic procedures. The effectiveness of politicians' joint actions is also enhanced by the expectation that in political perseverance, knowledge, contacts and judgment they are likely to prove vastly superior to electors. Hence given only that their internal support of democratic principles is great—as it has been shown to be—their role in defending democracy is likely to be vital regardless of how pro-democratic electoral preferences and appraisals may be. For the significance of action undertaken on the basis of such preferences and appraisals will vary with its effectiveness. Other things being equal, the more effective group will spearhead the defense of democratic procedures. Thus the examination of comparative political effectiveness provides another test of the assertion of the generalized Dahl-Key theory that the politicians play a special and essential role in maintaining democratic procedures.

There is a further point to this comparison. Because the measures of political effectiveness will be used in the next chapter to identify the political stratum, it is also necessary to be sure of their validity, and this can best be ascertained by discovering whether the initial prediction is upheld. For if it were overturned, the natural reaction would be to doubt the measures rather than to accept that electors were really more effective than politicians.

THE MEASURES OF POTENTIAL EFFECTIVENESS

These measures were constructed from the replies made to questions about various aspects of the nine political issues described in Appendix C. The best measure of effectiveness would, of course, have consisted of behavioral observations of the actions undertaken by politicians and electors and of how far they were successful in achieving the desired goals. Those who took action and succeeded in getting their own way upon the issue to a greater extent than others would then have been judged more effective.

Because present day techniques of social investigation are primitive and resources for the study, limited, this behavioral method of measuring effectiveness could not be adopted. Instead respondents were classified, on the basis of their replies to various questions, into those at least potentially capable of taking action on the issue and those who lacked even this potential. For example, people who had not heard about the issue were obviously incapable of taking action upon it. People who did not think that they were affected by the issue or who anticipated only slight effects were similarly unlikely to be aroused to action. Persons who saw themselves as affected in a variety of ways by the issue were more likely to act than those who felt they were affected in only one way. The same is true of people who felt more strongly about the issue than others.

An additional dimension was introduced into the measurement of effectiveness by considering the likely success of the action once undertaken. It can be plausibly argued that those who see a wide range of alternatives open to pursuit on any issue are more likely to decide on one that is well suited to their purposes than those who can think of only one and who are consequently bound to adopt that alternative or none at all. Similarly interviewees who adopt reasonably specific and concrete courses of action as their preferences are more likely to succeed in carrying them through than persons who adopt only vague and general policy alternatives. Also, people able to apply a reasonably broad frame of reference to the consideration of the issue—*i.e.*, to place the alternative policies they discuss in a broad context of economic, social or political theory, in a sequence of historical events, or in relation to other issues and other alternative policies on the same issue—are less likely to be tempted to hasty and ill-considered action than those persons who view it from no such general perspective. Finally some knowledge of the precise positions of the political parties (and the Trades Union Congress) in regard to these nine issues is necessary to undertake effective political action at the very minimal level, to give one's vote some effect on the resolution of the issue.[1]

Of course the people who emerge from these nine measures as more potentially effective than others may not necessarily take action

---

[1] A more detailed account of the construction of these measures is given in Appendix E.

Table 10.1: Politicians and Electors Compared on Political Effectiveness

	WAGE PAUSE	TRANSPORT BILL	GREATER LONDON GOVERNMENT	MONOPOLIES	IMMIGRATION BILL	COMMON MARKET	BERLIN NEGOTIATIONS	HOUSING SHORTAGE	EDUCATION SHORTAGES
Perception of issue	Sig. diff. χ^2 8.265 p < .005	Sig. diff. χ^2 67.622 p < .0005	Sig. diff. χ^2 18.768 p < .0005	Sig. diff. χ^2 18.327 p < .0005	Sig. diff. χ^2 7.338 p < .005	Sig. diff. χ^2 4.197 p < .025	Sig. diff. χ^2 8.686 p < .005	No sig. diff. χ^2 0.794 p > .05	Sig. diff. χ^2 4.591 p < .025
Number of alternatives perceived	Sig. diff. χ^2 59.600 p < .001	Sig. diff. χ^2 46.515 p < .001	Sig. diff. χ^2 69.263 p < .001	Sig. diff. χ^2 36.309 p < .001	Sig. diff. χ^2 23.758 p < .001	Sig. diff. χ^2 53.045 p < .001	Sig. diff. χ^2 41.859 p < .001	Sig. diff. χ^2 17.006 p < .001	Sig. diff. χ^2 24.486 p < .001
Frame of reference	Sig. diff. χ^2 28.949 p < .0005	Sig. diff. χ^2 46.720 p < .0005	Sig. diff. χ^2 69.949 p < .0005	Sig. diff. χ^2 46.678 p < .0005	Sig. diff. χ^2 35.580 p < .0005	Sig. diff. χ^2 19.639 p < .0005	Sig. diff. χ^2 25.219 p < .0005	Sig. diff. χ^2 43.574 p < .0005	Sig. diff. χ^2 27.302 p < .0005
Perception of effect	Sig. diff. χ^2 27.396 p < .0005	Sig. diff. χ^2 8.225 p < .005	Sig. diff. χ^2 36.633 p < .0005	Sig. diff. χ^2 8.287 p < .005	Sig. diff. χ^2 19.218 p < .0005	Sig. diff. χ^2 8.432 p < .005	Sig. diff. χ^2 11.915 p < .001	Sig. diff. χ^2 7.388 p < .005	Sig. diff. χ^2 12.741 p < .001
Number of effects perceived	Sig. diff. χ^2 20.485 p < .001	Sig. diff χ^2 10.759 p < .01	Sig. diff. χ^2 35.659 p < .001	Sig. diff. χ^2 8.910 p < .02	Sig. diff. χ^2 17.455 p < .001	Sig. diff. χ^2 11.949 p < .01	Sig. diff. χ^2 8.929 p < .02	No sig. diff. χ^2 3.103 p > .05	Sig. diff. χ^2 13.195 p < .001

Magnitude of effect	Sig. diff. χ^2 19.963 p < .001	Sig. diff. χ^2 7.871 p < .02	Sig. diff. χ^2 39.345 p < .001	Sig. diff. χ^2 8.951 p < .02	Sig. diff. χ^2 21.549 p < .001	Sig. diff. χ^2 12.894 p < .01	Sig. diff. χ^2 8.929 p < .02	No sig. diff. χ^2 3.370 p > .05	Sig. diff. χ^2 11.184 p < .01
Specific preferences	Sig. diff. χ^2 11.181 p < .0005	Sig. diff. χ^2 21.288 p < .0005	Sig. diff. χ^2 40.436 p < .0005	Sig. diff. χ^2 46.678 p < .0005	Sig. diff. χ^2 7.908 p < .005	Sig. diff. χ^2 6.476 p < .01	Sig. diff. χ^2 22.849 p < .0005	Sig. diff. χ^2 11.876 p < .0005	Sig. diff. χ^2 17.379 p < .0005
Strength of feeling	No sig. diff. χ^2 5.253 p > .05	Sig. diff χ^2 15.079 p < .001	Sig. diff. χ^2 39.492 p < .001	Sig. diff. χ^2 17.159 p < .001	No sig. diff. χ^2 0.909 p > .05	Sig. diff. χ^2 17.258 p < .001	Sig. diff. χ^2 12.912 p < .01	No sig. diff. χ^2 3.050 p > .05	No sig. diff. χ^2 5.338 p > .05
Correct perception of Party stands	Sig. diff. χ^2 17.363 p < .001	Sig. diff. χ^2 54.572 p < .001	Sig. diff. χ^2 19.632 p < .001	Sig. diff. χ^2 33.571 p < .001	Sig. diff. χ^2 21.86 p < .001	Sig. diff. χ^2 51.607 p < .001	No Sig. diff. χ^2 1.010 p > .05	Sig. diff. χ^2 33.418 p < .001	Sig. diff. χ^2 23.243 p < .001

NOTE: Details of these measures of effectiveness are given in Appendix E. The tests which produced the chi-square values reported in this and following tables were the 2×2 chi-square test of departure from statistical independence in the cases of Perception of the issue, Frame of reference, Perception of effect and specific preferences; and the Kolmogorov-Smirnov test in the case of Number of alternatives perceived, Number of effects perceived, Magnitude of effect, Strength of feeling and Correct perception of party and Trade Union Congress stands on issues. The level of significance in assessing results is taken as .05, with direction predicted.

on the issue. But it seems plausible to hypothesize that they are more likely to take action and that their action is likely to be better considered and more likely to achieve their ends than is the action of their fellows. Minimal measures constructed from survey data in the way outlined above have been quite widely used in political research and may be said to have proved their worth in discussions closely allied to the present one.[2]

SURVEY FINDINGS ON POTENTIAL EFFECTIVENESS OF POLITICIANS AND ELECTORS

Table 10.1 reports the results of comparisons between all politicians and all electors on all the measures of effectiveness outlined above. The table summarizes the eighty-one overall comparisons (a comparison on each measure of effectiveness for each issue) between the body of politicians and the body of electors.

In seventy-three out of eighty-one cases the politicians prove significantly more likely than electors to be effective on the measures employed in the table. Because of their superior effectiveness, therefore, as well as their higher agreement on the factual appraisals discussed previously, politicians seem likely to take the most prominent and significant part in maintaining democratic procedures. Any pro-democratic action on their part will prove vastly more weighty than any similar action undertaken by an elector.

Conversely since the measures of effectiveness reported in the table have produced the expected results on these comparisons of electors and politicians, more confidence can now be put in their ability to reveal differences in political effectiveness among the electors themselves.

COMPARISONS OF EFFECTIVENESS AMONG VARIOUS SUB-GROUPS OF POLITICIANS AND ELECTORS

It is interesting not merely to contrast the effectiveness of all politicians with that of all electors, but also to contrast the effectiveness of various sub-groups of each. The most obvious sub-groups to compare are, of course, politicians and electors of the same political parties. In the previous discussion of democratic preferences it was discovered that some contrasts between the body of politicians and the body of

---

[2] See the discussion in A. Campbell, P. Converse, W. Miller, and D. Stokes, *The American Voter* (New York: Wiley, 1960), Chap. 8, and in J. Rosenau, *National Leadership and Foreign Policy* (Princeton, N.J.: Princeton University Press, 1963), pp. 5–6.

electors disappeared when the politicians who paid a great deal of attention to political issues (and who were, therefore, described as exhibiting a high issue orientation) were compared with the corresponding group of electors. Contrasts in political effectiveness may similarly disappear when these sub-groups are contrasted. This appears all the more likely because electors who pay a great deal of attention to issues are likely to score highly on the various measures of political effectiveness employed in Table 10.1. Electors who follow the political messages of the mass media more closely than others are also more likely to have heard of issues, to be able to place them in a broad context, to "place" the parties in relation to them, etc. Hence a comparison between politicians of "high T.V. exposure" and electors of the corresponding group also seems appropriate. Lastly older electors are likely to have acquired a greater experience and knowledge of politics than are younger electors and therefore form another group that is more likely to score highly on political effectiveness.

Table 10.2 reports the results of comparisons between the eight groups of politicians and electors distinguished by their age, party, television exposure and issue orientation. Since the table embodies the results of 648 comparisons between different distributions of electors and politicians, it has not been possible to report the statistics obtained from the comparison in each cell of the table, nor to give the separate distributions in any of the Appendices. All that appears in each cell of the table is the final result of these comparisons. The first line of each cell entry repeats the result of the overall comparison between all politicians and electors already given in Table 10.1. The second line reports the result of the comparison of sub-groups of politicians and electors: either "Fails" (to repeat the contrast in effectiveness between all politicians and all electors in the comparison of sub-groups distinguished by) Age, Party, T. V. Exposure or Issue Orientation or "Sig-(nificant) Diff(erence) under all controls." The same statistical tests have been applied for comparisons on each measure as on the overall comparisons of all politicians with all electors.

The comparison between the effectiveness of the various sub-groups of politicians and corresponding sub-groups of electors results in a different pattern of findings from those encountered when all politicians were compared with all electors. The striking superiority of politicians is much less in evidence in Table 10.2 than in Table 10.1.

It will be remembered that in eight cases on the latter table there existed no significant difference in the effectiveness of politicians compared with that of electors. Out of the remaining significant differences fifty-one break down when various sub-groups of politicians are compared with corresponding sub-groups of electors. Thus in only twenty-

Table 10.2: Politicians and Electors Compared on Political Effectiveness under Various Controls

	WAGE PAUSE	TRANSPORT BILL	GREATER LONDON GOVERNMENT	MONOPOLIES	IMMIGRATION BILL	COMMON MARKET	BERLIN NEGOTIATIONS	HOUSING SHORTAGE	EDUCATION SHORTAGES
Perception of issue	Sig. diff. Fails Issue orientation	Sig. diff. under all controls	Sig. diff. Fails Issue orientation	Sig. diff. Fails Issue orientation	Sig. diff. Fails Issue orientation, T.V. exposure	Sig. diff. Fails Party, T.V. exposure, Issue orientation	Sig. diff. Fails Age, Party	No sig. diff.	Sig. diff. Fails T.V. exposure, Issue orientation
Number alternatives perceived	Sig. diff. under all controls	Sig. diff. Fails Issue orientation	Sig. diff. under all controls	Sig. diff. under all controls	Sig. diff. Fails T.V. exposure, Issue orientation	Sig. diff. under all controls	Sig. diff. under all controls	Sig. diff. Fails T.V. exposure, Issue orientation	Sig. diff. Fails Party, Issue orientation
Frame of reference	Sig. diff. under all controls	Sig. diff. Fails Age, T.V. exposure, Issue orientation	Sig. diff. under all controls	Sig. diff. under all controls	Sig. diff. under all controls	Sig. diff. Fails Party, T.V. exposure, Issue orientation	Sig. diff. under all controls	Sig. diff. under all controls	Sig. diff. under all controls
Perception of effect	Sig. diff. under all controls	Sig. diff. Fails Age, T.V. exposure, Issue orientation	Sig. diff. under all controls	Sig. diff. Fails Party Issue orientation	Sig. diff. under all controls	Sig. diff. Fails Party, T.V. exposure, Issue orientation	Sig. diff. Fails Party, Issue orientation	Sig. diff. Fails Issue orientation	Sig. diff. Fails Age, Issue orientation

	1	2	3	4	5	6	7	8	9
Number effects perceived	Sig. diff. Fails Issue orientation	Sig. diff. Fails Age, T.V. exposure, Issue orientation	Sig. diff. Fails Issue orientation	Sig. diff. Fails Age, Issue orientation	Sig. diff. Fails Age, T.V. exposure, Issue orientation	Sig. diff. Fails Age, Party, Issue orientation	Sig. diff. Fails all controls	No sig. diff.	Sig. diff. Fails Age, Party, T.V. exposure, Issue orientation
Magnitude of effect	Sig. diff. Fails Issue orientation	Sig. diff. Fails Age, T.V. exposure, Issue orientation	Sig. diff. Fails Issue orientation	Sig. diff. Fails Age, Party, Issue orientation	Sig. diff. Fails T.V. exposure, Issue orientation	Sig. diff. Fails Age, Party, T.V. exposure, Issue orientation	Sig. diff. Fails all controls	No sig. diff.	Sig. diff. Fails Age, Party, T.V. exposure, Issue orientation
Specific preferences	Sig. diff. under all controls	Sig. diff. Fails Issue orientation	Sig. diff. Fails Issue orientation	Sig. diff. under all controls	Sig. diff. Fails Party, T.V. exposure, Issue orientation	Sig. diff. Fails Party, T.V. exposure, Issue orientation	Sig. diff. Fails Issue orientation	Sig. diff. Fails T.V. exposure	Sig. diff. Fails Issue orientation
Strength of feeling	No sig. diff.	Sig. diff. Fails T.V. exposure, Issue orientation	Sig. diff. Fails Issue orientation	Sig. diff. Fails Party, Issue orientation	No sig. diff.	Sig. diff. Fails Party, T.V. exposure, Issue orientation	Sig. diff. Fails Party, T.V. exposure, Issue orientation	No sig. diff.	No sig. diff.
Correct perception of Party stands	Sig. diff. Fails T.V. exposure, Issue orientation	Sig. diff. under all controls	Sig. diff. under all controls	Sig. diff. Fails T.V. exposure	Sig. diff. Fails Issue orientation	Sig. diff. under all controls	No sig. diff.	Sig. diff. Fails T.V. exposure	Sig. diff. Fails Party, T.V. exposure

137

Table 10.3: All Politicians and Sub-Group of Electors Highly Oriented to Issues Compared on Political Effectiveness

	Wage Pause	Transport Bill	Greater London Government	Monopolies	Immigration Bill	Common Market	Berlin Negotiations	Housing Shortage	Education Shortages
Perception of issue	No sig. diff. χ^2 0.071 $p > .05$	Sig. diff. χ^2 29.576 $p < .0005$	Sig. diff. χ^2 2.880 $p < .05$	Sig. diff. χ^2 3.003 $p < .05$	Sig. diff. χ^2 2.830 $p < .05$	No sig. diff. χ^2 0.001 $p > .05$	No sig. diff. χ^2 1.232 $p > .05$	No sig. diff. between Politicians and all Electors	No sig. diff. χ^2 0.000 $p > .05$
Number alternatives perceived	Sig. diff. χ^2 27.607 $p < .001$	Sig. diff. χ^2 7.535 $p < .025$	Sig. diff. χ^2 38.160 $p < .001$	Sig. diff. χ^2 8.196 $p < .025$	No sig. diff. χ^2 3.039 $p > .05$	Sig. diff. χ^2 9.853 $p < .01$	Sig. diff. χ^2 24.163 $p < .001$	No sig. diff. χ^2 3.927 $p > .05$	Sig. diff. χ^2 6.409 $p < .05$
Frame of reference	Sig. diff. χ^2 10.422 $p < .005$	No sig. diff. χ^2 2.666 $p > .05$	Sig. diff. χ^2 23.645 $p < .0005$	Sig. diff. χ^2 13.010 $p < .0005$	Sig. diff. χ^2 5.675 $p < .013$	No sig. diff. χ^2 0.601 $p > .05$	No sig. diff. χ^2 2.572 $p > .05$	Sig. diff. χ^2 11.672 $p < .0005$	Sig. diff. χ^2 6.795 $p < .013$
Perception of effect	Sig. diff. χ^2 6.332 $p < .005$	No sig. diff. χ^2 .093 $p > .05$	Sig. diff. χ^2 9.332 $p < .005$	No sig. diff. χ^2 0.717 $p > .05$	Sig. diff. χ^2 6.793 $p < .005$	No sig. diff. χ^2 0.002 $p > .05$	No sig. diff. χ^2 0.345 $p > .05$	Sig. diff. χ^2 3.863 $p < .05$	No sig. diff. χ^2 1.998 $p > .05$
Number effects perceived	No sig. diff. χ^2 1.256 $p > .05$	No sig. diff. χ^2 0.798 $p < .05$	Sig. diff. χ^2 8.141 $p < .025$	No sig. diff. χ^2 3.545 $p > .05$	Sig. diff. χ^2 6.675 $p < .05$	No sig. diff. χ^2 2.344 $p > .05$	No sig. diff. χ^2 0.250 $p > .05$	No sig. diff. between Politicians and all Electors	Sig. diff. χ^2 6.185 $p < .05$

								No sig. diff. between Politicians and all Electors
Magnitude of effect	No sig. diff. χ^2 4.094 p > .05	No sig. diff. Direction of diff. reversed	Sig. diff. χ^2 9.351 p < .01	No sig. diff. Direction of diff. reversed	Sig. diff. χ^2 7.278 p < .05	No sig. diff. χ^2 0.909 p > .05	No sig. diff. χ^2 0.25 p > .05	No sig. diff. χ^2 2.159 p > .05
Specific preferences	Sig. diff. χ^2 8.187 p < .005	No sig. diff. χ^2 0.858 p > .05	Sig. diff. χ^2 7.658 p < .005	Sig. diff. χ^2 17.280 p < .0005	No sig. diff. χ^2 0.292 p > .05	No sig. diff. Direction of diff. reversed	No sig. diff. χ^2 0.140 p > .05	Sig. diff. χ^2 4.907 p < .025
Strength of feeling	No sig. diff. between Politicians and all Electors	No sig. diff. χ^2 0.947 p > .05	Sig. diff. χ^2 6.106 p < .05	No sig. diff. χ^2 1.004 p > .05	No sig. diff. between politicians and all Electors	No sig. diff. χ^2 0.909 p > .05	No sig. diff. χ^2 2.581 p > .05	No sig. diff. between politicians and all Electors
Correct perception of Party stands	Sig. diff. χ^2 2.176 p > .05	Sig. diff. χ^2 23.227 p < .001	Sig. diff. χ^2 8.348 p < .01	Sig. diff. χ^2 13.890 p < .001	Sig. diff. χ^2 6.940 p < .01	Sig. diff. χ^2 28.037 p < .001	No sig. diff. between Politicians and all Electors / Sig. diff. χ^2 20.503 p < .001	Sig. diff. χ^2 8.524 p < .025

139

two cases is there a significant difference in potential effectiveness for all comparisons of politicians and electors for the overall groups, and all sub-groups alike. On the other hand it must be remembered that controls reduce the number of cases being compared and thus make it more difficult to obtain significant chi-square values in any case.

The different types of final results from these comparisons are scattered sufficiently broadly over the cells of Table 10.2 to eliminate the possibility that significant differences or a lack of significant differences in the various comparisons are confined to a certain issue or to a certain measure of effectiveness.

If we examine the table in more detail, it emerges that the contrast in effectiveness most often breaks down on the comparison between electors and politicians of high issue orientation. In fact the contrast breaks down on this comparison in forty-six out of the fifty-one cases where it breaks down at all. The reason for the disappearance of the contrast in effectiveness is not that politicians of high issue orientation and those of low issue orientation differ at all from each other in their political effectiveness; rather, the essential difference in effectiveness is between electors of high issue orientation and other electors.[3]

Here then is a group of electors who seem likely to come closer to the whole body of politicians in their political effectiveness than any other electors. To discover whether a close resemblance between all politicians and this sub-group of electors does exist it is, however, necessary to contrast it with the body of politicians rather than simply with the corresponding sub-group. This comparison is summarized in Table 10.3.

In some cells of Table 10.3 the entry indicates that no significant difference in effectiveness existed between all politicians and electors.

---

[3] Issue orientation is measured on the standard open questions on likes and dislikes about parties and party leaders developed by the Survey Research Center, University of Michigan. Each reference to a political issue in reply to these questions is scored one. The purpose of the measure is to estimate the tendency of respondents to react to political events in terms of their effects upon policy and governmental action, and it is adapted from the similar procedure described in A. Campbell, G. Gurin, and W. Miller, *The Voter Decides* (Evanston, Ill.: Row, Peterson, 1954), pp. 112–15. Electors with a high issue orientation are those who make three or more references to issues. From one point of view both the measure of issue orientation and many of the effectiveness measures could be regarded as direct derivatives of interest in and attention to political events. This does not make the connection between these variables uninteresting, however, for the status of M.P. and Parliamentary Candidate could similarly be regarded as a direct derivative of interest in political events; yet the contrast in the potential effectiveness of politicians and electors is highly relevant for purposes of testing the generalized Dahl-Key theory. As will appear the contrast in potential effectiveness between electors of high and low issue orientation opens up one mode of analyzing the political stratum, which is investigated in Chapter 11.

The other entries report the appropriate statistic derived from the comparison of electors of high issue orientation with all politicians.

If we compare Table 10.3 with Table 10.2, it is evident that when the whole sample of politicians is contrasted with electors highly interested in issues, the number of cases where there is no significant difference in effectiveness declines to thirty-four. This contrasts with the forty-six cases where no difference in effectiveness appeared between these electors and the sub-group of politicians with a high interest in issues. The reason for the decline lies in the fact that politicians of high and low issue orientation do not differ in their effectiveness. Therefore when the combined groups of politicians are compared with electors of high issue orientation, the previous differences in political effectiveness are markedly increased.

Although electors of high issue orientation resemble the body of politicians in their political effectiveness less than they do the sub-group of politicians similarly concerned with issues, it should be noted that in thirty-four cases no significant differences appeared in Table 10.3. To these thirty-four cases must be added the eight cases where no significant difference separated the total samples of politicians and electors and where, therefore, there could also be no significant difference between politicians and these electors. Thus in forty-two cases out of a total of eighty-one comparisons there were no differences in effectiveness between politicians and this particular set of electors.

This finding upholds Dahl's and Key's assertion that electors cannot be regarded as an undifferentiated mass. There are some electors who resemble politicians more closely than others in their potential effectiveness as well as in their pro-democratic preferences. These variations in political weight and outlook among electors themselves require further investigation, since they point to the expected differences between the "political stratum" and other electors. Chapter 11 will examine the exact nature of the political stratum's democratic preferences and appraisals and explore its leading characteristics.

CONCLUSIONS:

The findings of this chapter:
1. Uphold the expectation that politicians are more politically effective than electors (Chapter 2, Prediction 1).
2. Show, however, that the group of electors distinguished by their high issue orientation resembles politicians more closely than do electors as a whole.

11

THE POLITICAL STRATUM: SUPPORT FOR DEMOCRATIC PRINCIPLES AND AGREEMENT ON FACTUAL APPRAISALS OF DEMOCRACY

Previous to this point discussion and analysis have focused upon contrasts between politicians and the body of electors. However a test of the initial theory that concentrated entirely on such contrasts would be incomplete.

In the first place some electors—the political stratum discussed in Chapter 2—are assumed to play an important role in supporting democratic procedures, even though this role may be passive in character and dependent upon a prior initiative by politicians. Resembling the latter more closely than other electors, they may also be capable to some extent of spontaneously recognizing threats to democracy and combining against them. The predictions derived from these expectations form explicit assertions of the generalized Dahl-Key theory: members of the political stratum are expected to agree more than ordinary electors on pro-democratic preferences and appraisals.

In the second place it has become increasingly apparent from previous analyses that straight comparisons between electors and politicians ignore the finding that important variations both in potential effectiveness and in support for democratic courses of action exist among electors themselves. The evidence suggests that the more politically effective sections of the electorate may be more strongly in favor of the maintenance of democratic procedures than the less politically effective. Such a finding would be of considerable relevance to the discussion, since it would show that the close similarity discovered between the support of politicians and electors for democratic procedures was, in fact, due to the presence among the latter of a group more strongly committed than the average elector to such procedures, rather than to an even spread of democratic support over the whole population.

IDENTIFICATION OF THE POLITICAL STRATUM

In attempting to test these predictions about pro-democratic feeling, one is faced by the preliminary question of how exactly to identify the political stratum. Obviously persons who undertake a greater number of political activities than the average have given the most solid proof of their orientation to politics. The actual behavior of electors, however, hardly suffices to allow some to be selected as more politically oriented than others. For example, only 14 percent engaged in anything more than minimal activities at elections. The best indicators to use, therefore, seem to be the various measures of potential effectiveness already employed in Chapter 10. They tap a potential ability to participate effectively in the resolution of issues, and can, therefore, be used as the most direct available operationalization of an orientation to politics. The predictions about the greater support for democratic procedures and the greater agreement on appraisals of democracy shown by the politically oriented electors can then be tested, using the electors who score more highly than others on the nine measures of potential effectiveness as the politically oriented sub-group of electors.

Methods of Comparing Potentially Effective Electors with Other Electors

It is possible to combine the nine measures of political effectiveness described in Chapter 10 into a single scale; however there is no way of determining at present whether any one of these measures has a more direct connection with effective political action than another. Therefore assignment of comparative weights to scores on these measures would be arbitrary, and it seems better to compare the high scorers on each measure separately with those electors who scored low, on their support for democratic principles.

On the other hand the decision to examine each group of potentially effective electors separately will involve an analysis of the replies of eighteen separate groups of electors (those who score as politically effective on each of the nine measures and those who do not). It is, therefore, difficult to examine the position of each group on each of the separate statements involving support for the democratic courses of action that were listed in the tables of Chapter 8. However use has already been made of scales that reveal the general tendency of politicians and electors to support or oppose the democratic position in the abstract or in specific situations. It will be remembered that such scales were formed by assigning a score of one to each pro-democratic answer on the statements on majority rule and minority rights. In the ensuing discussion scales indicating support or opposition to majority rule and minority rights in the abstract and to the application of each of these principles to specific situations will be employed. Use will also be made of a scale of "Support for specific applications of democratic principles," which combines the scales of support for majority rule and minority rights in specific situations.

GENERAL PRINCIPLES OF DEMOCRACY

As with politicians, all that can be required of the effective electors is that they support general principles as much as other electors. In fact when the various groups are compared on a general scale of support for the abstract principles of democracy, in eight out of nine cases no difference did appear between the potentially effective electors and others. Only when the electors who placed their views about any issue in a broader context were compared with those who had not done so did any significant difference in support emerge between any of the elector groups.

From the table it will be seen that the difference between this particular group of potentially effective electors and other electors is only significant in any sense if the distributions are dichotomized into those scoring highest in support of abstract democracy and those making any other score (*i.e.*, those scoring four v. the rest). This dichot-

Table 11.1: Support for General Democratic Principles of Electors Who Place Their Views About Any Issue in a Broad Context and Electors Who Do Not

SUPPORT FOR GENERAL DEMOCRATIC PRINCIPLES Score	ELECTORS WHO PLACE VIEWS ABOUT ANY ISSUE IN A BROAD CONTEXT		OTHER ELECTORS	
	N	(percent)	N	(percent)
Low				
One	0	0	0	0
Two	1	1	4	10
Three	11	11	9	22
Four	84	87	28	68
High				
TOTAL	96	100	41	100

omy was imposed on all nine comparisons of potentially effective electors and others. Even though this procedure substantially increases the chance of discovering a difference between the groups, it will be seen that very little difference exists between the potentially effective electors and the rest of the sample in their support of abstract democratic procedures. On the other hand when agreement with the statement that "Democracy is the best form of government" was examined among the various groups, significant differences were discovered between five sets of effective electors and other electors. A comparison of answers for all groups is given in Table 11.2.

Table 11.2: Agreement of Potentially Effective Electors and
Others with Statement that Democracy is Best Form of Government

ELECTORS	AGREE (percent)		
Who perceive existence of six			
or more issues	88	(111)	S.
Others	55	(29)	
Who perceive three or more policy			
alternatives on five or more issues	91	(64)	S.
Others	74	(76)	
Who place views about any			
issue in a broad context	88	(96)	S.
Others	66	(44)	
Who perceive most party policies			
correctly on five or more issues	94	(50)	S.
Others	74	(90)	
Who adopt concrete preferences			
on five or more issues	88	(85)	S.
Others	71	(55)	
Who feel affected by six			
or more issues	88	(52)	N.S.
Others	77	(88)	
Who perceive two or more effects			
from four or more issues	84	(45)	N.S.
Others	80	(95)	
Who perceive effect of issue as			
great on five or more issues	84	(76)	N.S.
Others	78	(64)	
Who feel strongly on six			
or more issues	85	(93)	N.S.
Others	74	(47)	

NOTE: Figures in parentheses are those on which percentages are based.
S. indicates that a comparison reveals a statistically significant difference between groups.
N.S. indicates that no such difference exists. The comparison in each case is between electors who agree to the statement and "others" ("disagree" and "D.K.").

The finding that some potentially effective electors show more support than other electors for the statement that democracy is the best form of government, although little difference appears between them in the support given to general democratic principles, compares interestingly with a similar finding when politicians were compared with the body of electors (Table 8.1). Support for democracy and for democratic norms in the abstract is at any rate widespread among electors (Table 8.1). We should not expect to find very marked differences here between potentially effective and other electors. The real test comes when we compare responses about specific applications of these democratic norms.

SPECIFIC PRINCIPLES OF DEMOCRACY

Table 11.3 compares the responses of potentially effective electors with those of other electors on a scale which combines answers to all the statements on specific applications of majority rule and minority rights. Again a score of one was given to each pro-democratic answer, and no score to any other response. On seven out of nine comparisons the groups taken as potentially more effective offer significantly more support for democratic statements.[1] This finding does on the whole uphold the initial expectations to the effect that in a stable democracy the more politically oriented electors will prove more consistent than the rest of the population in their support of democratic procedures.

When we examine the differences between the groups of the politically effective and other electors more closely, it is evident that the differences between the two groups are greater on the question of minority rights than on majority rule; that is, that compared to other electors, the potentially effective electors are relatively more attached to minority rights than to majority rule. On a scale which summarizes support for specific applications of majority rule,[2] only three significant differ-

---

[1] In all comparisons of support for specific applications of democratic principles in Table 11.3 distributions were dichotomized between those scoring seven and above and those scoring six and less. The comparison was thus essentially between those endorsing a very high proportion of democratic courses of action in the specific cases presented in the statements and those endorsing a rather low proportion. Scores were dichotomized in this way because the analysis deals with "potentially effective" electors who are only marginally distinguishable from other electors. In contrast, therefore, to the previous analyses when conservative assumptions were adopted in the estimation of relative agreement among politicians, every effort is made in this section of the discussion to point up the characteristics which distinguish these potentially effective electors from their fellows.

[2] The construction of this scale is reported in full in Appendix G of I. Budge, *Patterns of Democratic Agreement* (Ph.D. dissertation, Yale University Library; also published by University Micro Films, Ann Arbor, Mich., 1967).

ences appear between potentially effective groups and others.[3] On a scale which summarizes support for specific applications of minority rights,[2] there are six such differences.[4]

So far as the evidence goes, therefore, it does seem that in Britain the politicians' extensive and consistent adherence to democratic principles is supported by a similar adherence on the part of more politically effective elements in the population.

Again the fact that potentially effective electors support specific applications of the principle of minority rights more consistently than they do the principle of majority rule recalls the pattern of responses encountered among politicians. It may be that the British political culture stresses the tolerance of minorities much more than it emphasizes the rule of majorities and that different emphases are reflected in the replies both of the politicians and of politically oriented electors. A more general explanation for the replies, however, is possibly that support for minority rights demands more knowledge and understanding of political complexities than is required by simple majoritarianism. At any rate it does appear that in Britain the politicians' ability to combine in defense of democratic procedures is supported by a stronger adherence to such procedures on the part of the political stratum. The fact that a pattern of relatively greater democratic support was discovered even among electors distinguished on minimal measures of effectiveness makes it likely that high level activists will support democratic principles even more consistently and widely.

THE POLITICAL STRATUM AND APPRAISALS OF DEMOCRACY

The argument of Chapter 2 asserted that an agreement to support democratic principles is not sufficient to ensure that group support will be given to the existent political regime of a stable democracy. It is also necessary to have agreement among the group that such principles are actually being put into practice in the political system under which they live. The argument was applied to the politicians but can also be

---

[3] *Viz:* Between electors who perceive three or more policy alternatives on five or more issues, and other electors.

Between electors who place their views about any issue in a broad context, and others.

Between electors who perceive the effects of an issue as great on five or more issues, and others.

[4] The comparisons where *no* significant difference was revealed were:

Between electors who feel affected by six or more issues, and other electors.

Between electors who perceive two or more effects from four or more issues, and other electors.

Between electors who perceive the effect of the issue as great on five or more issues, and other electors.

Table 11.3: Support of Potentially Effective Electors and Others for Specific Applications of Democratic Principles

ELECTORS	High Ten/Nine	Eight/Seven	Six/Five (percent)	Four/Three	Low Below Two	
Who perceive existence of six or more issues	29	33	25	11	2	(110) S.
Others	8	27	27	27	11	(26)
Who perceive three or more policy alternatives on five or more issues	34	39	17	8	2	(64) S.
Others	17	25	33	19	5	(72)
Who place views about any issues in a broad context	30	38	21	8	2	(96) S.
Others	12	15	37	27	7	(40)
Who feel affected by six or more issues	29	44	13	11	2	(52) S.
Others	23	24	33	15	5	(84)
Who adopt concrete preferences on five or more issues	27	36	26	8	2	(84) S.
Others	21	25	25	23	6	(52)

Who feel strongly on six						
or more issues	28	36	23	12	1	(92) S.
Others	18	23	32	18	9	(44)
Who perceive most party policies						
correctly on five or more issues	36	34	22	8	0	(50) S.
Others	19	30	28	17	6	(86)
Who perceive two or more effects						
from four or more issues	18	43	27	11	0	(44) N.S.
Others	28	26	25	15	5	(92)
Who perceive effect of issue as						
great on five or more issues	29	28	25	17	1	(76) N.S.
Others	20	37	27	10	7	(67)

NOTE: Figures in parentheses are those on which percentages are based.
S. indicates that a comparison reveals a statistically significant difference between groups.
N.S. indicates that no such difference exists. The comparison in each case is between electors who agree to the statement and "others" ("disagree" and "D.K.").

149

applied to the political stratum. We should expect, therefore, to find the political stratum relatively more highly agreed than other electors about the existence of democracy in Britain and about the application of democratic procedures in the handling of political affairs.

Moreover we also anticipate that the political stratum will be more capable than other electors of acting together as a group in support of the democratic principles upheld by the politicians. This expectation requires some realization by potentially effective electors that their agreements outweigh their disagreements and that, consequently, there does exist some basis for combination in defense of these principles. The potentiality for such combination is assumed to be higher among members of the political stratum than among other members of the population. Therefore agreement on the factual appraisals that agreements exist in Britain, that they are more important than disagreements, and that they involve democracy should be greater among potentially effective electors than among others.

Again the potentially effective electors with whom the discussion will be concerned are those distinguished as such on the various issue responses used in the previous section. The questions on which the groups will be compared are those that were previously employed in the comparison of politicians and electors reported in Chapter 9.

First, therefore, we shall contrast the replies of "politically effective" electors and others to various statements about the consideration of government for the views of ordinary citizens.

Table 11.4 reports the percentages in each group making a reply that indicates a belief that the British political system is responsive to the desires of its citizens. From the replies it appears that there is no general difference between potentially effective electors and the other electors in their assessments of British democracy. Substantial numbers of potentially effective electors share the same misgivings as other electors about the ability of the political system to represent the views of ordinary people and also distrust the motives of persons in power. In some cases a majority of the potentially effective hold this view.

These findings certainly go against the expectations put forward at the beginning of this section of the discussion. However Table 11.4 compares the responses of the various groups to specific questions; it may give a fairer idea of the trends at work to compare their positions on a more general scale or combination of questions, a scale that has already been employed in Table 9.2 to summarize differences between politicians and electors as a whole. The scale of political efficacy attempts to estimate the strength of feeling among the various groups that the political system is responsive to their preferences. The scale combines some of the individual questions employed in Table 11.4 with others.[5]

The impression given by this comparison is rather different from that given by the previous comparison of responses to specific questions. On the political efficacy scale five of the potentially effective groups are significantly distinguished from other electors by their optimism about getting things done, although four are not so distinguished.

In a sense, of course, it is not surprising that these five groups should feel more able to get things done in politics. They *are* potentially effective electors: it is not remarkable that they themselves feel so. But the two characteristics—feeling politically effective and being so—are not exactly the same, although they are obviously connected. In some countries the more politically effective elements of the population might not, in fact, feel themselves to be particularly effective, and this contrast between their actual potentiality for political action and their subjective feelings of ineffectiveness might have its bearing upon democratic stability. We are thus left with two sets of findings from this analysis which can support rather different interpretations of how potentially effective electors regard the workings of British democracy.

Perhaps, however, there is only an apparent contradiction between these sets of findings. The potentially effective electors may feel that the political system is not equally open to all citizens but rather only to those with sufficient determination and energy—the effective citizens, in fact. The findings themselves of Table 11.4 offer some support to this interpretation. It is noteworthy that the significant differences that do occur between potentially effective electors and the other electors in this table are on two statements that concern the responsiveness of local and national government to the citizen. Thus if the politically effective are just as cynical as anyone else about the idealism of political decision-makers, some among them feel that the system offers themselves, at any rate, a chance to make their preferences felt.

The question arises, however, of whether this limited belief in the responsiveness of the system is sufficient to permit their support of democratic principles to urge them into action in the event of any erosion of democratic processes.

AGREEMENT ON THE EXTENT TO WHICH DEMOCRATIC PREFERENCES ARE SHARED

If a group is to undertake combined action, considerable numbers of its members must see that there is a base for such action, that some

---

[5] For the construction of these measures, see Appendix D.

Table 11.4: Percentages of Potentially Effective Electors and Others Who Believe that Democracy Exists in Britain

ELECTORS	Do you think you can trust local councillors or that they become tools of special interests? (percent)	I don't think local councillors care much about what people like me think (percent)	People who go into public office usually think of the good of the people more than of their own good (percent)	If people really knew what was going on in high places in the government it would blow the lid off things (percent)	It doesn't matter which Party wins elections, the interests of the little man don't count (percent)
Who perceive existence of six or more issues	(110) 41 N.S.	40 N.S.	58 N.S.	32 N.S.	71 N.S.
Others	(26) 30	36	65	35	61
Who perceive three or more policy alternatives on five or more issues	(64) 36 N.S.	30 N.S.	61 N.S.	39 N.S.	81 S.
Others	(72) 43	29	59	26	59
Who place views about any issue in a broad context	(96) 35 N.S.	48 S.	58 N.S.	63 N.S.	76 S.
Others	(40) 42	20	64	83	53
Who feel affected by six or more issues	(52) 41 N.S.	48 N.S.	56 N.S.	35 N.S.	78 N.S.
Others	(84) 38	34	62	31	64

Who perceive two or more effects from four or more issues	(44)	37 N.S.	52 S.	49 N.S.	39 N.S.	70 N.S.
Others	(92)	41	33	65	29	69
Who perceive effect of issue as great on five or more issues	(76)	42 N.S.	42 N.S.	56 N.S.	33 N.S.	74 N.S.
Others	(60)	36	36	64	32	64
Who adopt concrete preferences on five or more issues	(84)	42 N.S.	43 N.S.	52 N.S.	36 N.S.	74 N.S.
Others	(52)	36	33	72	27	63
Who feel strongly on six or more issues	(92)	40 N.S.	41 N.S.	56 N.S.	37 N.S.	75 S.
Others	(44)	39	36	67	24	57
Who perceive most party policies correctly on five or more issues	(50)	41 N.S.	37 N.S.	56 N.S.	58 N.S.	76 N.S.
Others	(86)	39	41	61	73	65

NOTE: Figures in parentheses are those on which percentages are based.
S stands for a significant difference between a potentially effective group of electors and other electors.
N.S. signifies that there is no significant difference.

Table 11.5: Sense of Political Efficacy of Potentially Effective Electors and Others

ELECTORS	SCORE					
	Low Nothing	One	Two (percent)	Three	*High* Four	
Who perceive existence of six or more issues	18	31	22	24	5	(109) S.
Others	28	36	32	4	0	(25) S.
Who perceive three or more policy alternatives on five or more issues	9	30	22	33	6	(64) S.
Others	30	34	26	9	2	(70) S.
Who place views about any issue in a broad context	13	34	22	26	5	(95) S.
Others	38	28	28	5	0	(39) S.
Who adopt concrete preferences on five or more issues	17	34	18	26	5	(83) S.
Others	25	29	33	10	2	(51) S.
Who feel strongly on six or more issues	15	32	21	27	4	(90) S.
Others	29	32	29	7	2	(44) S.

Who feel affected by six						
or more issues	13	29	27	27	4	(52) N.S.
Others	24	34	22	16	4	(82)
Who perceive two or more effects						
from four or more issues	20	29	20	23	7	(44) N.S.
Others	20	33	25	19	2	(92)
Who perceive effect of issues as						
great on five or more issues	21	32	21	24	3	(76) N.S.
Others	19	33	28	15	5	(58)
Who perceive most party policies						
correctly on five or more issues	16	30	24	26	4	(50) N.S.
Others	23	33	24	17	4	(84)

NOTE: Figures in parentheses are those on which percentages are based.
S. stands for a significant difference between a potentially effective group of electors and other electors.
N.S. signifies that there is no significant difference. For the statistical test, scores were dichotomised into 'low scores' (two and below) and 'high scores' (three and above).

preferences are shared, and that in importance to group members the shared preferences outrank those preferences which are not shared. We can again compare the replies of the potentially effective groups of electors with other electors to see if their perceptions on these matters were shared to a significantly greater extent than among other electors. Since the political stratum is expected to be more capable of acting as a cohesive group, the agreement of potentially effective electors on these points should also be greater if initial assumptions are valid. Table 11.6 gives the proportions of electors in each group who thought that agreement existed in Britain, that democracy or established institutions were among the agreed topics, and that agreements in Britain were more or as important as disagreements.

Again we are presented with mixed findings pointing in rather different directions. Almost all electors in the potentially effective groups share to a greater extent than others the belief that agreements exist in Britain. On the other hand there is practically no greater agreement among potentially effective electors on the appraisal that agreements outweigh disagreements. While the absence of superior agreement on this appraisal parallels a similar absence when politicians were compared with all electors, it is also present on appraisals of whether the agreed topics include democracy and established institutions. This is an appraisal on which politicians were more agreed than the body of electors. It is true that among a substantial number of the potentially effective electors there is a more widespread opinion than among other electors that topics of agreement in Britain include democracy or established government. But though it is a substantial number, it still constitutes only a minority.

The overall conclusion to be drawn is, therefore, that some of the factual agreements deemed necessary to joint pro-democratic action on the part of the political stratum do exist and some do not. Agreement on these appraisals is markedly less extensive and consistent than among the politicians. Certainly over the whole range of appraisals which have been examined the potentially effective groups do incline more than other electors to judgments that would favor their combined pro-democratic action. But the total number of agreements relative to those of other electors on these points do not seem enough to uphold the original prediction, since agreement is absent from many appraisals where it seems an essential requirement for cohesive action.

Because of this negative conclusion, it is necessary to re-interpret the role played by these lower elements of the political stratum in the disturbed periods of a stable democracy. The previous analysis has shown that politicians have all the prerequisites for taking spontaneous combined action in defense of democratic procedures. Not only do they share a high internal agreement on such procedures, but they also share an agreement on practically all the factual appraisals that would facilitate the building of a pro-democratic coalition.

Perhaps, therefore, it is not necessary for democratic stability that the potentially effective electors be so capable of acting as a group on their own account as the politicians. So long as the latter are capable of taking a democratic initiative, the only role these electors need be called upon to play is that of supporters, of followers. What is required from them is not so much spontaneous action on their own account as a ready response to the politicians' claim that democracy is in danger. Group awareness and cohesion in supporting democracy need not, therefore, emerge spontaneously from the political stratum but can be sparked by politicians if there is need.

What is important is the potential ability of these electors to respond to the initial actions of politicians. And this rests much more upon their greater agreement on democratic principles, uncovered in the first section of the chapter, than on any superior consensus on factual appraisals.

OTHER CHARACTERISTICS OF
THE POLITICAL STRATUM

The use of nine separate measures of potential effectiveness is unsatisfactory because of the difficulty of saying at any point "These are the potentially effective electors." For electors who are admitted on the basis of one set of issue-responses as effective are excluded on others. An attempt was accordingly made, on the basis of the present survey data, to discover whether any one criterion of political orientation or political weight existed among the electors.

The easiest way to find this single criterion of effectiveness is to isolate various groups on all the characteristics that might possibly be conceived of as distinguishing the politically weighty elements and compare their issue responses relating to potential effectiveness with those of a group whose weight is undoubted, *i.e.*, the politicians. If one group of electors comes noticeably nearer the politicians than any other, it may be concluded that the characteristic by which that group was distinguished is a leading characteristic of the political stratum, at least so far as Britain is concerned. There is reason also to recognize

Table 11.6: Agreement of Potentially Effective Electors and Others on Existence, Democratic Nature and Importance of Agreements in Britain

ELECTORS	Agreements exist in Britain (percent)	AMONG TOPICS OF AGREEMENT IN BRITAIN ARE:		COMPARED WITH DIS-AGREEMENTS, AGREE-MENTS IN BRITAIN ARE:	
		*Democracy (percent)	*Established institutions (percent)	More important (percent)	As important (percent)
Who perceive existence of six or more issues	(111)	81 S.	6	46 N.S.	26
Others	(29)	62	19 N.S.*	0	52	17
Who perceive three or more policy alternatives on five or more issues	(64)	85 S.	26 S.	9	48 N.S.	26
Others	(76)	70	14	1	47	23
Who place views about any issue in a broad context	(96)	81 S.	21 N.S.	6	45 N.S.	26
Others	(44)	67	15	2	52	20
Who feel affected by six or more issues	(32)	87 S.	24 N.S.	5	53 N.S.	24
Others	(88)	71	16	4	44	24
Who perceive two or more effects from four or more issues	(45)	85 N.S.	24 N.S.	4	39 N.S.	28
Others	(95)	72	17	5	50	22

Who perceive effects of issue as great on five or more issues	(76)	91 S.	25 S.	6	54 N.S.	21
Others	(64)	60	13	3	40	28
Who adopt concrete preferences on five or more issues	(85)	82 S.	24 S.	6	52 N.S.	26
Others	(55)	67	12	3	41	22
Who feel strongly on six or more issues	(93)	80 N.S.	21 N.S.	4	49 N.S.	26
Others	(47)	69	16	6	44	21
Who perceive most party policies correctly on five or more issues	(50)	92 S.	30 S.	6	56 S.	24
Others	(90)	68	13	4	42	24

NOTE: Figures in parentheses are those on which percentages are based.
S. stands for a significant difference between a potentially effective group and others.
N.S. signifies that there is no significant difference.
* Mutually exclusive categories. Electors are enumerated under "Established Institutions" only if they had not already mentioned "Democracy."

159

such a characteristic as the cause of these electors' greater support of democracy.

Thirty-six groups of electors were chosen for comparison with politicians. They were selected on the basis of all available criteria included in the survey and not already used to measure potential effectiveness.

Three out of the thirty-six groups emerged as closest to politicians on the measures of potential effectiveness: those who felt a strong interest in issues; those who were confident of their own political efficacy, and those who were distinguished by considerable conceptual ability and high political information. None of those three groups was noticeably closer to politicians than the others, nor did the support given to democratic procedures differ significantly between them. This fact aroused the suspicion that they consisted of the same electors, since they were not mutually exclusive. However the greatest overlapping membership was only 53 percent (between the group with high feelings of efficacy and the group with high conceptual ability and information).

What one can say from this is that a strong psychological involvement in politics seems to be associated both with potential effectiveness and with support of democratic principles. Perhaps it may even be a cause of effectiveness and pro-democratic sentiment. However there seem to be different types of involvement—three different types in the present case. This result confirms Dahl's assertion that "there are various ways in which individuals may be psychologically 'involved' in politics; these different forms of involvement usually run together but they need not."[6] There seems, in fact, to be no single criterion by which the potentially effective can be isolated and no single cause that can be assigned as an explanation for their support of democratic procedures. All that can be said is that a greater than average orientation to politics seems to lead to a greater appreciation of and adherence to the actual operating procedures under which politics is carried on.[7]

CONCLUSIONS

Findings presented in this chapter:

1. Uphold the expectation that the potentially more effective electors

---

[6] R. A. Dahl, *Modern Political Analysis* (Englewood Cliffs, N.J.: Prentice-Hall, 1963), p. 56.

[7] A much fuller account of the analysis described in this section is contained in Chapter 20 and Appendix J of Budge, *op. cit.*

support democratic procedures to a greater extent than less effective electors (Chapter 2, Predictions 3 and 5).

2. Do not uphold the expectation that the potentially more effective electors agree in their factual appraisals of democracy to a greater extent than less effective electors (Chapter 2, Prediction 9).

12 CONCLUSIONS

The major modification undergone by initial expectations can now be briefly summarized. In Britain politicians are distinguished from electors to some extent by their agreement on preferences, both procedural or substantive, but most markedly by their agreement on factual appraisals. This finding has been upheld under different methods of estimating agreement and over a variety of political topics. It can be readily evaluated against the generalized Dahl-Key theory, and its implications can be clearly spelled out. However the analysis has also raised a number of points that were not considered in the introductory discussion and whose theoretical bearings need to be assessed here. After these assessments have been made, it will be easier to say where the analysis has left the original explanation of democratic stability in terms of differential agreement and how unanticipated results fit with such an explanation.

SURVEY FINDINGS ON THE SIGNIFICANCE OF PARTY AS A SOURCE OF DISSENSUS AMONG POLITICIANS

It is striking that the factual appraisals on which politicians were relatively least agreed were those involving the political parties, *i.e.*, general appraisals of parties and party leaders and appraisals of party policies on issues. The fact that relative consensus is least on these appraisals brings to mind the important effect that parties have in dividing politicians into sharply defined groups with mutually exclusive loyalties and opposing aims.

The prediction that politicians would be relatively agreed on a substantial minority of issue preferences may similarly have foundered on a party split. In putting forward a consensual theory of democratic stability, therefore, one must constantly guard against the danger of minimizing the partisan conflicts and political divisions that exist inside a democratic system, conflicts in which the politicians themselves are most heavily involved. If politicians and electors of the same party agree more with each other than politicians do among themselves, then the assertion that politicians are more capable of united effective action than other groups in the population is immediately made doubtful. For the politicians and electors of each party would, on the assumption that higher agreement is associated with the ability to cooperate more effectively, achieve a higher degree of unity than the body of politicians. Even if it were only the politicians of each party who agreed more among themselves than did the body of politicians, this would still indicate that the party tie was stronger than the links uniting all politicians. This stronger intra-party agreement would count against the assumption that politicians could be regarded in most respects as a distinct group on their own account.

It is then to avoid understressing the divisive influence of party loyalties that explicit consideration has been given in each chapter to the question of relative agreement among politicians and electors of the same party. It has been argued that if the party tie does have any effect, it will be that of increasing agreement either among politicians *and* electors or among politicians alone. In the first case the contrast in agreement between politicians and electors of the same party should become less; in the second case it should become greater.

The findings show that the second of these anticipated results generally occurs in the case of the Labour Party; *i.e.*, the agreement of Labour electors remains the same and the agreement of Labour politicians increases. But neither possible consequence of the common party tie is discovered in the case of the Conservative Party. Here the contrast between the agreement of politicians and the agreement of electors diminishes not because electors agree more, but because politicians agree less: when agreement within this party is investigated, dissensus among Conservative politicians becomes more marked in many cases than it was among the whole body of politicians.

While found in opinions on topics of dissensus in Britain, likes and dislikes about the parties and party leaders, attitudes to equality of opportunity and appraisals of party stands, the contrast between the agreement of politicians in the two parties becomes most striking and significant in regard to preferences on issues. Labour politicians were more agreed than their electors in preferences on six issues; Conservative politicians were more agreed than Conservative electors in preferences on only two issues—as few as when the body of politicians was compared with the body of electors. A positive dissensus—a lack of overlap between two relatively equal groups with different opinions—

occurs among Conservative politicians on preferences about six issues. The bearing on the wider discussion of this lack of agreement among Conservative politicians is simply that the party division cannot of itself be regarded as promoting the disagreement in the views of the body of politicians which has been discovered to exist. For if the extensive dissensus among politicians in their preferences on issues had been caused principally by the party tie, agreement among the politicians in each party would have increased on the removal of the main cause of dissensus. Thus party loyalties do not unite politicians and electors who share the same party identification nor even the party groupings of politicians as such sufficiently for either to rival the body of politicians as groups capable of united effective action. It is true that Labour politicians are much more closely agreed in their preferences than the body of politicians. But since the Conservatives are not so agreed, the body of politicians is not split between two highly integrated groups. The opposite view may be taken that the high agreement of the Labour group forms a focus around which agreement may cohere as it seems to do in the case of most factual appraisals.

THE CONTRAST IN AGREEMENT AMONG CONSERVATIVE AND LABOUR POLITICIANS

The contrast between the agreement of Conservative and Labour politicians is also of interest for its own sake. The shape taken by the contrast—greater agreement among Labour politicians, lesser agreement among Conservative politicians—is all the more surprising since the major unfavorable attribute of the Labour Party among all politicians (44 percent) was considered to be its members' tendency to disunity and disloyalty. At the very time that this evaluation was being voiced, Labour politicians were, in fact, in greater agreement than Conservative politicians.

Part of the explanation for Labour agreement may well lie in the fact that the issues on which the preferences of the Labour politicians so strikingly concurred were almost all traditional rallying-points for members of their party (all except the question of negotiations over Berlin). Questions of British prestige and power, questions on which the Conservatives might have rallied, were, on the other hand, not among those chosen for study.

This is perhaps the best available explanation for the interesting contrast between the patterns of consensus among the two groups. It is indeed tempting to claim that these patterns foreshadow all the political developments of the three years subsequent to the survey (1962).

From Conservative dissensus one could trace the increasing discontents which first prompted the Macmillan Cabinet purges of the summer of 1962 and which, exacerbated by the failure of the Common Market negotiations and the Profumo scandal, subsequently forced Macmillan out. In Labour consensus one could see the genesis of the uncharacteristic unity that survived the leadership struggle between Wilson and Brown and that was later instrumental in gaining the precarious election victory of October 1964.

Such attempts at hindsight on the basis of the present distributions of opinion would, however, be extremely rash. It is very possible that these disagreements were reversed on the issues which came to the focus of politicians' attention in the next four months. Only if replications of the present study were instituted over a considerable period of time could the connection between such disagreements and party fortunes be tested. The more modest explanation that the issues examined in this time-period happened to be congenial to Labour politicians is more congruent with the available evidence.

TYPES OF AGREEMENT AND DISAGREEMENT

The survey findings have also helped to reveal the variety of senses in which agreement and disagreement may be said to exist among the British population. Each has a different implication for democratic stability which can now be summarized below.

1. Relative and 'Hypothetico-Deductive' Agreement

In the course of examining and comparing responses to democratic statements, it became evident that politicians were not notably more agreed than electors. Nevertheless it is still possible to talk about politicians' (and electors') high consensus on democratic norms. It appears from this fact that "agreement" or "consensus" can be used other than in a comparative sense. To emphasize the contrast between the two concepts of "agreement" this may be termed its "hypothetico-deductive" form. It can be assumed in this study that "high" agreement in a "hypothetico-deductive" sense represents a very close conformity to certain abstract statements about democracy, and that a group can be regarded as "agreed" (whatever its position *vis-à-vis* another group) if most of its members endorse the (previously determined) "democratic" answers to these statements.

This is the sense in which consensus was originally discussed by Prothro and Grigg. Here therefore the existence of internal agreement but not agreement relative to that of another group, is crucial in the assessment of the politicians' role. However that role could not be regarded as at all unique if agreements in the comparative sense had not been discovered on their factual appraisals of issues and of British democracy.

2. Non-Directed and Directed Agreement

Concurrence in naming the same aspects (whatever these aspects may be) of political issues means that the politicians can be regarded as being particularly equipped for handling policy questions through free negotiation and debate. Had their preferential and factual agreements about democracy not been "pro-democratic," however, it would have been impossible to view them as the leading practitioners and defenders of democratic procedures.

3. Conscious and Unconscious Agreement

It may be that politicians are unaware of their concurrent on their factual appraisals of issues. It hardly seems to matter if they are, for the easing of negotiation through such agreements can proceed whether they are consciously shared or not. A bold political initiative, such as the defense of democratic procedures in a crisis, would require, it seems, that politicians be conscious that a widespread agreement on democracy exists. Lacking this belief, they might hesitate to lead a defense of democratic procedures for fear of the consequences to themselves if their initiative was not followed.

4. Disagreement with Opposing Preferences and Disagreement with Compatible Preferences

The important difference between these types of dissensus has been noted at various points throughout the discussion. Disagreement where sizable groups of politicians endorse opposing preferences provides at least a favorable milieu for the development of a zero-sum clash of interests, a winner-take-all contest in which the losers face the total negation of their preferences. One or two such situations may be tolerated. But if all policy questions were of this type, an intolerable strain would seem likely to be imposed upon all the contestants, winners and losers alike. Relations between the competitors would deteriorate, for it would seem difficult to remain friendly with a man whose advantage was your disadvantage. Disagreements where sizable groups endorse compatible preferences seem, on the other hand, to provide a favorable milieu for negotiation since most persons' preferences can be satisfied through the adoption of a composite policy on the question.

INFORMATION AND AGREEMENT AMONG POLITICIANS

To what extent does agreement among politicians on factual appraisals result from the simple fact that they are better informed on all political matters than the general population? The better informed any group is about a factual situation, the more likely its members are to agree on certain facts simply because they are more likely to name the correct facts. Hence politicians *vis-à-vis* electors may be in the position of any group of specialists, discussing their chosen subject, *vis-à-vis* laymen.

To make the point that politicians may resemble other specialized experts, such as scientists, when they discuss their own field is not, of course, to demonstrate that the politicians' superior consensus on factual appraisals is irrelevant to the functioning of democracy. The way in which agreement is reached does not affect the consequences its existence may have on tendencies to negotiate, to debate and ultimately to compromise.

It should, however, be noted that politicians are not in exactly the same position as scientists and other academic specialists, or even as technologists and applied specialists. They have incomparably less knowledge about their subject and no universally accepted criteria for validating the knowledge they have. Their success may depend on accommodating (quite unconsciously and without hypocrisy) their personal views to those of constituents or of influential persons with whom they are in contact, rather than in independently applying their special knowledge in such a way as to arrive at the 'correct' facts of a situation.

We have no direct evidence bearing on the relationship between political knowledge and agreement; but we did discover that political efficacy and interest brought electors' issue-responses closer to politicians' to exactly the same extent as did information and political conceptual ability. On the basis of this finding it seems plausible to argue that factors other than specialist information prompt politicians' agreement. It thus seems unlikely that any superior consensus found among politicians can be attributed solely to their ability as specialists to mention "correct" political facts. Their sensitivity to each others' opinions and their constant discussion and interaction may also act powerfully to promote common views. Of course the influence of these factors may vary between different appraisals. Agreement on the extent to which one is affected by an issue probably depends less on a common stock of specialist knowledge than on shared identifications and the tendency of discussion and interaction to produce similar judgments. Where the attribution of party support or opposition to a policy may help one's own electoral chances, it would also be unrealistic to expect most politicians to apply their specialist knowledge with the sole aim of arriving at the correct facts.

Such expertise, however, could be almost the sole influence prompting agreement on the question of whether issues exist or not. For the definition put forward previously implies that a problem that qualifies as a political issue has been taken up by a significant number of political activists. Otherwise courses of action relating to it would not be urged in the press or through representative bodies or by pressure groups. Given this situation, in which some feeling already exists about the problem among politically significant groups, it is likely that most of the time most politicians will agree that the issue is live, simply because of their expert sensitivity to strong currents of feeling among those people with whom they come in contact.

DEMOCRATIC AND A-DEMOCRATIC AGREEMENT

Agreements of various kinds have been described as existing among the politicians of unstable democracies such as the France of the Fourth Republic, not to mention politicians of an authoritarian regime.[1] Obviously the existence of a special body of mutual "understandings" among these politicians did not contribute to the maintenance of democratic procedures in their respective countries. Can a claim really be made that the existence of the agreements just described contributes to British democratic stability?

It must be realized, however, that the "agreements" described as existing among the French and Russian politicians are not the same as those analyzed in the present study. The former refer to a common style of playing the game of politics, but the same political tactics were employed (in the Fourth Republic at any rate) for mutually exclusive political ends, namely the substitution of oneself in office in the place of one's rivals. None of the agreements uncovered among French *Deputés* referred to policy matters, and thus they stood in quite a different category from the substantive agreements described here. It is quite true that a majority of *Deputés* might have supported the estab-

---

[1] N. Leites, *On the Game of Politics in France* (Stanford, Calif.: Stanford University Press, 1959), and N. Leites, *A Study of Bolshevism* (Glencoe, Ill.: Free Press, 1953).

lished procedures and system which benefited them, but there would have been a significant dissidence among Communists and Gaullists, not to mention the opposition of the latter groups to many aspects of majority rule or minority rights.

Thus the agreements discussed here are not the same as those which seem to have existed in unstable democracies or in authoritarian regimes; and until substantive and procedural agreements of the type of those described are discovered under those systems it seems legitimate to regard their existence in a stable democracy as significant for the functioning of that political system.

WAYS IN WHICH DEMOCRATIC AGREEMENTS MIGHT BE WEAKENED

It was suggested in the opening discussion that the main threat to consensus on democratic procedures comes from ongoing political controversies, even though the procedures themselves are not directly involved in the conflict. Perhaps this is so because the losing side tries to avert its defeat by attacking the rules which ensure its defeat.

The survey findings, however, bear upon this point only inferentially, first by showing that politicians' feelings about substantive policy questions tend to be very strong, strong enough that they are certainly not inhibited by apathy or inertia from carrying their policy disputes over into procedural matters. Second one can deduce from Labour politicians' reluctance to let the B.M.A. organize its members that their attitudes toward procedures have been influenced by the hostility between them and B.M.A. over substantive issues.

The more direct evidence of the survey findings testified, however, to a different sort of interplay between substantive disputes and adherence to democratic procedures. In the case of some Conservative politicians one democratic procedure seems to form part of a general constellation of attitudes which they oppose: namely, the principle of equal opportunities for all. In opposing political equality of opportunity, they do not seem to be trying to change the procedural rules to benefit their own case, for on many matters they might expect the support of the B.M.A. yet oppose its right to organize its membership electorally. Their opposition seems to stem not from political self-interest, but from a general attitude that is applied consistently to substantive and procedural matters alike. They simply oppose equality of opportunity in all spheres of life, social and political.

One can envisage few conflicts, other than the one over equality of opportunity, that directly focus upon procedural points as well as substantive policy matters. But possibly the whole question of the place of minorities in British society might constitute a topic capable of engendering substantive controversy over social policies and political procedures at the same time. In the same way that the politicians' dispute over educational opportunity and equal access to public jobs was accompanied by opposition to political equality, so the dispute over immigration into Britain had at least a potential for engendering opposition to immigrants' political rights. But if the topic had the potentiality for engendering procedural disagreement, that potentiality was not fulfilled: the politicians were unanimous in upholding the political rights of West Indians in spite of their disagreement over the Immigration Bill.

Controversies that involve procedural principles other than the one over equality of opportunity seem, therefore, to be absent among British politicians, at least for the period during which the survey was conducted.[2]

A MODIFIED EXPLANATION OF DEMOCRATIC STABILITY IN TERMS OF DIFFERENTIATED AGREEMENT

Looking at the survey findings as a whole it is obvious that differentiated agreements have been found and that they can plausibly be connected with pro-democratic action. Politicians and political stratum support democratic procedures more strongly and consistently than the less involved electors. Politicians share factual agreements about democracy that are likely to sensitize them to threats to democracy and to facilitate their united defense of the established system. To this extent the generalized Dahl-Key theory has been upheld. However it has to be modified slightly to take account of the absence of markedly higher agreement among the politicians compared with other groups on both democratic and issue preferences.

Although the survey relates to only a single point in time, the probable interaction between general and differentiated agreements of the kinds uncovered is best illustrated by extrapolating over time. For the number and scope of agreements and disagreements in Britain might vary widely between different periods. At some points the number of zero-sum conflicts of preference between politicians might be very much greater than at the time of the present survey; consensus on factual appraisals might also be very much less. At other points in time, such as the period examined, zero-sum conflicts might be minimal and agreement on factual appraisals widespread.

---

[2] For an explanation as to why this might be so, see the end of Chapter 8.

If the overall extent of agreement on substantive political issues fluctuates over time, it is possible to postulate a dynamic relationship between this substantive consensus and consensus on democratic norms. When the number of zero-sum conflicts was very high and agreement on factual appraisals low, a very strong commitment to democratic norms on the part of politicians would be needed to keep the system stable. In a situation where zero-sum conflicts were largely absent and factual agreements high there would be relatively little strain on procedural agreements. Such periods (similar to the one on which we have the present survey evidence) would facilitate the building-up of agreements on procedures which would carry through times of severe substantive disagreements.

The absence of zero-sum disagreement and the presence of extensive factual agreements attach politicians to democratic procedures first through the probability that policy disagreement would not typically take the form of a direct clash of preferences, a clash that could end only in the rejection of some and the adoption of others. Rather it consists in the endorsement of different policies by different groupings of politicians. And these different preferences could quite conceivably be included in a combined final program on the issue, a possibility that offers some satisfaction to all significant groups.

Thus the situation that normally exists with regard to most of the politicians' preferences over policy questions seems one in which even strong political feeling is more likely to prompt discussion, negotiation and bargaining than a flouting of established rules. Everybody can hope for a slice of the cake by working within the established procedures in order to bring about a compromise. Flouting these procedures is likely to result in loss of the whole cake.

Second there is the consideration that politicians, practical men concerned with the day-to-day running of a society, are likely to stick to democratic courses of action and to the debating and negotiating procedures that they guarantee so long as these channels are found effective in settling political problems. When that effectiveness decreases, it is likely that attachment to them will decrease as better modes of handling disputes are sought.

It has been a leading assumption of the whole analysis that the more extensive the initial area of agreement, the more likely negotiation and discussion are to lead to accepted settlements of substantive matters under dispute. More will be said about this assumption later in the chapter. If we accept its truth for the moment, however, we can see from the survey findings how democratic procedures continue to be employed by politicians in the handling of policy questions. For the overwhelming number of agreements uncovered in politicians' factual appraisals of politics and of policy matters under dispute seem capable of lending focus and coherence to democratic persuasion and bargaining such that democratic methods emerge a most efficient way of procuring compromise and ultimate consensus on the question. The agreements on factual appraisals seem particularly likely to produce results given the predominance of such relatively mild preferential disagreements as these just discussed. For where compromise on different preferences is possible, it must be a great help in reaching it to share the same opinions about the effects they will have as well as to see much the same range of policies as open to pursuit on the question.

The relevance of this condition to adherence to democratic procedures is more evident when it is noted that the politicians' attachment of democratic procedures is in normal times under a much severer strain than that of the rest of the population. Their greater political effectiveness exposes them to a continuous pressure of political problems, to the passions of the moment, and to constant irritation at the slowness and cumbrousness of bargaining tactics. The mass of the population are insulated from these feelings by the fact that the politicians undertake the arduous political task of handling controversies in such a way.

Thus although the politicians' attachments to democratic procedures are not very much greater in extent than those of the rest of the population, such attachments cannot be explained simply as factors at work among the population as a whole, such as the lack of bitter preferential disagreements on substantive policy matters. Some condition must be present which eases the work of persuasion and discussion, and that condition seems to lie in the agreements on appraisals mentioned above. They seem to form the main reason why politicians could not simply be replaced by other groups in the population without its resulting in serious damage to democracy. For any other group that lacked the understanding of one another's positions, an understanding that politicians have, would in all likelihood prove unable to resolve by democratic means the questions facing them.

The absence of bitter substantive disagreement may help to ensure that normal adherence to established democratic practices represents a habitual reaction which is largely unconsidered by participants. But as soon as any upheaval occurs, some readjustments have to take place. Such an upheaval may constitute much less than a direct challenge to democratic principles, no more of a challenge, for example, than an upsurge in the number of zero-sum conflicts over policy or the replacement of one party which has had a long tenure of office by another. The point has already been made that democratic processes are subject to erosion in a variety of ways other than through direct attack (a turn of events that is unlikely in Britain anyway). At any difficult juncture there are likely to be temptations and pressures to cut through problems by action that denies some minority its rights, that thwarts majority powers of decision-making, or that undermines the rules that preserve these. The upheavals in Britain during the twentieth century which have imposed these pressures and temptations would include the House of Lords crisis in 1910, the Irish question prior to 1914, the experience of total war in both the First and Second World Wars—especially the replacement of Asquith by Lloyd-George and of Chamberlain by Churchill—the formation of the first Labour Party Government in 1923–24, the General Strike, the Depression, the sweeping socioeconomic reforms of the post-War Labour Government, the Suez crisis, and the related problems of immigration and civil rights in the 'sixties.

Under the stresses imposed by these problems it seems likely that conscious adherence to certain principles assumes more importance as an explanation of action undertaken. Although such conscious adherence may be powerfully supplemented by various issue agreements, ingrained habits of action and complementary role-expectations in normal times, these can hardly stand as the sole explanations of continued adherence to democratic practices during a period when issue agreements are diminishing and when ingrained habits and role-expectations are being changed. Of course it is conceivable that some habits and role-expectations could be changed without affecting those that relate to democratic procedures, but this is unlikely to be an unconscious distinction mutely accepted by participants. Conscious considerations surely play a major part in limiting the changes which people are willing to accept.

How exactly does the relationship between democratic agreements and adherence to democratic practices seem to function during a period of change? Preferences are the opinions that have probably the strongest and most immediate association with actual behavior. Therefore the relevance for democratic stability of the widespread attachment of politicians and electors to democratic procedures can hardly be over-emphasized. Given a suitable stimulus, this attachment seems capable of motivating strong support for democratic courses of action whenever it is aroused. The interesting question is how it can be aroused.

To say that of all opinions preferences are probably the most closely related to action is not to imply that they are synonymous with action. This is especially true where action is not guided by well-established precedent and set rules (as with voting) and where it depends for success on the cooperation of large numbers of people and not simply on the impulses of one individual. The findings replicate much other empirical evidence in demonstrating that the majority of the population has little political information or interest or intense feeling. Under these conditions it is likely that the pro-democratic preferences of electors—if the latter were left to themselves—would not avail in most situations to stimulate counter-action in the presence of a threat to democratic procedures. In the first place electors' widespread political apathy and ignorance would mean that the threat if it was at all insidious would simply not be recognized for what it was. And even if the threat was so obvious and blatant as to force itself on everyone's attention, there might well be a general tendency in such a situation to await a lead from others, since taking the first step would leave one open to the possibility that one's action would after all be unsupported, which, in turn, would leave one open to reprisals.

The stimulus that is required to translate the democratic preferences of the general population into pro-democratic action seems, therefore, to depend upon the presence of people who do pay close attention to politics, who are capable of recognizing threats to democratic procedures in specific policy proposals, who are sure that their pro-democratic preferences are widely shared, and who are used to coalition-building in pursuit of political objectives. And this kind of person is most completely typified by the politician.

Even though the only agreements which emphatically set politicians apart from the general population are those on factual appraisals, it is precisely such agreements that are capable of triggering their pro-democratic preferences into collective action. And it is their collective action which, in turn, can trigger the pro-democratic preferences of electors into action. For it is probable, according to the survey evidence that if the politicians find it necessary to raise the cry of "Democracy in danger," others will respond—not only other politicians and high-level activists, but the more politically knowledgeable and potentially effective elements in the population as a whole. It is true that the latter have grave doubts about the extent to which democracy actually functions in Britain, but their stronger democratic preferences seem to make them more susceptible than the other sections of the population to the politicians' appeals, while their own experience with the working of the political system has not been unfavorable. Their lack of agreement on factual appraisals about democracy seems to make the translation of their democratic preferences into pro-democratic action dependent on a prior initiative by the politicians. But their stronger democratic preferences are there and available for such translation.

The pattern of agreements among British politicians explains therefore, why both in routine and exceptional political periods these figures play a unique and vital role in maintaining democratic procedures. This conclusion confirms the main initial assertion of this study about the role of politicians during routine political periods and the expectations put forward by Dahl about their role in periods of up-heaval.[3] They are the group continuously concerned with using and upholding democratic procedures, and they are the only group in the democratic population that, by virtue of its various understandings and agreements, is fully capable of undertaking this task.

SUMMARY OF FINAL CONCLUSIONS

At the outset of Chapter 2 the generalized form of the original Dahl-Key theory was presented in a series of numbered statements. It may prove helpful at this point to state the main conclusions of the present research in the form of a similar paradigm. This will permit a rapid assessment of the modifications undergone by these initial expec-tations and will, at any rate, succinctly present the view of agreement and stability that we derive from our findings. As a preliminary one should note the extent to which investigation has upheld the utility of the initial analytic division of political participants into politicians, political stratum, and politically uninterested and uninvolved citizens: interesting differences occur between the three groups which can read-ily be interpreted as significant for democratic stability. Moreover party differences within these groups are less important than the differences between them.

Our findings indicate that:

1. The politicians agree highly (but with some inconsistencies) on the specific operating norms of democratic behavior and on the more abstract democratic norms. They are highly agreed (and more con-sistently than on actual democratic norms) that established institutions are democratic, that support for these institutions is widespread and more important than any political cleavages may otherwise exist.

2. The politically oriented citizens are highly agreed on the more abstract norms of democratic behavior and also (but somewhat inconsistently) on relatively specific procedures derived from the gen-eral norms. Their agreement and consistency are slightly less than ap-pears among politicians. Politically oriented citizens agree with con-siderable inconsistency, that established institutions are responsive to citizens with sufficient perseverance to make themselves heard, but not that they are fully democratic nor that they attract any widespread support which outweighs other divisions.

3. The politically uninterested citizens agree highly on the more abstract norms of democratic behavior and agree somewhat less than

---

[3] R. A. Dahl, *Who Governs?* (New Haven, Conn.: Yale University Press, 1961), pp. 321–24.

politically oriented citizens on specific applications of these norms. They do not see established institutions as democratic in any way whatsoever; consequently they fail to recognize the existence of any widespread democratic support or to see that democratic agreements outweight disagreements.

4. On non-procedural substantive issues any distribution of preferential agreement or disagreement among the politicians may be accompanied by any distribution of agreement or disagreement among the general population. Agreement-disagreement is not, however, a dichotomy, but a continuum: certainly the existence of mutually-exclusive groups with opposing preferences must be distinguished from a situation where the different groups have compatible, though different, preferences.

5. Zero-sum disagreements of the former type are normally in a small minority among politicians and electors. Other issue preferences may be the subjects of agreement or negotiable disagreement. On factual judgments of issue characteristics the politicians are distinguished from electors by their widespread agreements.

6. The system works in normal times because politicians are strongly attached to both specific and abstract democratic ideas, see established institutions and procedures as putting these ideals into practice, and have few political goals which are completely blocked under present procedures (of the sort which would arise from extensive zero-sum disagreements). Politicians have most weight in the discussion and resolution of issues because of their high interest and activity in politics, and because of their extensive factual agreements and political understandings. Their use of democratic procedures is unchallenged because the most politically effective citizens support these procedures; even the more apathetic are extensively, although inconsistently, attached to the specific operating rules. In case of a challenge to democratic norms the politicians can thus trigger a strong counter-response on the part of the whole population.

RELATIONSHIP OF OTHER INFLUENCES
UPON DEMOCRATIC STABILITY TO
THE ABOVE PATTERNS OF AGREEMENT

Various attempts have been made, either speculative or empirical, to link the operation of certain factors to the maintenance of democratic stability. Some of these factors were discussed in Chapter 1, and others have been cited at various points in the analysis. Their relationships to the agreements uncovered by the present survey are considerd separately below.

1. Existence of Issues upon Which Attention and Feeling Are Focused to the Exclusion of Other Issues

Schattschneider suggests that some questions so focus attention and interest as to prevent other potential cleavages from having any political effects. The survey provides evidence on this point in producing data that show how far the attention and feeling of respondents is concentrated on some of the nine political issues examined and how far other issues are ignored.

The patterns that seem to emerge among electors differ from those found among politicians. Among the former there is a definite tendency to exclude one or two issues from their attention: the Transport Bill is a prime example of such an exclusion. There is a marked tendency to feel strongly about a limited range of issues. Out of the nine issues considered, only four arouse widespread feeling: the housing problem, Immigration Bill, the Wage Pause and education shortages. So far as electors go, therefore, a concentration of attention and particularly of feeling upon some issues does seem to exist, and Schattschneider's contention that some potentially divisive questions are pushed aside by others is upheld by this British data. Among politicians, however, variations in attention and intensity of feeling from one issue to another exist only to a very limited extent.

While this absence of variation probably results from the questions' being too crude to tap finer variations of feeling, it is probably in fact true that politicians do feel strongly about most political matters. In such an apparently dull and technical matter as the Transport Bill they are, for example, much better able to discern a clash over two opposing conceptions of the whole role of transport—social service or money-spinner—and behind that a clash of utterly different political *Weltanschauungen*. This ability to generalize politically would thus seem to encourage strong feeling on most political topics that one hears about, and politicians hear about most issues. Schattschneider's explanation of how one conflict pushes out others does not seem to apply to British politicians therefore—at least in normal times. Other factors must be invoked to explain their crucial adherence to democratic procedures.

2. Cross-Cutting Conflicts

The idea that cross-cutting conflicts of equal intensity could play a powerful part in promoting mutual tolerance was discussed at the very outset of this study. The Greater London survey provides evidence that supports this idea. One major finding was that politicians' agreements and disagreements on current policy matters (whether in regard to preferences or appraisals) did not coincide with party divisions. The major line of opinion cleavage seemed to run through one of the party groups of politicians, rather than between the two groups. Not only did this non-party cleavage hold in relation to current policy matters, it also applied to a general point of view (that of equality of opportunity) that seems to lie behind many current policy disputes, and that represents the only procedural principle on which some tendency to division appeared among the politicians.

Now it is indubitable that divergent party loyalties constitute a major line of division among British politicians. The importance of the finding that divisions of opinion divide one of the party groups internally is, therefore, that it reveals the existence of a cross-cutting cleavage between politicians' party loyalties and opinions.[4] It may be assumed that these politicians are very strongly committed to their parties, and the survey shows that they entertain strong feelings about their position on issues. This additional piece of evidence, therefore, seems to support the possibility that these cross-cutting conflicts are of equal intensity. A linkage between these cross-cutting conflicts (at least at the politicians' level) and democratic stability does, consequently, seem to exist so far as the present evidence can indicate.

3. Limited Coalition-Building

A temporary and limited consensus of pragmatic politicians arrived at only in order to get immediate policies pushed through was suggested by Friedrich as being the only type of agreement that could exist in a democracy, agreement on more fundamental topics being considered impossible.[5] The survey evidence has shown this last assertion to be wrong, for widespread agreement upon fundamental political procedures does exist among both politicians and population. It has, however, been suggested at various points that this fundamental procedural consensus needs to be supplemented (at least at certain times) by broad substantive agreements among the politicians over policy matters. Moreover the common situation in which the political preferences of the sizable groups of politicians are mutually compatible seems one that offers great encouragement to attempts at compromise and limited coalition-building on each issue. Such activities would also seem

---

[4] This parallels the situation that seems to prevail among British electors where issue opinions coincide only to a limited extent with party loyalties.

[5] C. J. Friedrich, *The New Image of the Common Man* (Boston: Beacon Press, 1950), Chap. 5.

to be facilitated by the extensive understandings on all aspects of politics, which exist among politicians.

4. Habits of Democratic Behavior

That democratic behavior becomes an unconscious habit is another of the factors that Friedrich advances as being responsible for democratic stability.[6] It was pointed out in Chapter 1 that people are usually aware of such widespread behavior patterns and infer agreements from them. Thus there may very well be an interplay between some of the agreements studied in this analysis and habits of behavior. Only it is not clear which is cause and which effect. For example, people may infer from their own and other peoples' habitual behavior that their agreements are more important than their disagreements. This consensus then becomes an additional factor capable of affecting their future behavior during a crisis in which normal behavior patterns are upset.

5. Macropolitical Socioeconomic Factors

In influential studies of a large number of countries in different parts of the world, S. M. Lipset and P. Cutright linked democratic stability to relative prosperity and to the relative absence of violent disparities between rich and poor.[7] A connection between such broad socioeconomic factors and democratic stability does, according to their studies, appear to exist. The present study also infers a connection between the stability of the British political system and the body of agreements and non-zero-sum disagreements existing among its British samples. If both lines of reasoning are correct, there should be a connection between such macropolitical factors and the agreements described above, a connection which ought to be discussed.

The most likely connection seems to be that summarized in Figure 12.1. Here the absence of zero-sum disagreements on preferences and the presence of agreements of various kinds are regarded as factors which are produced by general economic prosperity and by the absence of violent disparities, and which, in turn, act to bring about democratic stability. Obviously an atmosphere of general prosperity and

---

[6] *Ibid.*

[7] S. M. Lipset, *Political Man* (Garden City, N.Y.: Doubleday, 1960), Chap. 2, and P. Cutright, "National Political Development: Economic and Social Correlates," in N. W. Polsby, R. A. Dentler, and P. A. Smith, eds., *Politics and Social Life* (Boston: Houghton Mifflin, 1963), pp. 569–82 *passim*.

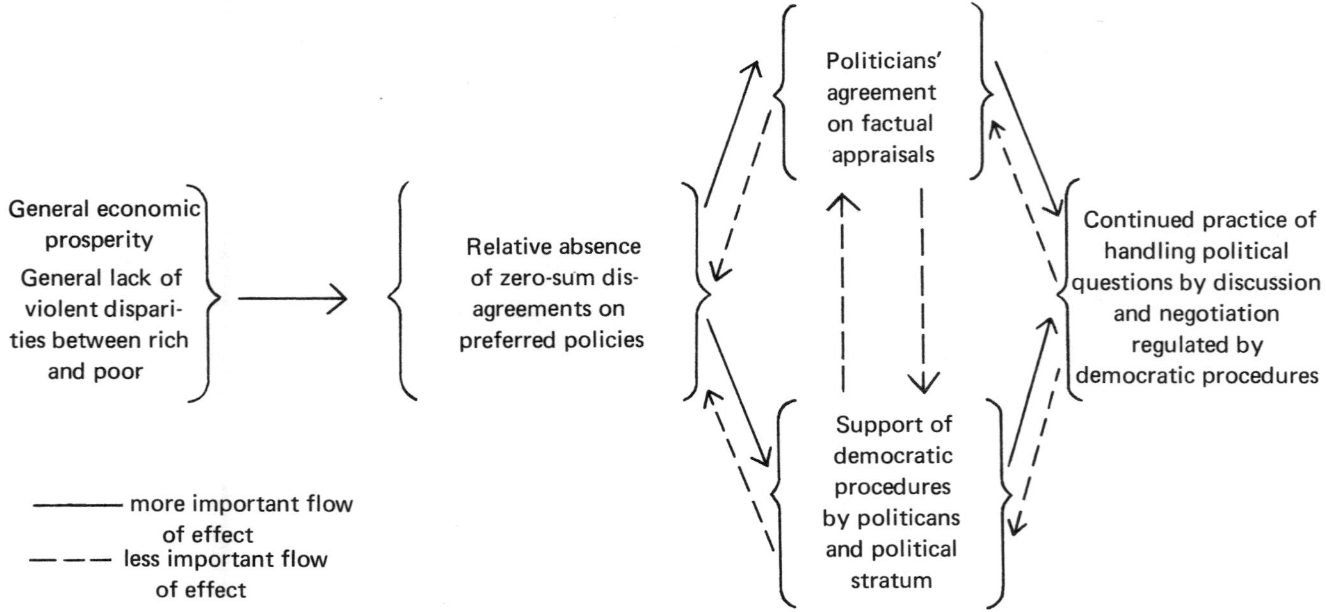

Figure 12.1. Hypothesized Connection Among Socioeconomic Factors, Non-Zero-Sum Preferential Disagreements, Consensus and Democratic Stability

economic expansion is highly conducive to the avoidance of zero-sum disagreement. Economic and social welfare questions are the issues on which policy positions are most closely related to party support among British electors;[8] consequently these are the issues most likely to generate cumulative instead of cross-cutting conflicts, and cumulative conflicts seem more likely to be zero-sum than cross-cutting conflicts.

They are also, as the present survey evidence shows, the issues most likely to produce strong feelings among electors (three out of the four issues on which electors had the strongest feelings were socioeconomic in character).[9] Should electors be bitterly divided on these issues, their opposing pressures would seem likely to pull the politicians sooner or later into similar opposing groups, perhaps through replacement of the old politicians by new men, as the Liberals were replaced by Labour. And electoral division is most likely to be produced by strikes and lock-outs, poverty and unemployment—all the accompaniments of economic depression. Expansion, on the other hand, produces a larger slice of the cake for everyone.[10]

These macropolitical factors, therefore, seem to minimize the head-on clashes of preferences among participants in the political system. Starting from what they feel to be a tolerable situation, people are less inclined to harbor preferences that are diametrically opposed to what their rivals want. This relative absence of zero-sum disagreement on preferences is regarded as a requisite condition for the existence of, first, the agreements among politicians on factual appraisals of all aspects of politics that were uncovered by the survey and, second, the general support given by both politicians and electors to democratic

---

[8] J. Blondel, *Voters, Parties, and Leaders* (Harmondsworth, England: Penguin, 1963), p. 77.

[9] Table 3.1.

[10] An objection may be made to our regarding "objective" economic factors as prime movers of agreement in this hypothetical scheme. For other factors such as religious or, indeed, political differences (Communists or Fascists opposing democrats) could conceivably operate to bring about zero-sum disagreement. As it stands the scheme seems to regard economic factors as solely capable of producing such situations. This is not, in fact, an implication meant to be drawn. Political, religious or other factors might in certain circumstances take the place of the economic factors shown there. Only economic factors are shown because only in the case of such factors has a connection with democratic stability been established through a systematic and comprehensive review of quantitative evidence such as the one undertaken by Lipset. It might also be said that "objective" economic factors could affect politics only through people's perceptions of their effects upon their own and the general well-being. (See A. Campbell, P. Converse, W. Miller, and D. Stokes, *The American Voter* [New York: Wiley, 1960], pp. 393–400.) While this is true, it is unlikely that people would for long remain unaware of economic depression or disparities. In the interest of simplification and clarity, therefore, this fine point can be omitted from the figure.

courses of action in most situations. Of course we suspect that these agreements also help to sustain one another in ways mentioned in previous parts of the discussion and that they help to prevent zero-sum disagreements from arising. But the main direction of effect is conceived as stemming from the absence of preferential zero-sum disagreement, rather than the other way around. For as has been emphasized throughout, preferences seem to be the opinions most directly related to action. It is doubtful that factual agreement would exist in the presence of bitter preferential disagreement, for it is a short step from condemning an opponent's policies as self-interested and opportunist to calling him a cheat and a liar.

Disputes over substantive policies also seem likely to involve procedures if they are bitterly and lengthily fought. Obviously a strong commitment to democratic procedures themselves can dampen substantive disputes. But the strain that the latter can place upon procedures seems the weightier factor to take into consideration.

The connection between politicians' agreements on factual appraisals, general support of democratic procedures, and democratic stability has been discussed at length throughout this study and in the previous sections of this chapter. It is worthwhile noting, however, that the very success that politicians have in employing democratic procedures may itself generate support and agreements on factual appraisals —for example, the judgment that everyone agrees about such procedures. This possibly less important but significant reverse flow of effect is also detailed in the figure.

SUGGESTIONS FOR FUTURE RESEARCH

Many of the statements and assumptions on the basis of which predictions were made in the initial discussion of Chapter 2 have themselves not been directly tested by the survey evidence that has been presented. Had the predictions not correctly anticipated some of the patterns into which the data fell, however, the whole structure of interrelated arguments put forward in Chapter 2 would have been rejected, whether particular assumptions contained in that structure were valid or not. The total theory behind the discussion has, therefore, been subjected to one series of checks by this study. The untested assumptions that it contains do, on the other hand, provide means of checking the validity of its arguments in the additional ways suggested below.

1. At previous points the opportunity has been taken of stressing the unproven nature of certain crucial assumptions used in most of the arguments of the study. These assumptions are:

a. That the initial existence of extensive political agreements among members of a group improves the chances of successful discussion, negotiation and compromise.

b. That extensive political agreements among members of a group make it easier for the group to act politically as a united body.

c. That the presence of roughly equal and mutually exclusive groups with opposing preferences among members of a body increases the chance that a zero-sum political situation will arise in which one group of participants will achieve their preferences only if another group is totally defeated. Conversely, it has been assumed that the absence of these roughly equal and mutually exclusive groups with opposing preferences will promote the possibility of political compromise.

d. That a prevalence of such zero-sum situations on most matters of substantive policy under discussion by members of the group will result in the prevalence of disagreement on most other political topics among members of the group. Conversely, it is assumed that the relative absence of zero-sum situations will, other things being equal, promote agreements on most other political topics among group members.

The points at which these assumptions have been employed in the preceding discussion will be obvious. Any test applied to them would severely probe the validity not only of the consensual theory of democratic stability advanced in the text, but of all such consensual theories. For all such theories rest on the assumption that agreement is ultimately related to the possibility of combined democratic action.

Further refinements would, of course, have to be introduced before the statements were ready for testing. For example a distinction would have to be drawn between the initial existence of agreement on factual appraisals and agreement on preferences, since the two might well prove to have different relationships to successful discussion and combined action.

The best way of checking these assumptions against actual political reactions is not through survey methods, but rather through intensive experiments with selected groups under laboratory conditions. The three basic types of groups would be politicians or very high-level activists, moderate activitists shading into electors more oriented to politics (on various measures) than the average, and the average electors without a high involvement in politics. Initial assessments of the state of opinion among different groups of these types could be followed by an assessment of their success in reaching accepted solutions to set problems under democratic conditions. Each of the members of such groups could be separately questioned about his reactions in past political crises and about the course of action he would take in hypothetical crises, in order to see whether his reactions in these two situations were the same or widely different. With other groups such hypothetical questions could be put to the group as a whole in order to see whether the group would divide or unite around pro-democratic courses of action.

From a wide selection of persons willing to participate groups could, furthermore, be made up of persons who would fall into roughly equal and mutually exclusive groups with opposing preferences; after subjecting the groups to varying periods of political discussion the extent of agreement among such groups could be assessed. Other groups could be formed whose preferences on substantive policy matters fell predominantly into the various other states outlined in Table 7.3, and these could be subjected to similar stimuli, with the object of seeing whether they were any more prone to form political and democratic agreements. In the same way the different tendency of various groups to arrive at zero-sum situations or compromises after discussion could be assessed.

2. These studies with experimental groups could be supplemented by further surveys. The most obvious need is for a survey of politicians' and electors' opinions and behavior during some sort of upset in the normal political routine of a stable democracy. This upset need not be a crisis, although an investigation of crisis reactions would probably be most valuable. Such questions as whether politicians are really more concerned about democratic procedures in times of crisis, and as whether they are consciously uniting with other politicians in order to uphold them could be investigated. If any electoral reactions appear at such a time, the direction of effect could be investigated, and it could be discovered whether these reactions were spontaneous or prompted by the politicians in the first place. If surveys of this type could be undertaken during different political upsets, the effect of politicians' agreement upon substantive policy questions outstanding at the time could be estimated. Procedural agreement might exist quite independently of any other type of agreement, or it might not. Only experimental studies and repeated surveys will provide the answers.

3. Further surveys of the present type during normal political periods are required to establish whether the patterns disclosed in this study are enduring or transient. For example, the question of the extent to which an internal party dissensus is linked to a decline in its political fortunes could be profitably studied. Questions that were not asked in the present survey because their relevance was not foreseen

could be put to respondents; *e.g.*, politicians could be directly asked to what extent they regard debate as effective, or to what extent they stick to it for other reasons. Surveys repeated in different time periods could also show whether substantive and procedural agreements had different effects at different times. Such surveys could also be designed to investigate agreement among the various levels of the political stratum more intensively than was permitted here.

4. The question of how far background homogeneity (such as similarities in class or educational background) stimulates various types of agreement and the relative absence of head-on clashes of preference between sizable groups is of considerable relevance to the consideration of consensus, for it offers the most plausible explanation of how some groups in the population might be united by more substantial bodies of agreement than others. Again the best way to investigate the topic more closely seems to be through experiments with groups of various types under laboratory conditions. An analysis of this kind would also enable the investigator to determine which background characteristics were linked most closely to which types of agreement. Groups that were homogeneous on one or on a selection of characteristics but heterogeneous on others could have their initial agreements compared with those of groups distinguished by homogeneity on other background characteristics. Agreements could also be compared after the groups had taken part in a discussion of various political topics.

Should these suggested lines of investigation be pursued, the link between democratic stability and agreement among various groups in a democratic population would be more vigorously probed than in the present study. The latter has, however, shown that the distributions of opinion in one stable democracy do not disprove this link, and it may also have contributed to the discussion of the influence of consensus by pointing to the variety of ways in which different types of agreement and disagreement might influence political reactions.

APPENDIX A | THE SURVEY AND ITS DESIGN

THEORETICAL BACKGROUND TO THE SURVEY

The design cannot be fully understood unless it is realized that the survey was expressly undertaken to uphold or disconfirm the series of detailed hypotheses developed from the generalized theories of Dahl and Key described in Chapter 2. The fact that the project is a part of a cumulative body of research confers upon it considerable methodological advantages. For one thing the questionnaire could be designed to focus upon the topics raised by the hypotheses in a narrower and more intense way than would have been possible had it tried to cover more diffuse interests. For the purpose of analysis considerably more statistical rigor could be obtained by predicting the direction as well as the existence of a difference between groups of respondents.

SURVEY DESIGN
A. General Nature

The general nature of the survey design was dictated by the considerations discussed in the first chapter. It seemed obvious that any test of the Dahl-Key theory must involve comparisons between two groups, *i.e.*, the electorate (who would include both the political stratum and others) and the professional politicians. It also seemed necessary for politicians and electors to be drawn from roughly the same geographical area so that they would have been exposed to much the same political problems and stimuli. Thus differences in their responses would seem more likely to proceed from differences in their political standing than from extraneous causes of any kind.

For theoretical reasons, national politicians—*i.e.*, politicians who aspired to or occupied some national office—were preferred to local politicians. It was felt that the major gap in the evidence cited by Dahl and Key in support of their theory lay in the lack of comparable data on the opinions of national politicians and of the general population. Key had data on the American population as a whole; Dahl, on the functioning of a local political system. But the most direct way of testing the theory seemed to be to obtain responses from national politicians and from electors to the same questions about agreements and issues.

B. Comparability of Responses

So strong indeed did the importance of comparability between politicians and electors seem that it dominated the methods of data collection employed in this survey. The questionnaires used with politicians and electors were identical in the wording and order of the questions and in every other respect. This decision was made even at the risk of injuring rapport with the politicians, although, in fact, it seemed to do so in only a few cases. Moreover all the respondents in this survey, politicians and electors alike, were interviewed by the investigator. There may well be some interviewer bias in the responses, but it is held constant throughout, and to the extent that the main interest lies in comparisons between the groups, its influence is eliminated. Of course the number of respondents who could be interviewed by one person were considerably smaller than the number whom a team might have covered. Here again relative advantages were weighed, and the theoretical considerations previously mentioned tipped the balance in favor of comparability. For the same reason the samples were interviewed concurrently—between 16th March and 12th July 1962—so that the effects of external political events would be the same for both sets of respondents.[1] Fortunately this period was one of relative political calm during which the relative importance of the issues to which attention was devoted in the questionnaire remained the same.

The stress on comparability continued after the survey had been conducted into the stage of ordering and coding the data. All answers from both samples were coded by the investigator. A 15 percent sample of questionnaires was then coded independently by another person using the same coding instructions. A comparison of the results obtained from these separate operations showed that the same coding decisions were reached for 75 percent of the sample on all questions, and for over 80 percent on most questions.

---

[1] For an assessment of these effects, see Appendix C.

C. Choice of Populations

The greatest concentration of national politicians is found in Greater London (as defined in the 1951 Census of Great Britain—*i.e.*, the former counties of London and Middlesex, with parts of Essex, Kent, Surrey, and Hertfordshire).[2] It was decided, therefore, to make a random selection of candidates and back bench M.P.s from the Greater London area. Frontbench M.P.s were excluded because it was felt that their commitments would make them almost impossible to interview. Candidates were included because it was anticipated that in such a geographically compact area they would mingle frequently with M.P.s through party organizations and local representative bodies (the county and borough councils and their committees) and thus form part of the group of active politicians. Subsequent analysis of their responses proved this assumption correct. Only four differences between M.P.s and candidates were discovered over the whole range of topics discussed in the study. The sheer size of the area made it impossible to draw a sample of electors from the total Greater London electorate. The alternative was to interview in a sub-area or areas. Because of the constitution of the electoral register from which the sample of electors must be drawn, such sub-areas have to be Parliamentary constituencies, whose boundaries may or may not coincide with those of Greater London boroughs. The fact that interviews were conducted by one interviewer meant that the sample of electors had to be drawn from a single sub-area.

It was not felt that a comparison of electors from a sub-area of Greater London with a sample of politicians from the whole area limited the general nature of the conclusions that could be drawn from the data, for the following reasons:

1. The purpose of the survey was to test previously formulated hypotheses, not to provide data for an exploratory analysis. Comparisons of these two samples are sufficient to disprove general statements about differences between leaders and electors, given the points made below.

2. The political boundaries of the Greater London area are even less than normally relevant to the social and economic life of this highly integrated region. To say that a person lives in a given area is not to say that most, or even many, of his contacts are with persons who live in that area. Evidence from another part of Greater London confirms

---

[2] L. J. Sharpe, "The Politics of Local Government in Greater London," *Public Administration Review* (Summer 1960), pp. 157–72.

this assertion: in Clapham only 20 percent of a sample of the population worked within the bounds of the area.[3]

3. However, if the fact of living in a sub-area exerted any influence at all, it must be to make the electors more homogeneous in their opinions and background than if they had been drawn from the whole of Greater London. But this effect works against both sets of hypotheses— those which predict that politicians will agree more than electors and those which predict that certain groups of electors will diverge from others in their responses. Any bias is therefore in a conservative direction.

4. It would, however, be more satisfactory to eliminate all such effects together. For the reasons given above—the small geographical size of Greater London and the high degree of interaction among all its inhabitants—the main effect one would anticipate from concentrating in a single area would be the predominance of one social class in the sample. Along with class distribution would go, among other things, certain distribution of party affiliation[4] and type and length of education of the respondents.[5] Because of these considerations, the constituency from which the sample of electors was drawn was not selected at random, but was chosen for its representativeness of Greater London as a whole in terms of social class. This selection could be carried out according to two criteria: census classifications and the J-index. The latter was the percentage of electors who, in effect, had the property qualifications that made them liable for jury service.[6] It was thus a useful guide to the proportions of socioeconomic groups in an area. The constituency (by chance also a borough) that came closest to the Greater London average on social class and very close on the J-index was that made up of Brentford and Chiswick.

The social and political characteristics of this area (where the electorate survey was conducted) are summarized through census and sample figures in Tables A.2, A.3 and A.4. One is more likely to meet respondents of the upper middle class in Chiswick, and respondents of the unskilled working class in Brentford. But most people in both belong to the lower middle class and upper working class. In local politics the Conservatives have been generally dominant; but the Labour Party came to power for a short period after the Second World War

[3] L. J. Sharpe, *A Metropolis Votes* (London: London School of Economics and Political Science, 1962), p. 63.

[4] J. Blondel, *Voters, Parties and Leaders* (Harmondsworth, England: Penguin, 1963), p. 57.

[5] *Ibid.*, p. 43.

[6] P. G. Gray, T. Coplett, and Pamela Jones, *The Proportion of Jurors as an Index of the Economic Status of a District* (London: Central Office of Information, 1951).

Table A.1: Class Composition of Brentford and Chiswick

	1951 Census Classification			
	Class I & II	Class III	Class IV & V	J-Index
Greater London	22.5	54.7	22.8	6.64
Brentford and Chiswick	21.8	54.7	23.5	6.85

NOTE: The results of the 1961 Census were not at the time available as a basis for decision. See Table A. 3 for figures on occupations.

Table A.2: Economic Standing of the Separate Wards in Brentford and Chiswick

WARDS	J-INDEX
Chiswick:	
Bedford Park	12.29
Turnham Green	8.64
Grove Park	7.47
Gunnersbury	7.05
Old Chiswick	5.28
Chiswick Park	4.36
Brentford:	
West	7.30
East	7.16
Central	1.23

Table A.3: Social Composition of the Electorate in Brentford and Chiswick

	SAMPLE 1962 (N = 147) (percent)	CENSUS 1961 (percent)
Sex		
Male	50	46
Female	50	54
Age		
21–29	13	19
30–39	25	16
40–59	44	40
Over 60	18	25
Occupation:		
Professional, admin., small		Not Comparable
business, clerical	49	because of
Skilled manual	30	Classification
Unskilled manual	22	
Marital Status		
Married	63	67
Not Married	37	33

and from 1958 to 1960. In the 1945 landslide the Parliamentary constituency was captured by Labour, but apart from that election it had (up to the period of interviewing) been consistently Conservative.

SAMPLING PROCEDURE
A. Electors

A systematic sample of electors was drawn by choosing a point on the first page of the electoral register at random and taking every 196th name after that. The total came to 203 names. Because the register had been compiled the previous October, it was to be expected that some of these 203 persons would have moved, become ill or died. However, most losses to the sample, as is usually the case with British surveys, occurred from direct refusals or from failure to contact potential respondents.

Table A.4: Voting in Brentford and Chiswick in 1959

	SAMPLE	RESULTS
Nonvoters	20	18
Voters	80	82
As percent of voters:		
Conservative	50	54.5
Labour	50	45.5

Seventy-two percent of the original sample of 203 were successfully interviewed—a result that compares with the 71.8 percent obtained by a survey conducted in London in April 1961.[7] The characteristics of those who were not successfully interviewed were the same as those noted in other surveys:[8] there were more women among them than men, more old persons than young, and more persons of lower than of higher social status.

B. The Sample of Politicians

In order to obtain the sample of M.P.s and candidates from Greater London, the entire population was numbered from 1 to 182. The first eighty numbers falling between 1 and 182 that were encountered in a table of random numbers then constituted the sample of politicians.

---

[7] Sharpe, *A Metropolis Votes, op. cit.,* p. 57.

[8] See, for example, J. Trenaman and D. McQuail, *Television and the Political Image* (London: Methuen, 1961), Appendix C.

Table A.5: Interviewing Losses in Electorate Sample

Successfully interviewed	147
Dead, ill, moved	20
Refused	27
Could not be contacted	9
	203

Fifty-nine of these politicians—74 percent, that is—were contacted and interviewed. Those candidates and M.P.s who refused an interview usually gave lack of time as their reason. Refusals numbered twelve candidates and nine M.P.s, fourteen of whom were Labour adherents and seven of whom were Conservatives. A few of the respondents successfully contacted failed to complete their interviews; even in those cases, however, the bulk of the questions were answered.

Table A.6: Characteristics of Politicians

	SAMPLE (N = 59) (percent)	POPULATION (N = 182) (percent)
Backbench M.P.s	39	43
Candidates	61	57
Conservative	58	48
Labour	42	52

RELIABILITY OF THE SAMPLE

The representativeness of the samples can be checked against certain data (sex, age, and the like) whose distribution is known for the total population. Information about the population of Brentford and Chiswick is contained in Tables A.3 and A.4 above. The sample percentages given beside those for the population fall within the limits of normal sampling errors. For politicians the most readily available statistics are the proportion of M.P.s to candidates, and of Conservatives to Labour. Percentages are given in Table A.6. These again do not diverge significantly from the figures for the population.

A FURTHER DISCUSSION
OF AGREEMENT
IN MULTIPLE-CHOICE SITUATIONS

OTHER DEFINITIONS OF "AGREEMENT"
IN CASES OF MULTIPLE RESPONSE

Other definitions of "agreement" than the one outlined in Chapter 3 could be adopted for cases of multiple responses. This is still true even when the dimension of intensity is ignored. Two other definitions of "agreement" in multiple-choice situations which refer simply to the clustering of respondents in terms of numbers are outlined below:

A. On the assumption already adopted in Chapter Three that the definition of agreement should bear upon the likelihood of members of a group adopting certain preferences or appraisals as the joint preferences or appraisals of the group (hence making it more probable that they will act in unity) it is still possible to come to an alternative definition of "agreement" to that chosen in that chapter. For it can be argued that the important influence bearing upon the readier acceptance of preferences or appraisals as common to a whole group is not whether higher proportions in one group than in another mention the most popular alternative. Instead the important question is whether a higher proportion in one group than in another hold a whole range of alternatives—say, three or four—in common. Any such cluster of alternatives held by a solid and cohesive bloc seems to be much more likely to be adopted as common policies or "facts" than others. A hypothetical comparison between politicians and electors in terms of the above definition is shown in Figure B.1.

We would on this definition of agreement have to say that no greater agreement existed among politicians than among electors since the proportions holding three alternatives in common were the same. This is a definition of "agreement" or "consensus" that is quite as plau-

Figure B.1. Hypothetical Distribution of Replies of Politicians and Electors in a Multiple-Response Situation

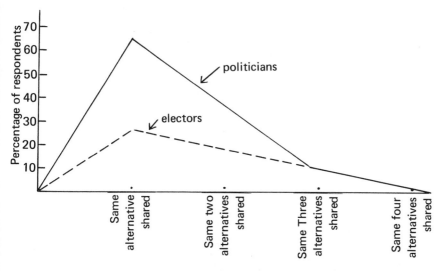

sible in terms of its effects on the possibility of combined action by a group as is the definition adopted in the text. Of course the two definitions are not entirely independent of each other, especially as agreement in a group becomes higher. For insofar as higher proportions of one group than of another do mention the most popular alternatives, there is a greater likelihood that higher proportions will mention the same three alternatives. For example, if fifty-six out of fifty-nine politicians mention one alternative, fifty-four mention another alternative and fifty a third alternative, one can at least be sure that forty-two politicians mentioned the same three alternatives. To this extent the definition of "agreement" given just above varies with the textual definition.

B. It could also be suggested that "agreement" refers to the tendency of the replies to share a more limited range of alternatives, while "disagreement," in contrast, implies a more or less random scatter of replies over all alternatives. It could be argued that the group that achieved a greater overlapping of replies in this sense would be better able to go on to achieve a greater concentration of preference or attention on the same alternatives and would thus be better fitted for unified group action than the group whose replies spread out over the whole spectrum of possibilities without including a common narrower range of alternatives. The difficulty with this definition is that a group is still regarded as quite highly agreed if 50 percent of its members happened to mention one alternative while the other 50 percent mentioned another without mentioning any of the alternatives put forward by the first group of members. Such a case is, of course, expressly guarded against in the procedure outlined in Chapter 3. Yet it is quite a plausible definition, especially where the alternatives are not necessarily incompatible with each other. A greater concentration of replies has been achieved by one group, and it may be that this would give them a better chance of adopting the same preferences or appraisals as joint premises for united group action.

Because of the necessity for clear exposition it is impossible to apply these different definitions to the data simultaneously. It is likely, however, that they would both tend to support similar conclusions about the relative agreement of politicians and electors. A formal treatment of the conception of agreement just described and an empirical test of the extent to which it varies with the textual definition is accordingly offered below.

ALTERNATIVE PROCEDURE FOR
ESTIMATING COMPARATIVE AGREEMENT
IN CASES OF MULTIPLE RESPONSES
Definition

A group is regarded as exhibiting more consensus than another group in relation to a given topic if a higher proportion of the members of the former mention at least one out of a limited range of factual appraisals or preferences.

This definition thus describes "consensus" as the situation in which a smaller number of alternatives is shared by members of a group, relative to the number shared by the other group in the comparison. The opposite situation—dissensus—would be one in which preferences or appraisals spread evenly over all alternatives. The question is, therefore, whether politicians' preferences and factual appraisals always include one or two that are widely shared among them and whether electors tend to ignore each other's choices. A procedure for estimating comparative agreement in this sense was suggested to the author by Professor D. E. Stokes. The replies to the question dealing with topics of consensus in Britain are used to illustrate the procedure.

This question, like other multiple-response questions, can be regarded as generating two cumulative distributions—one for politicians and one for electors. The first possible topic is mentioned by a certain proportion of the (politicians' or electors') sample; the first *or* the second is mentioned by a somewhat larger proportion; the first *or* second *or* third is mentioned by a rather larger proportion, and so forth. There is no reason why the topics cannot be ordered (the order *may* differ for politicians and electors) in such a way that the one mentioned by the largest proportion is first, the one mentioned by the largest proportion of *additional* respondents (*i.e.*, those who have not mentioned the first topic) is second, and so on. For practical reasons the distributions cover only the first three topics.

The hypothesis that politicians are more agreed than electors can now be expressed operationally in terms of a lag between the cumulative distributions for politicians and for electors. The first three categories shown in Figure B.2 should (if the hypothesis is correct) contain a higher number of politicians than electors.

Figure B.2. Cumulative Distribution Showing Extent of Relative Agreement of Politicians and Electors on Perceived Topics of Consensus in Britain

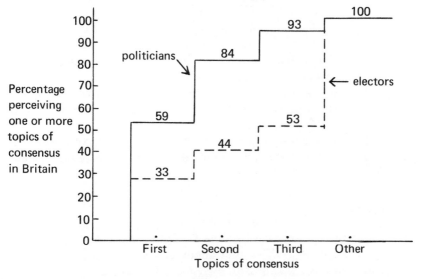

Because of the greater agreement among politicians (in this case), their cumulative distribution rises more quickly than that for electors. More members of the more agreed sample mention the most popular topic, and more among those who do not mention the more popular topic mention the next topic. The proportion of politicians who mention the first *or* second *or* third topic is thus 93 percent compared to the 53 percent of electors who mention the same range of topics. In this case the replies of the politicians almost always contain one or two topics in common, as compared to the much more even spread of electors' replies over all topics. Had there been little difference in the agreement of the samples in this sense, the two distributions would have more closely approached each other. The goodness of fit between the two distributions as a whole can be tested by means of the chi-square test of goodness of fit.

The results of the application of this test to the overall comparisons between politicians and electors in cases of multiple responses which are carried out in the text are reported below. In each case it is noted whether the estimation of comparative agreement that this procedure yields corresponds to that reached in the text through the alternative procedure adopted there.

OVERALL COMPARISONS OF "AGREEMENT" AMONG POLITICIANS AND ELECTORS

NOTE: B   denotes result of procedure described in Appendix B.
       T   denotes result of procedure described in text.
      B+ signifies that politicians are more agreed than electors according to the present procedure and
      B− signifies that they are not more agreed according to that procedure.
      T+ signifies that politicians are more agreed according to the textual procedure and
      T− that they are not.

The value of chi-square required to uphold the hypothesis at the .05 level (similar to that applied in the text) at two degrees of freedom is 5.991.

Chapter Four

Topics of Consensus in Britain—Tables 4.1 and 4.2
    Chi-square 27.690 significant at .05 level B+ T+
Topics of Dissensus in Britain—Tables 4.1 and 4.2
    Chi-square 3.734 not significant at .05 level B− T+

Chapter Five

Likes Labour Party—Table 5.2
    Chi-square 10.809 significant at .05 level B+ T−
Dislikes Labour Party—Table 5.2
    Chi-square 12.347 significant at .05 level B+ T+
Likes Conservative Party—Table 5.2
    Chi-square 1.430 not significant at .05 level B− T+
Dislikes Conservative Party—Table 5.2
    Chi-square 9.208 significant at .05 level B+ T+

Chapter Six

Wage Pause: Alternatives Open to Pursuit—Table 6.2
    Chi-square 16.806 significant at .05 level B+ T+
Transport Bill: Alternatives Open to Pursuit—Table 6.2
    Chi-square 24.798 significant at .05 level B+ T+
London Government: Alternatives Open to Pursuit—Table 6.2
    Chi-square 30.555 significant at .05 level B+ T+
Monopolies: Alternatives Open to Pursuit—Table 6.2
    Chi-square 41.913 significant at .05 level B+ T+
Immigration Bill: Alternatives Open to Pursuit—Table 6.2
    Chi-square 0.226 not significant at .05 level B— T—
Common Market: Alternatives Open to Pursuit—Table 6.2
    Chi-square 18.488 significant at .05 level B+ T+
Berlin Negotiations: Alternatives Open to Pursuit—Table 6.2
    Chi-square 14.138 significant at .05 level B+ T+
Housing Problem: Alternatives Open to Pursuit—Table 6.2
    Chi-square 10.485 significant at .05 level B+ T+
Education Shortages: Alternatives Open to Pursuit—Table 6.2
    Chi-square 2.536 not significant at .05 level B— T—
Wage Pause: Effects—Table 6.6
    Chi-square 3.205 not significant at .05 level B— T+
Transport Bill: Effects—Table 6.6
    Chi-square 26.603 significant at .05 level B+ T—
London Government: Effects—Table 6.6
    Chi-square 7.431 significant at .05 level B+ T+
Monopolies: Effects—Table 6.6
    Chi-square 49.067 significant at .05 level B+ T+
Immigration Bill: Effects—Table 6.6
    Chi-square 1.706 not significant at .05 level B— T+
Common Market: Effects—Table 6.6
    Chi-square 2.641 not significant at .05 level B— T+
Berlin Negotiations: Effects—Table 6.6
    Chi-square 22.666 significant at .05 level B+ T+
Housing Problem: Effects—Table 6.6
    Chi-square 34.082 significant at .05 level B+ T—
Education Shortages: Effects—Table 6.6
    Chi-square 9.750 significant at .05 level B+ T—

Chapter Seven

Wage Pause: Preferences—Table 7.1
    Chi-square 1.577 not significant at .05 level B— T—

Transport Bill: Preferences—Table 7.1
　　Chi-square 0.507 not significant at .05 level B— T—
London Government: Preferences—Table 7.1
　　Chi-square 12.656 significant at .05 level B+ T—
Monopolies: Preferences—Table 7.1
　　Chi-square 2.099 not significant at .05 level B— T—
Immigration Bill: Preferences—Table 7.1
　　Chi-square 3.200 not significant at .05 level B— T—
Common Market: Preferences—Table 7.1
　　Chi-square 3.523 not significant at .05 level B— T—
Berlin Negotiations: Preferences—Table 7.1
　　Chi-square 5.304 not significant at .05 level B— T+
Housing Problem: Preferences—Table 7.1
　　Chi-square 2.819 not significant at .05 level B— T+
Education Shortage: Preferences—Table 7.1
　　Chi-square 1.581 not significant at .05 level B— T—

The cases in which the two procedures produce the same result outnumber those in which different results are reached: in twenty-one cases the same finding emerges; in 12, a different finding. And even though conclusions in some specific cases may be different, overall conclusions about the pattern of agreement that exists on each set of appraisals or preferences remain the same. Politicians tend to be more agreed than electors in their appraisals of the effects of issues and of the alternatives open to pursuit on issues; they tend to be somewhat more agreed in their appraisals of topics of consensus and controversy and in their likes and dislikes about the parties; and they tend not to be much more agreed than electors in their issue preferences. The confirmation of these findings by this second procedure serves to increase confidence in their validity.

A POSSIBLE OBJECTION TO ALL DEFINITIONS OF "AGREEMENT" PROPOSED HERE

It may be objected that higher proportions of politicians may mention the most popular topics—or may overlap in their replies—in the case of multiple-response questions for reasons that do not intuitively suggest agreement. A higher proportion of politicians than electors, for example, mention topics of consensus in Britain (see Figure 3.5). Is the greater clustering of politicians on certain topics not partly due to their greater ability and predisposition to talk at length about politics? In such a case they would tend to cluster not because they were more agreed, but because they talked more about the issues.

Such an objection rather misses its point, however, because agreement has been defined in terms of one group's clustering more than another. On distributions such as that given in Table 4.1 the greater loquacity of politicians may thus appear as one explanation for their greater agreement, but it cannot affect the fact that they are more agreed. Nor is this a definitional evasion of the real point. The tendency of politicians to talk at greater length enables them to explore points of understanding better and thus to establish agreements to a greater extent than electors. Certainly the politicians' greater eloquence—their ability to use longer words and more sophisticated language as distinct from their actually mentioning more topics and possibilities—might have constituted an artificial distinction between the samples: for electors might in essence have been saying substantially the same things but in less eloquent and expressive language.

However this possibility has been allowed for and, it is hoped, overcome in coding. The degree of talkativeness does, however, seem to constitute a genuine difference between the two samples and can be accepted as a possible substantive reason for the greater agreement that exists among politicians.

APPENDIX C

BACKGROUND AND SELECTION OF THE POLITICAL ISSUES

THE POLITICAL BACKGROUND

The period from February to July in 1962 during which all respondents were interviewed was one of the quietest in recent British political history.[1] This was extremely fortunate, for it meant that there was little chance that various predictions upon which the selection of issues was based would be falsified.

In early 1962 the Conservative government was only just beginning to seem insecure in its eleven-year tenure in office, but it was still fortified by the massive electoral victory of 1959. The Labour Party under the leadership of Gaitskell was just emerging from a period of acute internal strife over the retention of nationalization as a domestic policy and over the question of Britain's unilateral nuclear disarmament in foreign affairs; behind these conflicts lay the tensions fostered by electoral defeat and personality clashes among the leaders.

The internal struggles of the Labour Party and the agitation created by the Campaign for Nuclear Disarmament and its offshoots had been the most spectacular political events of 1960 and early 1961. Various initiatives of the government had, however, by late 1961 begun to appear at the center of controversy.

DESCRIPTION OF THE ISSUES

In response to a balance of payments crisis in the autumn of 1961, the government had attempted to restrict wage awards to government

---

[1] It was abruptly terminated by Macmillan's wholesale dismissals of cabinet ministers in the summer of 1962, seemingly in response to demands by the rank and file of Conservative candidates and M.P.s for "young blood" in the government. Some rumblings of the Conservative discontents that resulted in the government purges were discernible in the interviews with politicians, but not to any great extent.

employees to within the limits of two and one-half percent of the current wage and to induce private employers to follow their example. This "Wage Pause," as it was colloquially termed, was somewhat relaxed after April 1962, but attempts were still made to steer wage awards by the government's "guiding light."

The attempts to regulate wage negotiations were resented by the Trades Unions and attacked by the Labour Party, who demanded to know why salaries as well as wages had not been regulated. Special causes such as the nurses' agitation for increases in their low rate of remuneration attracted widespread newspaper support.

Perhaps in order to offset the negative action of the Wage Pause, the government pressed ahead with its negotiations to enter the Common Market. This initiative also provoked widespread, or at least vociferous, objections. Some Conservative M.P.s and others prominent in the councils of the party opposed entry into the European trade group because of the danger to Commonwealth links and to Britain's political independence. Influential sections of the Labour Party shared these fears and also saw a threat to working conditions and wage standards in unlimited immigration from the Continent. Gaitskell was widely thought to be hostile to the European idea. Officially, however, the Labour Party assumed a "wait and see" posture on the terms that might be obtained from the Common Market countries.

The Immigration Bill probably surpassed both the previously mentioned issues in generating intense political heat in a short period of time. This bill was a government measure designed to place restrictions upon the hitherto unlimited right of entry to Britain of Commonwealth immigrants (mainly West Indians, Indians and Pakistanis; the Southern Irish were completely excluded from its provisions). The first Commons debates on the bill were held before Christmas, 1961, and generated unusual bitterness among Parliamentarians. Gaitskell pledged that the bill, if it became law, would be withdrawn when Labour returned to power. The bill passed its formal readings during the interviewing period, but passions by that time had been spent and the readings hardly affected the temperature of the political climate at all.

Among issues which had arisen just before the interviewing was that of the reorganization of London government.[2] In a White Paper of 1961 the government proposed to abolish a large number of the existing local authorities in Greater London (including the London and Middlesex County Councils) and to replace them by larger local boroughs

---

[2] For a full discussion of this measure, see F. Smallwood, *The Politics of Muncipal Reform* (Indianapolis: Bobbs-Merrill, 1965).

and a new Greater London Council. Some Labour politicians saw in this a Conservative scheme to destroy the Labour-dominated London County Council.

Similarly the Transport Bill, which was being seen through Parliament during the interviewing period, arose from a relatively new determination on the government's part to eliminate the financial deficit incurred from nationalized transport undertakings—particularly the railways. The bill abolished the central transport board, which had the effect of separating the management of the railways from that of the other forms of nationalized transport. It was largely intended to free Dr. Beeching, the government's nominee as chairman of the board, to close uneconomic railway lines and services.

The bill was one move in a long political controversy between government and the opposition. The latter had consistently urged that transport be run as a social service. The government did not reject this argument entirely, but urged that the profitability of a service was the best indication of when it was required on social grounds. The clash of philosophies over transport and the controversial figure of Dr. Beeching had for an extended period attracted considerable newspaper attention, attention that continued during the interviewing period. The Transport Bill itself, however, was so technical that little newspaper coverage was devoted to its specific and detailed proposals or to the Parliamentary debates in which these were discussed.

The question of economic monopolies was also one that had been the subject of sporadic political attention over the last sixty years. In January 1962 the question was dramatically re-opened by the attempted takeover of Courtaulds, a giant of the man-made–fiber industry in Britain, by Imperial Chemical Industries, the other giant in that industry. The battle lasted about a month during which time many other aspects of the tendency to industrial concentration received newspaper attention. After Courtaulds had defeated the I.C.I. bid, the issue began to fade. However demands for an investigation of monopolies continued to be made by various bodies and individuals right up to July.

Monopoly thus can be considered an issue that was alive during the interviewing period, but one that was by then receiving a low degree of coverage from the mass media. This very fact made it representative of many political issues being debated during the period and, for this reason, an interesting topic to investigate.

The other three issues that have been selected were all staples of British politics which had been with politicians since the Second World War, if not before. None had lost their habitual urgency, and normal demands for rapid settlement were being made.

The first of these issues was the housing problem. The shortage of living accommodation and the high prices and high rents that resulted from it were particularly acute problems in areas of high immigration such as Greater London where interviewing of both electors and politicians took place.

The second issue concerned shortages in education. The government cut-back on public expenditure—designed, as was the Wage Pause, to ease the balance of payments—applied to education as well as to other services; the resulting shortages in that field brought on a flood of complaints. However the question of education expenditures had not returned by the time of the interviewing to the center of attention though it did so spectacularly with the Education Reports of 1963 and 1964.

The last topic was that seemingly permanent focus of Western diplomacy—Berlin. Many ingenious suggestions had been made for solving the impasse between West and East Germans, between the NATO allies and the Russians. Most were, as always, being canvassed during this period although seventeen years of stalemate tended to engender pessimism about the chances of any solution. A mild flurry of newspaper comment on the Berlin situation was produced by a Russian initiative in the middle of the interviewing period. And the human interest situations that arose out of the division of the city provided good newspaper material which kept spilling over to the front page.

GROUNDS FOR THE SELECTION OF ISSUES

Why were these and no other issues selected from the hundreds of topics upon which various courses of action were being urged by or upon the government through representative bodies, pressure groups or the mass media? At the time of interviewing the British government was, for example, deeply concerned with the situations in Central Africa and in the Congo. At home a Road Traffic Bill was being passed in the interest of road safety, and the question of consumer protection was being aired along with proposals for regulating Trade Union elections. And a problem that exercised government and Parliament very deeply, judging from their spokesmen's public remarks, was that of increasing recruitment to the Regular Army in order to meet British commitments abroad.

It was, of course, impossible to examine all issues, and some mode of selection had to be devised that would ensure that the issues actually studied were in some sense representative of all issues current during the interviewing period. The chosen issues must be representative because people's reactions to them would be used as data to test hypotheses that purported to apply to all issues, not just to issues of certain special types. The simplest way of ensuring that a representative selection of issues was obtained would have been to employ random sampling methods. The whole "universe" of topics that qualified as political issues in terms of the definition could have been listed, numbered, and certain numbers drawn out by means of tables of random numbers. The topics so selected would have constituted a truly representative selection of current issues.

Unfortunately the drawing up of an exhaustive list of issues current at a particular time is sufficiently difficult to make this approach impossible. Issues are constantly arising and disappearing to that such a listing—and, therefore, the sample drawn from it—would be obsolete and unrepresentative almost from the moment it was made. And the complexity of government and the multiplicity of bodies and channels through which action might be urged are such that it would be a full-time task to trace all issues current at one moment of time.

If random sampling methods could not be employed, the quota sample could be and was approximated. In order to derive a quota sampling of people, a number of personal and social characteristics are picked that are likely to have most influence upon an individual's reactions to the subject about which the sample is to be interviewed (for example, characteristics like sex, age and class if voting or buying habits are being investigated). The sample is made up of people who exhibit these characteristics in proportion, usually, to the numbers of people having these characteristics in the total population.

In applying this technique to issues it was not possible to choose issues in proportion to the number of issues with the same characteristics in the whole population of issues. Given the difficulty outlined above it was difficult to know anything about the population. But certain characteristics of issues likely to affect responses could be isolated and issues could be chosen so that they reflected most of the possible variations in these characteristics.

Three characteristics recommend themselves on the basis of both theory and previous research findings. The finding that electors' reactions to issues vary with the nature of the issue has been encountered both in the United States[3] and Britain.[4] Electors seem better able to relate economic and social welfare matters than issues of a more ab-

---

[3] B. Berelson, P. F. Lazarsfeld, and W. McPhee, *Voting* (Chicago: University of Chicago Press, 1955), pp. 184–85; A. Campbell, P. Converse, W. Miller, and D. Stokes, *The American Voter* (New York: Wiley, 1960), p. 197.

[4] J. Blondel, *Voters, Parties, and Leaders* (Harmondsworth, England: Penguin, 1963), pp. 76–87.

stract nature to their own personal interests and to their support of a particular party. Their attitudes about economic and social welfare matters are, therefore, more consistent and more firmly held than are their attitudes on the less personal or more theoretical matters such as civil liberties, procedural issues or foreign affairs. The nature of an issue was, therefore, one of the characteristics on the basis of which issues were selected.

Intuitively it seems likely that the coverage of an issue by the mass media will have some effect on reactions to it. It is true that a mass of evidence attests to the average person's well-developed capacity for evading political news or discussion.[5] Nevertheless a British voting survey has shown that television exposure (in an election at any rate) increases political information as measured by knowledge of the parties' policies on issues.[6] Since most people read at least parts of newspapers and watch some T.V. programs, it is probable that some information reaches them this way. And, of course, this impact would be very much greater in the case of politicians. Extensive coverage by the mass media was accordingly another characteristic on the basis of which the selection of issues was made.

The third characteristic was the policy adopted by the political parties on the issues. Here it is true that some electors' lack of knowledge about party stands will prevent such stands from having any effect upon those electors' reactions[7] on some issues. But since the majority of the population identify[8] with political parties, the parties do form salient and conspicuous political reference groups. When, therefore, electors do have knowledge of the party position, that position is likely to have some effect. And the politicians are likely to take the parties' attitudes explicitly into their calculations. The important factor from the point of view of the investigation as a whole was not, however, the specific stand taken in itself, but rather how the stand of one party compared with that of the other party. This seemed to have a more direct effect on the degree of partisan bitterness and strength of feeling on the issue.

Other characteristics of political issues could undoubtedly have

---

[5] For the United States, see the figures reported in Berelson, *et al., op. cit.,* pp. 240–241. For Britain, see J. Trenaman and D. McQuail, *Television and the Political Image* (London: Methuen, 1961), Chap. 5 *passim.*

[6] *Ibid.,* p. 187.

[7] Campbell, *et al., op. cit.,* pp. 182–87.

[8] For the United States, see *ibid.,* p. 124. The present London survey of electors and a Glasgow survey (reported in I. Budge, "Political Behaviour and Attitudes of Glasgow Electors," *Political Studies,* 13 [1965], 386–92) indicate that most British electors similarly identify with political parties.

been taken as criteria for selection. It was felt, however, that these three were among the most important and that, in the interests of clarity and simplicity, the criteria should be limited as far as possible.

POSITION OF SELECTED ISSUES
IN REGARD TO SUBJECT–MATTER
MEDIA COVERAGE AND PARTY RELATIONSHIPS

The selection of issues had, of course, to be made in advance. The application of the criteria to the issues in the selection process was carried out with the guidance of a panel made up of three Members of Parliament, a Parliamentary official, a journalist specializing in Parliamentary affairs, and an academic political expert. Members of the panel were asked to forecast the shape that current topics of debate would assume in the course of the next six months. Because politics were quiet during the period and because the panel was apparently well informed, the shape actually taken by the issues did not vary substantially from the predictions according to which they were chosen.

The tables which follow summarize the way in which the issues are characterized on the various criteria.

Table C.1: Subject Matter of the Selected Issues

SUBJECT MATTER	ISSUES
Style:	
Foreign Policy	Berlin question
Civil Liberties	Immigration Bill
Procedural	Reorganization of London government
Position:	
Welfare	Housing
Economic	Wage Pause
	Transport Bill
	Common Market
	Monopolies
Education	Education shortages

NOTE: Some of the assignments may be queried. The Immigration Bill was regarded as falling in the area of Civil Liberties, because it was widely castigated as a color-bar bill and did provoke a debate on the position of colored immigrants in British society. The reorganization of London government represented a modification of political procedures, although only at the local level; as such it clearly stood in a different category from the other issues. The Common Market could well be regarded as a foreign policy and not as an economic issue. It has been classed as the latter because most respondents talked about it in economic terms.

Table C.2: Party Controversy over the Selected Issues

DEGREE OF PARTY CONTROVERSY	ISSUES
Parties clearly opposed	Transport Bill Reorganization of London government
One or both parties divided	Common Market Education shortages Monopolies Housing shortage Wage Pause
Parties clearly agreed	Berlin negotiations

NOTE: Degree of party controversy is determined by reference solely to the Conservative and Labour parties. An issue was assigned to the "divided" category if one or the other party (or both) suffered a degree of internal division on the question which prevented its assignment to a category implying their clear-cut confrontation or agreement. The placing of issues in these categories was done by a panel of political scientists after the interviews had been taken. Consequently they had the benefit of hindsight in judging this dimension of the issues. The fact that most issues fall in the "divided" category probably reflects the usual reality of the party debate.

From the previous description of the issues and from the fact that they spread over all categories in the three dimensions on which they were selected it is at least evident that they represent more than a single type of issue. Issues that were regarded (at least by the politically articulate) as important were included along with others that made less impact, but all were topics of current debate at the time when in-

Table C.3: Newspaper Coverage of the Selected Issues

NEWSPAPER COVERAGE	ISSUE
High	Common Market (11,521.95) Wage Pause (9,362.38)
High medium	Berlin negotiations (3,601.39) Education shortages (3,560.96) Housing shortage (3,531.34)
Low medium	Transport Bill (2,842.97) Monopolies (2,333.26)
Low	Immigration Bill (1,536.75) Reorganization of London government (633.80)

NOTE: Actual coverage of each issue in square inches is given in parentheses.

Table C.4: Television Coverage of the Selected Issues

TELEVISION COVERAGE	ISSUE
High	Common Market (134.0)
High medium	Education shortages (66.5) Housing shortage (52.0) Wage Pause (45.0)
Low medium	Transport Bill (23.0) Berlin negotiation (22.0) Immigration (14.0)
Low	Monopolies (none) Reorganization of London government (none)

NOTE: The selected programs for which minutes of viewing time are given are B.B.C. T.V.—Panorama, Gallery, Tonight; I.T.V.—This Week.

Actual coverage of each issue in minutes of viewing time is given in parentheses.

terviews were taken. Furthermore each is concerned with a relatively specific policy question; they are not vague, global antitheses between the parties but are meant to be representative of the day-to-day topics —some of greater and some of lesser importance—that have to be settled by political bargaining and negotiation and that may have repercussions upon the democratic procedures in accordance with which they are discussed. Consequently it is hoped that the findings drawn from the selected issues have some claim to apply to the total genus of British political issues rather than to a restricted species.

APPENDIX D

THE MEASURES OF POLITICAL EFFICACY AND POLITICAL ALIENATION

SENSE OF POLITICAL EFFICACY

Questions

(Q8 h) I don't think local councillors care much about what people like me think. (Agree, Disagree).

(Q19 j) Sometimes local politics and government seem so complicated that a person like me can't really understand what's going on. (Agree, Disagree).

(Q20 c) People like me don't have any say about what the local government does. (Agree, Disagree).

(Q20 n) Voting is the only way that people like me can have a say about how the borough council runs things. (Agree, Disagree).

Construction of Index

"Disagree" responses to (Q8 h), (Q19 j), (Q20 c), (Q20 n) each score one. All other responses score nothing.

Source

Questions (adapted to meet British conditions) from A. Campbell, G. Gurin and W. Miller *The Voter Decides* (Appendix A).

Purpose

To measure respondents' feelings about whether they can get things done through politics if they wish.

Distribution of Samples

	POLITICIANS		ELECTORS	
	N	Percent	N	Percent
Low				
Score nothing	0	0	27	20
Score one	0	0	43	32
Score two	2	4	32	24
Score three	16	34	27	20
Score four	29	62	5	4
High				
Total	47	100	134	100

For comparisons the electors' distribution has been collapsed into:
High Political Efficacy (Score three and above)
Low Political Efficacy (Score two and below)

SENSE OF POLITICAL ALIENATION
Questions

(Q8 a) People who go into public office usually think of the good of the people more than of their own good. (Agree, Disagree).

(Q8 k) Local councillors soon lose touch with the people who elected them. (Agree, Disagree).

(Q19 a) If people really knew what was going on in high places in the government, it would blow the lid off things. (Agree, Disagree).

(Q20 l) It doesn't matter which party wins elections, the interests of the little man don't count. (Agree, Disagree).

(Q3) Some people say you can usually trust local councillors because they are your neighbors and friends; others say that elected councillors become tools of special interests no matter who they are. What do you think?

Construction of Index

"Agree" responses to (Q8 k), (Q19 a), (Q20 l), the "Disagree" response (to Q8 a) and the response to (Q3) that elected councillors become tools of special interests, each score one. All other responses score nothing.

Source

Questions (reworded to suit British conditions and one original question dropped) are taken from C. McCall's study of political recruitment in New Haven, Conn. Original source is W. E. Thompson and J. E. Horton "Political Alienation as a Force in Political Action," *Social Forces*, Vol. 38 (1960), pp. 190–95.

Purpose

To measure a feeling of bitterness and frustration with ordinary political processes among respondents.

Distribution of Samples

	POLITICIANS		ELECTORS	
	N	Percent	N	Percent
Low				
Score nothing	31	66	21	15
Score one	10	21	24	18
Score two	4	9	31	23
Score three	1	2	24	18
Score four	1	2	21	15
Score five	0	0	15	11
High				
TOTAL	47	100	136	100

For comparisons the electorate distribution has been collapsed into:
High Political Alienation (Score three and above)
Low Political Alienation (Score two and below)

APPENDIX E | MEASURES OF POTENTIAL EFFECTIVENESS

The same sequence of questions was used on each issue to measure potential effectiveness. The measures are listed below, each alongside the question which was designed to tap them.

Table E.1

Measure of Potential Effectiveness	Interview Question
1. Perception of issue	Have you heard anything about the (political issue)?
2. Number of alternatives perceived on the issue*	Not speaking now only about the present British Government, what different kinds of action do you think any British government could take on this question of the (political issue)? (Anything else?)
3. Frame of reference	
4. Perception of effect	Do you feel that the (political issue) affects you at all? (IF NO) Do you feel that the (political issue) affects anyone or anything in which you take an interest?
5. Number of effects perceived from issue	How does it affect you (OR person/thing in which you take an interest)? (Any other effect?)
6. Magnitude of effect	Would you say its effect on this is very great, moderate, or rather slight?
7. Specific alternatives preferred	Not necessarily excluding anything you've said before, what would *you* *like* to see done about this (political issue)?
8. Strength of feeling	How strongly do you feel this should be done—do you feel very

Table E.1 (cont.)

Measure of Potential Effectiveness	Interview Question
	strongly it should be done, moderately strongly, or do you not particularly care?
9. Perception of party stands	Please indicate by a tick in the appropriate place for each of the parties—Conservative, Labour and Liberal—whether they are in your view for or against (specific issues).

* Alternatives that were not mentioned in response to this question, but that were later introduced in reply to the question on preferences were also counted in Number of Alternatives perceived.

CONSTRUCTION OF MEASURES OF POLITICAL EFFECTIVENESS

Perception of Issue Perception of Effect	Responses to the questions on which these measures are based consist of simple affirmatives or negatives (Table E.1)
Magnitude of Effect Strength of Feeling	In their replies to the questions on which these measures are based respondents mark their own perceptions/feelings. (Table E.1)
Number of Alternatives Perceived on the Issue Number of Effects Perceived from Issue	Responses were coded into conceptually distinct alternatives and effects.* Then a count of the numbers of conceptually distinct effects and alternatives was made. This procedure guarded against the possibility of a loquacious respondent mentioning a large number of hardly differing alternatives or effects for when coded into a broad category all these counted as one.
Specific Alternatives Preferred	After coding the final preferences of respondents into the various categories for the nine issues it could be seen whether no alternatives or only vague alternatives had been preferred, or on the other hand whether concrete proposals had been advanced.

* For full details of coding instructions and procedures see Budge, *Patterns of Democratic Agreement* (Appendices D and E).

FRAME OF REFERENCE†

Coding instructions for the broadness of the frame of reference applied to the discussion of viable alternatives were constructed as follows: Code for highest level of sophistication, given the nature of the master code materials.

Relation of issue to a wider context.

1. Explicit placing of the issue in a broad theoretical, causal, temporal, geographical or political context, *i.e.*, viewing the particular issue as one manifestation of a wider process.

EXAMPLES: "Essentially a matter of allocating priorities between this and other areas." "With the continuing change in the conception of government responsibilities, reforms in the structure and methods of government are always necessary." "This situation is only one outcrop of the world-wide struggle between East and West."

2. Implicit placing of the issue in a wider context, assumption of knowledge of East-West relations and economic theory by use of terms drawn from these fields, without spelling them out.

Relation of alternatives to each other within the issue.

3. The issue is regarded as posing a specific problem, and all alternatives mentioned are regarded as attempts of varying orders of merit to solve the single problem posed by the issue. But the problem is *not* placed in a wider context as is the case in the higher categories. (More than one reason or alternative is given.)

4. One alternative is explicitly contrasted with other alternatives; respondent clearly distinguishes between the various courses of action he outlines, or rejects one of the alternatives he mentions.

No structuring of answer.

5. Specific reasons are given for advancing (every) alternatives mentioned, but these reasons do not form a connected argument, (must be two reasons or above).

6. One isolated reason is given for action on the issue (reason is taken as being some justification advanced for pursuing some course of action on an issue).

7. No reasons are given although alternatives are mentioned.

8. D.K., irrelevant answer altogether.

---

† The derivation of this measure from the "Level of Conceptualization" employed in Campbell, Converse, Miller, Stokes *The American Voter, op. cit.,* pp. 216–56 will be obvious.

CORRECT PERCEPTION OF PARTY
AND T.U.C. ISSUE-STANDS

Correct perceptions of Party and T.U.C. issue-stands were measured by means of a special index constructed from responses to the following questions:

Q.9. Please indicate by a check in the appropriate place for each of these parties—Conservative, Labour and Liberal—whether they are in your view for or against:

(a) Britain joining the European Common Market

Conservative	FOR ✓	AGAINST	DIVIDED ✓
Labour	FOR	AGAINST	DIVIDED ✓
Liberal	FOR ✓	AGAINST	DIVIDED

(b) Immediately opening negotiations with the Russians over Berlin

Labour	FOR ✓	AGAINST	DIVIDED
Liberal	FOR ✓	AGAINST	DIVIDED
Conservative	FOR ✓	AGAINST	DIVIDED

(c) Splitting the British Transport Commission

Conservative	FOR ✓	AGAINST	DIVIDED
Labour	FOR	AGAINST ✓	DIVIDED
Liberal	FOR ✓	AGAINST	DIVIDED

(d) Immediately spending more money to make up shortages in education

Liberal	FOR ✓	AGAINST	DIVIDED
Conservative	FOR	AGAINST ✓	DIVIDED ✓
Labour	FOR ✓	AGAINST	DIVIDED

(e) Preventing the creation of private monopolies in any products in Britain

Conservative	FOR	AGAINST ✓	DIVIDED ✓
Labour	FOR ✓	AGAINST	DIVIDED
Liberal	FOR ✓	AGAINST	DIVIDED

(f) Tightening up restrictions on immigrants from the Commonwealth

Labour	FOR	AGAINST ✓	DIVIDED
Liberal	FOR	AGAINST ✓	DIVIDED
Conservative	FOR ✓	AGAINST	DIVIDED ✓

(g) Making the building of houses the top priority in domestic affairs

Conservative	FOR	AGAINST ✓	DIVIDED ✓
Labour	FOR	AGAINST ✓	DIVIDED
Liberal	FOR	AGAINST ✓	DIVIDED ✓

(h) Reorganizing local government in Greater London

Liberal	FOR √	AGAINST ___	DIVIDED ___
Conservative	FOR √	AGAINST ___	DIVIDED ___
Labour	FOR ___	AGAINST √	DIVIDED ___

(i) Keeping wages steady for a time

Conservative	FOR √	AGAINST ___	DIVIDED ___
Labour	FOR ___	AGAINST √	DIVIDED √
Liberal	FOR ___	AGAINST √	DIVIDED √

Q. 10. Please indicate in the same way whether, in your opinion, the T.U.C. (Trades Union Congress) was for or against:

(a) Tightening up restrictions on immigrants from the Commonwealth

FOR ___   AGAINST √   DIVIDED ___

(b) Splitting up the British Transport Commission

FOR ___   AGAINST √   DIVIDED ___

(c) Making the building of houses the top priority in domestic affairs

FOR ___   AGAINST √   DIVIDED ___

(d) Britain joining the European Common Market

FOR ___   AGAINST ___   DIVIDED √

(e) Immediately opening negotiations with the Russians over Berlin

FOR √   AGAINST ___   DIVIDED ___

(f) Keeping wages steady for a time

FOR ___   AGAINST √   DIVIDED ___

(g) Immediately spending more money to make up shortages in education

FOR √   AGAINST ___   DIVIDED ___

(h) Preventing the creation of private monopolies in any products in Britain

FOR √   AGAINST ___   DIVIDED ___

The positions checked in the example of the questions given above each score one, if endorsed by respondents. All other endorsements score nothing. The positions taken as correct perceptions of party and T.U.C. stands were selected by a panel of experts independent of the investigator, at the end of the period of interviewing.

INDEX